"There are a lot of WordPress books out there, but Head First WordPress once again proves that [this] series is the gold standard for smart, readable, easy-to-use reference guides for creative web users everywhere."

> **— Paul Andrews**
> **Blogger, author, and journalist; editor of bikeintelligencer.com**

"This friendly book offers tips that I haven't seen in other books, and features useful, real-world scenarios to help get you up to speed with the latest version of WordPress quickly. "

> **— Jim Doran**
> **Software engineer at Johns Hopkins University**

"Administering and managing a WordPress blog can be daunting for the uninitiated. *Head First WordPress* walks you through the basics to help you ramp up your WordPress site quickly. "

> **— Ken Walker**
> **Business analyst**

Praise for other *Head First* books

"Building websites has definitely become more than just writing code. *Head First Web Design* shows you what you need to know to give your users an appealing and satisfying experience. Another great Head First book!"

> **— Sarah Collings**
> **User experience software engineer**

"*Head First Web Design* really demystifies the web design process and makes it possible for any web programmer to give it a try. For a web developer who has not taken web design classes, *Head First Web Design* confirmed and clarified a lot of theory and best practices that seem to be just assumed in this industry."

> **— Ashley Doughty**
> **Senior web developer**

"I ❤ *Head First HTML with CSS & XHTML*—it teaches you everything you need to learn in a 'fun-coated' format!"

> **— Sally Applin**
> **UI designer and artist**

"The Web would be a much better place if every HTML author start off by reading *Head First HTML with CSS & XHTML*."

> **— L. David Barron**
> **Technical Lead, Layout & CSS, Mozilla Corporation**

"*Head First HTML with CSS & XHTML* is a thoroughly modern introduction to forward-looking practices in web page markup and presentation. It correctly anticipates readers' puzzlements and handles them just in time. The highly graphic and incremental approach precisely mimics the best way to learn this stuff: make a small change and see it in the browser to understand what each new item means."

> **— Danny Goodman**
> **Author of *Dynamic HTML: The Definitive Guide***

"Oh great, you made an XHTML book simple enough a CEO can understand it. What will you do next? Accounting simple enough my developer can understand it? Next thing you know we'll be collaborating as a team or something."

> **— Janice Fraser**
> **CEO, Adaptive Path**

"Behind the Ajax ball? Get out of the shadows with *Head First Ajax*. You'll wrap your mind around the core concepts, and have some fun in the process."

> **— Bear Bibeault**
> **Web application architect**

"Ajax is more than just revisiting existing technologies, making some small changes to your web application and then delcaring it Ajax-enabled. Rebecca M. Riordan walks you through all of the steps of building an Ajax application in *Head First Ajax*, and shows you that Ajax is more than 'that little asynchronous part', but a better approach to web design altogether."

> **— Anthony T. Holdener III**
> **Author of *Ajax: The Definitive Guide***

"*Head First Design Patterns* manages to mix fun, belly laughs, insight, technical depth and great practical advice in one entertaining and thought-provoking read."

> **— Richard Helm**
> **Coauthor of *Design Patterns***

"*Head First Design Patterns* is close to perfect, because of the way it combines expertise and readability. It speaks with authority and it reads beautifully. It's one of the very few software books I've ever read that strikes me as indispensable. (I'd put maybe 10 books in this category, at the outside.)"

> **— David Gelernter**
> **Professor of Computer Science, Yale University**

"*Head First Rails* continues the tradition of the Head First series, providing useful, real-world information to get you up and going quickly. [It] is an excellent book for people learning Rails, as well as those brushing up on the latest features."

> **—Jeremy Durham**
> **Web developer**

"*Head First Rails* is a great, broad introduction to iterative Web 2.0 development. This book will show you how quick and easy it is to develop robust, next-generation websites."

> **— Matt Proud**
> **Systems administrator and developer**

Other related books from O'Reilly

Learning Web Design

Website Optimization

CSS: The Definitive Guide

Creating a Web Site: The Missing Manual

Other books in O'Reilly's *Head First* series

Head First C#

Head First Java

Head First Object-Oriented Analysis and Design (OOA&D)

Head First HTML with CSS and XHTML

Head First Design Patterns

Head First Servlets and JSP

Head First EJB

Head First SQL

Head First Software Development

Head First JavaScript

Head First Physics

Head First Statistics

Head First Ajax

Head First Rails

Head First Algebra

Head First PHP & MySQL

Head First PMP

Head First Web Design

Head First Networking

Head First WordPress

Wouldn't it be dreamy if there was a book to help me learn how to build WordPress sites that was more fun than going to the dentist? It's probably nothing but a fantasy...

Jeff Siarto

O'REILLY®

Beijing • Cambridge • Köln • Sebastopol • Taipei • Tokyo

Head First WordPress

First Edition

by Jeff Siarto

Published by O'Reilly Media, Inc., 1005 Gravenstein Highway North, Sebastopol, CA 95472.

O'Reilly Media books may be purchased for educational, business, or sales promotional use. Online editions are also available for most titles (*http://my.safaribooksonline.com*). For more information, contact our corporate/institutional sales department: (800) 998-9938 or *corporate@oreilly.com*.

Series Creators:	Kathy Sierra, Bert Bates
Editors:	Courtney Nash
Cover Designer:	Karen Montgomery
Production Editors:	Kristen Borg, Scott Delugan, and Rachel Monaghan
Indexer:	Julie Hawks
Proofreader:	Nancy Reinhardt
Page Viewers:	Henry and Romulus

Printing History:

July 2010: First Edition.

Henry, Jeff's nephew

Romulus

ISBN: 978-0-596-80628-6

[M]

To Allie, for putting up with the late nights and busy weekends.
This would not have been possible without you.

Jeff

Jeff Siarto is a user experience and web designer currently calling Chicago home. He has two degrees from Michigan State University and was a student of the standards-based web design movement—aspiring to the likes of Cederholm, Zeldman, and Meyer.

Jeff is a die-hard coworker and helps organize Jelly Chicago, a coworking group that meets twice a week in Chicago's Lincoln Park neighborhood.

When Jeff isn't pushing pixels, he enjoys cooking and eating (OK, mostly eating) and spending time with his wife on Chicago's west side and in Michigan with friends and family.

Table of Contents (Summary)

Table of Contents (the real thing)

Intro

Your brain on WordPress. Here *you* are trying to *learn* something, while here your *brain* is doing you a favor by making sure the learning doesn't *stick*. Your brain's thinking, "Better leave room for more important things, like which wild animals to avoid and whether naked snowboarding is a bad idea." So how *do* you trick your brain into thinking that your life depends on knowing enough to create your own WordPress site?

getting started

WordPress from scratch
You've got something to say.

Whether it's just you and your desire to let everyone know about your growing collection of hand-crocheted *Star Wars* figures, or a big company with hundreds of products, **blogging** let's anyone publish online without having to be a genius about **HTML**, **CSS**, or any other *programming*. In this chapter, you'll learn how to get **hosting** for your blog, **install** WordPress, and **create and publish** your *first* blog post.

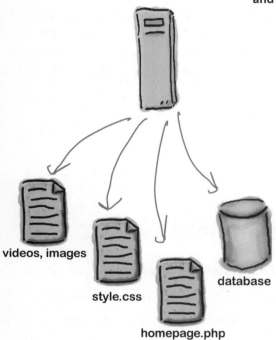

videos, images

style.css

homepage.php

database

changing your blog's look and feel

2 A question of style

You've finally got your own blog. But it looks so…generic.

Time to make it your own. WordPress comes preloaded with lots of **themes** you can apply to your blog, but we're going to go one step further and make our own *custom* theme. Along the way, you'll learn some basic **HTML** and **CSS** to really make your blog look exactly how you want. We'll also delve into CSS **rules**, which allow you to *quickly* change how your blog looks, and take advantage of WordPress **widgets** to easily add sidebar content to the blog..

Template Files
Up Close

```
#header {
        background: #ddd;
        height: 50px;
}
#nav ul {
        float: right;
        margin: 17px 0 0 0;
}
```

content management with wordpress

Beyond the blog

3

You're starting to outgrow the blog.

Maybe your business is growing, maybe you need more control of what shows up where on your blog, and *when*. Luckily, WordPress handles a lot more than just chronological blog posts. We'll start to tap into its **content management system** capabilities by creating **static pages** like on a regular website, adding **navigation** for the new pages, and changing the home page of your new site so it isn't your blog. Get ready to build a full-fledged *website* practically without writing a single line of HTML or CSS.

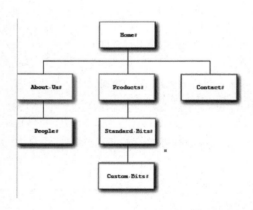

users, categories, and tags

Keeping things organized

4

It's time to invite some friends to the party.

Blogging (or managing a WordPress site) doesn't *have* to be a solitary venture. Loads of well-know blogs out there feature multiple user **roles**, from **writers** to **editors** and **administrators**. In this chapter, you'll learn how to get **multiple people** posting on the same blog, manage the **workflow** across all those people, and put **categories** and **tags** to work in organizing your site's content.

We all use the same login because it's easy—you never forget the password!

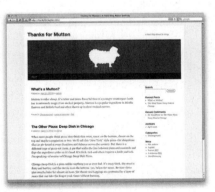

video and plug-ins

Getting things moving

5

Video can add a whole other dimension to your blog. For nearly any kind of content, video makes your site more *engaging*, and gives you readers plenty more to comment on and share with their friends. In this chapter, you'll learn how to **host your videos** online and include them (along with other **downloadable files**) in your blog posts. We'll introduce **plug-ins**, which do a lot of heavy lifting (and *coding*) for you, and use **categories** to create a consistent, easy-to-find home for all the videos on your site.

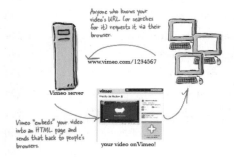

Anyone who knows your video's URL (or searches for it) requests it via their browser.

www.vimeo.com/1234567

Vimeo server

Vimeo "embeds" your video into an HTML page and sends that back to people's browsers.

your video on Vimeo!

Plug-ins Up Close

6
podcasting and syndication
Spreading the word

It's time more people knew about your awesome site.

Your blog is humming along, and you've already figured out how to expand WordPress to manage an *entire website*. Now that you've got **video** playing there too, why not *expand* your audience base? In this chapter, we'll discover how to **distribute** videos through Apple's iTunes store as **podcasts**, and how to **syndicate** your content so that a ton more people will find out about your site (and *keep coming back* for **more**).

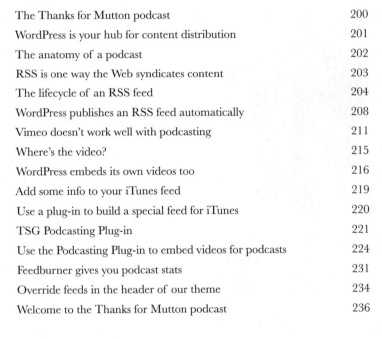

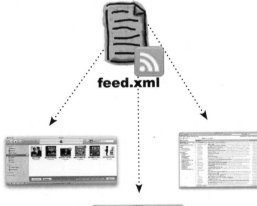

feed.xml

securing wordpress

Locking things down

Not everyone on the Internet is nice.

It's a fact of modern life on the Internet: there are people who spend their time trying to break into, or *hack*, other people's websites. Some do it just for the thrill, others to cause chaos, and some are simply after *sensitive information* like **credit card numbers**, social security numbers, and other **personal information**. Now, you'll learn how to make your WordPress site *more secure*, with unique **usernames**, **strong** passwords, and more. You'll also kick off **automatic backups** of all your WordPress files so you can **restore your site** if it ever does get hacked, or goes down for other reasons.

Hackers Exposed

This week's interview:
We interview a hacker serving
time for credit card theft

making wordpress fast

Time for the passing lane

8

Speed is important online.

A fast-loading site isn't just about keeping visitors around. Yes, if your site doesn't load quickly then people might just wander off, but a slow site also gets dinged in search results from the likes of Google, meaning fewer people will actually find your site in the first place. Beyond just increasing your horsepower, you'll also learn how to use caching, database optimization, and additional hosting options to beef up your site to handle more traffic, too.

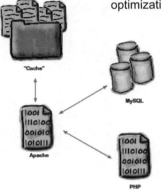

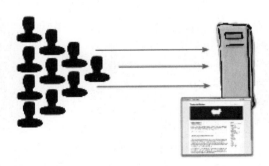

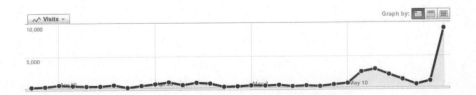

appendix: leftovers
Top ten things (we didn't cover)
We've really covered a lot of ground in this book.

The thing is, there are some important topics and tidbits that didn't quite fit into any of the previous chapters. We feel pretty strongly about this, and think that if we didn't at least cover them in passing, we'd be doing you a disservice. That's where this chapter comes into the picture. Well, it's not really a chapter, it's more like an appendix (OK, it *is* an appendix). But it's an awesome appendix of the top ten best bits that we couldn't let you go without.

how to use this book

Intro

In this section, we answer the burning question: "So why _DID_ they put that in a WordPress book?"

Who is this book for?

If you can answer "yes" to all of these:

① Are you familiar with blogs in general, or currently use WordPress to publish and manage blogs and websites?

② Are you familiar with the concepts of web hosting, file transfer (FTP) and have a basic understanding of HTML and CSS? Do you want to learn how to build not just a blog, but a full-fledged WordPress site?

It definitely helps if you've already got some solid web development chops too, but it's certainly not required.

③ Do you prefer **stimulating dinner party conversation** to **dry**, **dull**, **academic lectures**?

this book is for you.

Who should probably back away from this book?

If you can answer "yes" to any of these:

① Are you **completely new** to blogging and how websites work?

Check out Head First HTML with CSS and XHTML for an excellent introduction to web development, and then come back and join us in WordPressville.

② Are you looking for a **reference book** on WordPress tools, plug-ins, and the like?

③ Are you **afraid to try something different**? Would you rather have a root canal than mix stripes with plaid? Do you believe that a technical book can't be serious if there's a foodie blog in it?

Thanks for Mutton

this book is not for you.

[Note from marketing: this book is for anyone with a credit card. Or cash. Cash is nice, too — EdJ

We know what you're thinking.

"How can *this* be a serious WordPress book?"

"What's with all the graphics?"

"Can I actually *learn* it this way?"

And we know what your *brain* is thinking.

Your brain craves novelty. It's always searching, scanning, *waiting* for something unusual. It was built that way, and it helps you stay alive.

So what does your brain do with all the routine, ordinary, normal things you encounter? Everything it *can* to stop them from interfering with the brain's *real* job—recording things that *matter*. It doesn't bother saving the boring things; they never make it past the "this is obviously not important" filter.

How does your brain *know* what's important? Suppose you're out for a day hike and a tiger jumps in front of you, what happens inside your head and body?

Neurons fire. Emotions crank up. *Chemicals surge.*

And that's how your brain knows...

This must be important! Don't forget it!

But imagine you're at home, or in a library. It's a safe, warm, tiger-free zone. You're studying. Getting ready for an exam. Or trying to learn some tough technical topic your boss thinks will take a week, ten days at the most.

Just one problem. Your brain's trying to do you a big favor. It's trying to make sure that this *obviously* non-important content doesn't clutter up scarce resources. Resources that are better spent storing the really *big* things. Like tigers. Like the danger of fire. Like how you should never again snowboard in shorts.

And there's no simple way to tell your brain, "Hey brain, thank you very much, but no matter how dull this book is, and how little I'm registering on the emotional Richter scale right now, I really *do* want you to keep this stuff around."

Your brain thinks THIS is important.

Great. Only 350 more dull, dry, boring pages.

Your brain thinks THIS isn't worth saving.

We think of a "Head First" reader as a <u>learner</u>.

So what does it take to *learn* something? First, you have to *get* it, then make sure you don't *forget* it. It's not about pushing facts into your head. Based on the latest research in cognitive science, neurobiology, and educational psychology, *learning* takes a lot more than text on a page. We know what turns your brain on.

Some of the Head First learning principles:

Make it visual. Images are far more memorable than words alone, and make learning much more effective (up to 89% improvement in recall and transfer studies). It also makes things more understandable. **Put the words within or near the graphics** they relate to, rather than on the bottom or on another page, and learners will be up to *twice* as likely to solve problems related to the content.

That's nice and all, but what about those tags?

Use a conversational and personalized style. In recent studies, students performed up to 40% better on post-learning tests if the content spoke directly to the reader, using a first-person, conversational style rather than taking a formal tone. Tell stories instead of lecturing. Use casual language. Don't take yourself too seriously. Which would *you* pay more attention to: a stimulating dinner party companion, or a lecture?

Get the learner to think more deeply. In other words, unless you actively flex your neurons, nothing much happens in your head. A reader has to be motivated, engaged, curious, and inspired to solve problems, draw conclusions, and generate new knowledge. And for that, you need challenges, exercises, and thought-provoking questions, and activities that involve both sidesof the brain and multiple senses.

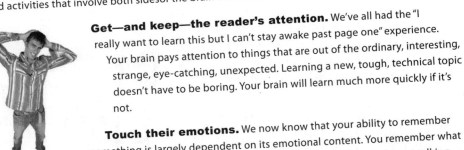

Get—and keep—the reader's attention. We've all had the "I really want to learn this but I can't stay awake past page one" experience. Your brain pays attention to things that are out of the ordinary, interesting, strange, eye-catching, unexpected. Learning a new, tough, technical topic doesn't have to be boring. Your brain will learn much more quickly if it's not.

Touch their emotions. We now know that your ability to remember something is largely dependent on its emotional content. You remember what you care about. You remember when you *feel* something. No, we're not talking heart-wrenching stories about a boy and his dog. We're talking emotions like surprise, curiosity, fun, "what the...?" , and the feeling of "I Rule!" that comes when you solve a puzzle, learn something everybody else thinks is hard, or realize you know something that "I'm more technical than thou" Bob from engineering *doesn't*.

Metacognition: thinking about thinking

If you really want to learn, and you want to learn more quickly and more deeply, pay attention to how you pay attention. Think about how you think. Learn how you learn.

Most of us did not take courses on metacognition or learning theory when we were growing up. We were *expected* to learn, but rarely *taught* to learn.

I wonder how I can trick my brain into remembering this stuff...

But we assume that if you're holding this book, you really want to learn about WordPress. And you probably don't want to spend a lot of time. And since you're going to build more apps in the future, you need to *remember* what you read. And for that, you've got to *understand* it. To get the most from this book, or *any* book or learning experience, take responsibility for your brain. Your brain on *this* content.

The trick is to get your brain to see the new material you're learning as Really Important. Crucial to your well-being. As important as a tiger. Otherwise, you're in for a constant battle, with your brain doing its best to keep the new content from sticking.

So just how *DO* you get your brain to think that WordPress is a hungry tiger?

There's the slow, tedious way, or the faster, more effective way. The slow way is about sheer repetition. You obviously know that you *are* able to learn and remember even the dullest of topics if you keep pounding the same thing into your brain. With enough repetition, your brain says, "This doesn't *feel* important to him, but he keeps looking at the same thing *over* and *over* and *over*, so I suppose it must be."

The faster way is to do **anything that increases brain activity,** especially different *types* of brain activity. The things on the previous page are a big part of the solution, and they're all things that have been proven to help your brain work in your favor. For example, studies show that putting words *within* the pictures they describe (as opposed to somewhere else in the page, like a caption or in the body text) causes your brain to try to makes sense of how the words and picture relate, and this causes more neurons to fire. More neurons firing = more chances for your brain to *get* that this is something worth paying attention to, and possibly recording.

A conversational style helps because people tend to pay more attention when they perceive that they're in a conversation, since they're expected to follow along and hold up their end. The amazing thing is, your brain doesn't necessarily *care* that the "conversation" is between you and a book! On the other hand, if the writing style is formal and dry, your brain perceives it the same way you experience being lectured to while sitting in a roomful of passive attendees. No need to stay awake.

But pictures and conversational style are just the beginning.

Here's what WE did:

We used *pictures*, because your brain is tuned for visuals, not text. As far as your brain's concerned, a picture really *is* worth a thousand words. And when text and pictures work together, we embedded the text *in* the pictures because your brain works more effectively when the text is *within* the thing the text refers to, as opposed to in a caption or buried in the text somewhere.

We used *redundancy*, saying the same thing in *different* ways and with different media types, and *multiple senses*, to increase the chance that the content gets coded into more than one area of your brain.

We used concepts and pictures in *unexpected* ways because your brain is tuned for novelty, and we used pictures and ideas with at least *some emotional* content, because your brain is tuned to pay attention to the biochemistry of emotions. That which causes you to *feel* something is more likely to be remembered, even if that feeling is nothing more than a little *humor*, *surprise*, or *interest.*

We used a personalized, *conversational style*, because your brain is tuned to pay more attention when it believes you're in a conversation than if it thinks you're passively listening to a presentation. Your brain does this even when you're *reading*.

We included loads of *activities*, because your brain is tuned to learn and remember more when you *do* things than when you *read* about things. And we made the exercises challenging-yet-do-able, because that's what most people prefer.

We used *multiple learning styles*, because *you* might prefer step-by-step procedures, while someone else wants to understand the big picture first, and someone else just wants to see an example. But regardless of your own learning preference, *everyone* benefits from seeing the same content represented in multiple ways.

We include content for *both sides of your brain*, because the more of your brain you engage, the more likely you are to learn and remember, and the longer you can stay focused. Since working one side of the brain often means giving the other side a chance to rest, you can be more productive at learning for a longer period of time.

Fireside Chats

And we included *stories* and exercises that present *more than one point of view,* because your brain is tuned to learn more deeply when it's forced to make evaluations and judgments.

We included *challenges*, with exercises, and by asking *questions* that don't always have a straight answer, because your brain is tuned to learn and remember when it has to *work* at something. Think about it—you can't get your *body* in shape just by *watching* people at the gym. But we did our best to make sure that when you're working hard, it's on the *right* things. That *you're not spending one extra dendrite* processing a hard-to-understand example, or parsing difficult, jargon-laden, or overly terse text.

We used *people*. In stories, examples, pictures, etc., because, well, because *you're* a person. And your brain pays more attention to *people* than it does to *things*.

Here's what YOU can do to bend your brain into submission

So, we did our part. The rest is up to you. These tips are a starting point; listen to your brain and figure out what works for you and what doesn't. Try new things.

cut this out and stick it on your refrigerator.

---

① Slow down. The more you understand, the less you have to memorize.

Don't just *read*. Stop and think. When the book asks you a question, don't just skip to the answer. Imagine that someone really *is* asking the question. The more deeply you force your brain to think, the better chance you have of learning and remembering.

② Do the exercises. Write your own notes.

We put them in, but if we did them for you, that would be like having someone else do your workouts for you. And don't just *look* at the exercises. **Use a pencil.** There's plenty of evidence that physical activity *while* learning can increase the learning.

③ Read the "There are No Dumb Questions"

That means all of them. They're not optional sidebars—*they're part of the core content!* Don't skip them.

④ Make this the last thing you read before bed. Or at least the last challenging thing.

Part of the learning (especially the transfer to long-term memory) happens *after* you put the book down. Your brain needs time on its own, to do more processing. If you put in something new during that processing time, some of what you just learned will be lost.

⑤ Drink water. Lots of it.

Your brain works best in a nice bath of fluid. Dehydration (which can happen before you ever feel thirsty) decreases cognitive function.

⑥ Talk about it. Out loud.

Speaking activates a different part of the brain. If you're trying to understand something, or increase your chance of remembering it later, say it out loud. Better still, try to explain it out loud to someone else. You'll learn more quickly, and you might uncover ideas you hadn't known were there when you were reading about it.

⑦ Listen to your brain.

Pay attention to whether your brain is getting overloaded. If you find yourself starting to skim the surface or forget what you just read, it's time for a break. Once you go past a certain point, you won't learn faster by trying to shove more in, and you might even hurt the process.

⑧ Feel something!

Your brain needs to know that this *matters*. Get involved with the stories. Make up your own captions for the photos. Groaning over a bad joke is *still* better than feeling nothing at all.

⑨ Create something!

Apply this to your daily work; use what you are learning to improve your own blog. Just do something to get some experience beyond the exercises and activities in this book. All you need is something to add to your blog, such that you're applying the tools and techniques from the book to your site (or maybe a friend's site!).

Read me

This is a learning experience, not a reference book. We deliberately stripped out everything that might get in the way of learning whatever it is we're working on at that point in the book. And the first time through, you need to begin at the beginning, because the book makes assumptions about what you've already seen and learned.

We start off by installing WordPress and creating a real post in your first chapter.

Believe it or not, even if you've never blogged or developed a website before, you can jump right in and starting blogging. You'll also learn your way around the main interface used for WordPress.

We don't cover all the ins and outs of getting hosting for your blog in the book.

In this book, you can get on with the business of learning how to create a full WordPress site (not just a blog) without all the complexity of hosting your blog on a hosting comany's web server. But, we know that getting hosting (and making sure it is exactly what you need and set up properly) can be daunting, so we've put together a quick screencast with way more detail and information that you can find at *www.headfirstlabs.com/WordPress*.

The activities are NOT optional.

The exercises and activities are not add-ons; they're part of the core content of the book. Some of them are to help with memory, some are for understanding, and some will help you apply what you've learned. ***Don't skip the exercises.***

The redundancy is intentional and important.

One distinct difference in a Head First book is that we want you to *really* get it. And we want you to finish the book remembering what you've learned. Most reference books don't have retention and recall as a goal, but this book is about *learning*, so you'll see some of the same concepts come up more than once.

The Brain Power exercises don't have answers.

For some of them, there is no right answer, and for others, part of the learning experience of the Brain Power activities is for you to decide if and when your answers are right. In some of the Brain Power exercises, you will find hints to point you in the right direction.

The technical review team

Paul Andrews

Jim Doran

Louis Rawlins

Ken Walker

Technical Reviewers:

For this book we had an amazing, elite group of tech reviewers. They did a fantastic job, and we're really grateful for their incredible contribution.

Co-author of *Gates: How Microsoft's Mogul Reinvented an Industry—and Made Himself the Richest Man in America*, career journalist **Paul Andrews** has been blogging for a decade and was an early adopter of WordPress. An avid cyclist, he writes a leading bike blog, BikeIntelligencer.com, dividing his time between Seattle and the San Francisco Bay Area with his wife Cecile and loyal but obstinate bichon frise, Maggie.

Louis Rawlins works with media as an educator, artist, and engineer. The forests and city streets of his neighborhood inform his perception of media and advertising which he shares through dialogue and community. He lives and works in Oakland, California..

As a web designer, teacher and speaker, **Jim Doran** loves open source technologies and web standards. He's currently a software engineer at Johns Hopkins University and a faculty member at the Community College of Baltimore County. When not hacking WordPress, Jim rides skateboards and makes art which he publishes at *http://jimdoran.net*.

Ken Walker has been passionate about building easy-to-use technology since he first learned how to type. He holds a bachelors degree in computer science from Rutgers University and works at a financial services firm in New York City. In the brief moments he's not working or raising his beautiful family—and probably should be sleeping—Ken shares the stories of the people who are making an impact in his hometown at *www.dailynewarker.com*.

Acknowledgments

My editor:

Courtney Nash has been a patient and brilliant editor. She has taken this book though lots of ups and downs and has been instrumental in helping me put together a title that looks at WordPress in a different, uniquely Head First way. Her input and guidance have been invaluable.

Courtney Nash

The O'Reilly team:

As always, the O'Reilly team has been extremely helpful and supportive. I'd like to thank everyone that had a hand in making this book great, including **Karen Shaner**, **Scott Delugan**, and **Laurie Petrycki**. I'd also like to thank **Brett McLaughlin**, a Head First master for teaching me the ways of the brain and taking a chance on a punk kid just out of college.

My friends and family:

Jelly Chicago has been the backbone of my time in Chicago and this book is better off because of the people that I've meet and worked with there. I'd also like to thank my **Loudpixel** colleagues, **Allie Osmar**, **Ryan Abbott**, and **Lesley Jones**, for keeping the business running smoothly while I was on deadline.

My wife (as of November 2010), **Allie**, has been amazingly supportive throughout this entire process. To my mom, **Jill**, and my dad, **Jeff**, for their endless support of my work and their willingness to listen to me ramble on about technology and all things geek. You guys mean the world to me!

Safari® Books Online

 Safari Books Online is an on-demand digital library that lets you easily search over 7,500 technology and creative reference books and videos to find the answers you need quickly.

With a subscription, you can read any page and watch any video from our library online. Read books on your cell phone and mobile devices. Access new titles before they are available for print, and get exclusive access to manuscripts in development and post feedback for the authors. Copy and paste code samples, organize your favorites, download chapters, bookmark key sections, create notes, print out pages, and benefit from tons of other time-saving features.

O'Reilly Media has uploaded this book to the Safari Books Online service. To have full digital access to this book and others on similar topics from O'Reilly and other publishers, sign up for free at *http://my.safaribooksonline.com/?portal=oreilly*.

1 getting started

WordPress from scratch

You know, I sure enjoy these made from scratch blogs...

You've got something to say.

Whether it's just you and your desire to let everyone know about your growing collection
of hand-crocheted *Star Wars* figures, or a big company with hundreds of products,
blogging let's anyone publish online without having to be a genius about **HTML**, **CSS**,
or any other *programming*. In this chapter, you'll learn how to get **hosting** for your blog,
install WordPress, and **create and publish** your *first* blog post.

Web publishing for the masses

With your own WordPress blog, you can easily—and for free—publish your own writing, pictures, movies, and even software. Before we dive in to getting WordPress installed and set up, let's take a look at an example to see what a real live blog looks like:

This is the Head First blog. It's incorporated into our main website, so it appears as a tab at www.headfirstlabs.com.

The blog displays a series of posts, or articles, in reverse chronological order. That means the most recent post shows up at the top of the page.

Each post has an author (and a link to their profile page), the date it was published, and "tags" that describe what the post is about (more on tags in Chapter 4).

This blog, like many others out there, has two columns. One bigger one for the content, and a smaller column, or a sidebar, that has a search box, links, and related content.

Over time, the posts start to accumulate. On the main page, only short snippets of each post is shown, and people have to click through to see the full post entries.

Further down the page, you can see monthly archives, which allow readers to find content organized by the month it was published.

Head First Labs

O'REILLY   Brain-Friendly Guides from O'Reilly Media, Inc.

Home   Books   Forums   Blog   About   write for us

ARCHIVES

The three phases of Government 2.0
By Mark Drapeau
May 10, 2010 | Comments: 4

As the program co-chair for the upcoming **Gov 2.0 Expo**, I've had a lot of time to learn about what's happening at the edges of the space. And through my experience working on the topic with the Department of Defense, and now through a different lens at Microsoft's public sector division, I've had a lot of time to think about where it's been, and where it is now. I've seen three phases in what most people would agree is "Government 2.0" -- a phase of surprise, a phase of experimentation, and a phase of solutions.

Tags: gov 2.0, gov 20, open government

Building Web sites optimized for the iPhone and Android OS 2
By Matthew David
May 10, 2010 | Comments: 7

Apple's iPhone 3.0 OS and Google's Android run recent branches of the Open Source WebKit browser. To this end, they are able to support technologies that are only just making it to desktop browsers. In this article you can learn how you can build Web sites that target iPhone and Android Web browsers.

Tags: android, iPhone, mobile

Gov 2.0 Week in Review
By Alex Howard
May 7, 2010 | Comments: 6

Topics in this week Gov 2.0 Week in Review include: Open 311, OGI, open government, open source, revisiting net neutrality and disaster response 2.0. If you have news and tips about the government 2.0 space, please let me know at

Search

Search Tips

Subscribe to our RSS feed

Follow us on Twitter

Visit our Facebook Page

Looking for source files, code, exercise answers, and other materials to go along with your Head First book? Go to this page, find your book on the list, and click on the title.

Get The Latest Head First Tweets!

RT @courtneynash Need tech reviewer 4 Head First iPhone & iPad Dev. Reqs: Previous OO dev exp, minimal or no Objective-C exp. #headfirst 5 days ago

RT @OReillyMedia: We just released Head First C#, 2nd Edition. You can read all about it here http://oreil.ly/bAyP8M 14 days ago

Medina, who recently retired from the CIA and will speak at next month's Gov 2.0 Expo, openness is just what the agency needs.

Tags: cia, gov2.0, gov20

State of the Internet Operating System Part Two: Handicapping the Internet Platform Wars
By Tim O'Reilly
April 30, 2010 | Comments: 44

As I wrote **last month**, it is becoming increasingly clear that the internet is becoming not just a platform, but an operating system, an operating system that manages access by devices such as personal computers, phones, and other personal electronics to cloud subsystems ranging from computation, storage, and communications to location, identity, social graph, search, and payment. The question is whether a single company will put together a single, vertically-integrated platform that is sufficiently compelling to developers to enable the kind of lock-in we saw during the personal computer era, or whether, Internet-style, we will instead see services from multiple providers horizontally integrated via open standards.

Tags: internet operating system, web 2.0, web2.0

Understanding the Cloud Landscape
By George Reese
April 29, 2010 | Comments: 11

Making sense out of all of the components of cloud computing confuses even many of the major analysts. It's easy to understand how Google, Amazon, or

Monthly Archives

January 2010 (1)
August 2009 (1)
July 2009 (1)
June 2009 (1)
March 2009 (2)
February 2009 (1)
January 2009 (6)
December 2008 (5)
November 2008 (3)
October 2008 (7)
September 2008 (5)
August 2008 (3)
July 2008 (7)
June 2008 (5)
May 2008 (7)
April 2008 (5)
March 2008 (7)
February 2008 (11)
January 2008 (27)
December 2007 (20)
November 2007 (22)
October 2007 (26)
September 2007 (4)

How WordPress works: the 30,000-foot view

WordPress is all about the browser. You don't need to install anything on your own actual computer—you do everything on another computer (called a web server, more on that in a minute) that you access over the Internet using your browser. You create your posts and manage all your WordPress files and settings through a browser, and on the other end, WordPress creates your blog as a collection of web pages that other people can view in their browsers, too.

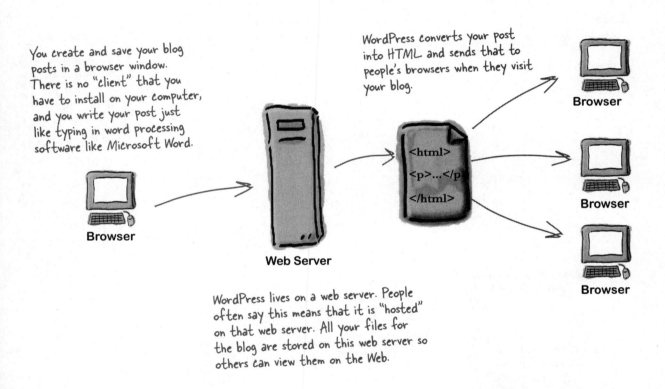

You create and save your blog posts in a browser window. There is no "client" that you have to install on your computer, and you write your post just like typing in word processing software like Microsoft Word.

Browser

Web Server

WordPress lives on a web server. People often say this means that it is "hosted" on that web server. All your files for the blog are stored on this web server so others can view them on the Web.

WordPress converts your post into HTML and sends that to people's browsers when they visit your blog.

Browser

Browser

Browser

Let's take a closer look at how this all works...

The lifecycle of a WordPress blog post

So we said that WordPress is installed on a web server. A web server is simply another computer somewhere that you can access over the Internet. At its most simplest, a web server delivers web pages to other computers over the Internet. But most servers also allow you to store/upload files, run programming scripts, and even allow other people (your site visitors) to contribute content as well (such as comments on your blog).

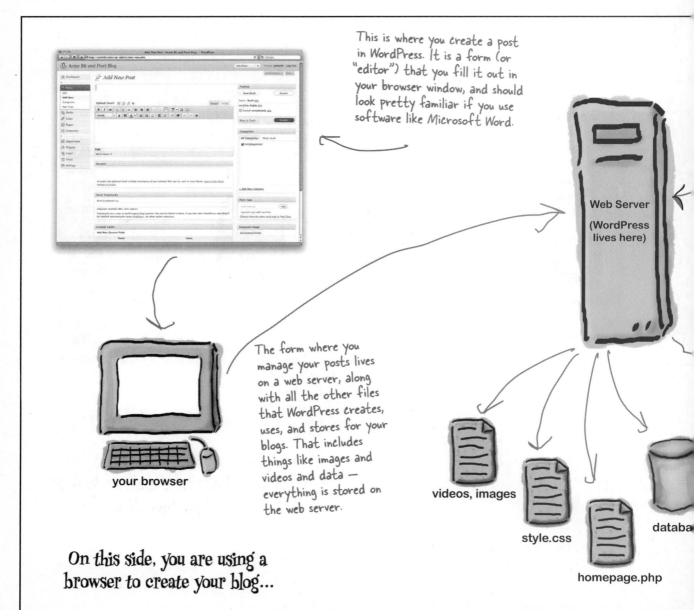

This is where you create a post in WordPress. It is a form (or "editor") that you fill it out in your browser window, and should look pretty familiar if you use software like Microsoft Word.

Web Server

(WordPress lives here)

your browser

The form where you manage your posts lives on a web server, along with all the other files that WordPress creates, uses, and stores for your blogs. That includes things like images and videos and data — everything is stored on the web server.

videos, images

style.css

homepage.php

databa

On this side, you are using a browser to create your blog...

... and over here, someone is typing your blog's URL into a browser.

When someone types in the URL of your blog, their browser sends a "request" to WordPress (on the web server).

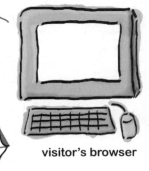

visitor's browser

On the web server, WordPress pulls the corresponding content, images, and data for that URL and sends the blog post (which is a web page) to the visitor's browser.

www.headfirstlabs.com/archive.php

These two parts—creating the blog and someone viewing the blog—happen *asynchronously*. That is, they don't necessarily happen at the same time. You create and publish your blog, and someone might come read it minutes, hours, or days later. In the middle of it all is the web server, which acts both as host for your blog's files, and as the mechanism that serves it all up to anyone who wants to read your blog.

Now let's see it in action...

The Acme Bit and Pixel Company

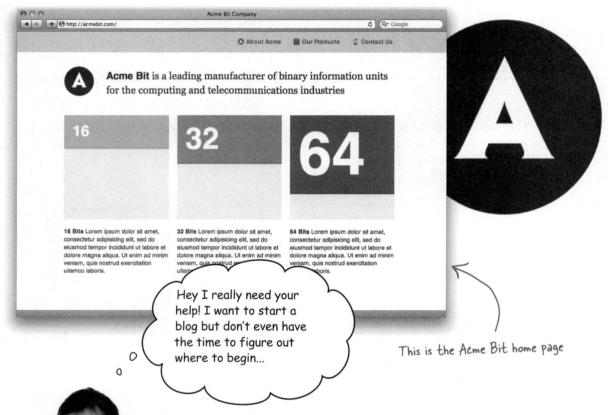

This is the Acme Bit home page

Acme Bit needs a blog, stat!

Acme Bit and Pixel has a basic website, but your friend Jay—the VP of Engineering—is also a big mover and shaker in the industry. He wants a way to share his neverending stream of ideas, and maybe even publish videos of his conference keynotes and lectures. He really wants a blog, but he's too swamped coming up with new Bits to do it himself. He's offered to pay you, so do you think you could help him out?

Before Jay can start blogging, we need to get WordPress set up.

Download WordPress

WordPress is free, open source software, meaning the code that runs it is freely available for anyone to download, install, and modify—it's one of the reasosns WordPress is so powerful. There are no paid licenses, fees, or "boxed copies" of the software. To get WordPress, you simply download it from their website, install it, and run it on a web server. (Don't worry, we'll explain the web server part in a minute.)

1 Point your browser at:
http://wordpress.org/download

2 Click the main download button. The WordPress ZIP file should download to your computer.

3 Find the downloaded ZIP file and double click it to unpack the contents. WordPress is now ready to be configured and uploaded to your hosting server.

A ZIP file is just a folder full of files that's been squashed down (compressed) into a single file. This makes the overall size decrease and makes the software easier and faster to download.

Relax

Don't worry about hosting or servers

We will cover all that a little later and help you get going with WordPress's 5-minute install. If you have web hosting already, great! Just hang tight and we'll help you set it up in just a minute.

The "famous" 5-minute WordPress Install®

There are two ways in install WordPress: The first is manually, by setting up a database, uploading the files and running through the install process step-by-step. Your other option is to use a "One-click Install" offered at many of the prefered hosting companies recommended by WordPress. These are automated processes that do all the necessary steps for you and email you when your blog is ready for use. They're quick, easy and alomst never fail. The problem is, you're not really learning what's going on under the hood—and the engine that runs WordPress is important. So, if you're in a hurry, go ahead and do the One Click Install. But we encourage you to stick around and install WordPress from scratch—at least once—so you can learn about all the cool stuff that make WordPress possible.

This is the "One Click" WordPress install from MediaTemple—
one of the hosting companies recommended by WordPress.

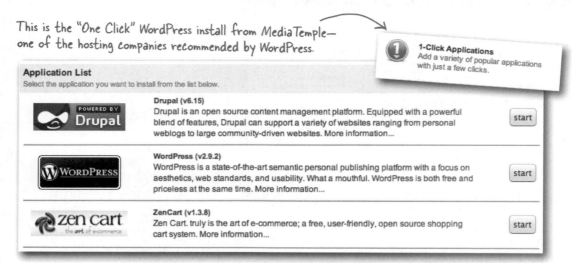

1-Click Applications
Add a variety of popular applications with just a few clicks.

Application List
Select the application you want to install from the list below.

POWERED BY Drupal

Drupal (v6.15)
Drupal is an open source content management platform. Equipped with a powerful blend of features, Drupal can support a variety of websites ranging from personal weblogs to large community-driven websites. More information...

start

WORDPRESS

WordPress (v2.9.2)
WordPress is a state-of-the-art semantic personal publishing platform with a focus on aesthetics, web standards, and usability. What a mouthful. WordPress is both free and priceless at the same time. More information...

start

zen cart the art of e-commerce

ZenCart (v1.3.8)
Zen Cart. truly is the art of e-commerce; a free, user-friendly, open source shopping cart system. More information...

start

To install WordPress from scratch, start with the readme.html

This file is located in the unzipped folder you downloaded earlier.

Check it out. We've already completed the first step. You did download WordPress, right?

5-min Install Steps
1. Unpack WordPress files
2. Complete config.php
3. Upload files to server
4. Choose a title for your blog and enter a valid email address
5. Install

Installation: Famous 5-minute install

1. Unzip the package in an empty directory.
2. Open up wp-config-sample.php with a text editor like WordPad or similar and fill in your database connection details.
3. Save the file as wp-config.php.
4. Upload everything.
5. Open /wp-admin/install.php in your browser. This should setup the tables needed for your blog. If there is an error, double check your wp-config.php file, and try again. If it fails again, please go to the support forums with as much data as you can gather.
6. Note the password given to you.
7. The install script should then send you to the login page. Sign in with the username admin and the password generated during the installation. You can then click on 'Profile' to change the password.

> Wait! I still don't get WHAT we are installing WordPress on. I thought you said I don't have to download anything on my computer—and what is this web server you keep talking about?

Use a web hosting company for your web server

Don't worry, this isn't as scary as it sounds. You just downloaded WordPress so you'll have all the files that you need to put up on your web server. There are thousands of companies out there that offer hosting on a web server, and you can get space on a server for less than a few trips to Starbuzz Coffee each month. We're going to use MediaTemple because they are one of the recommended hosting providers for WordPress. You can use any host you want, just make sure that they support WordPress. You should be able to find an FAQ or section on their website that lists support for blogging and content management systems.

In this book we will use the Media Temple Grid Service (http://mediatemple.net/webhosting/gs/) for all hosting, server and database examples. However, any hosting that supports WordPress will work just fine.

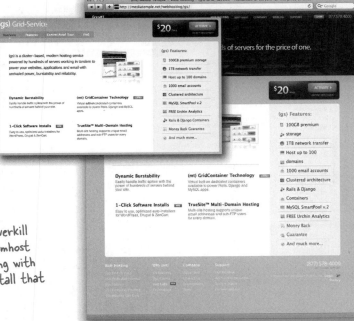

If Media Temple is overkill for your needs, Dreamhost offers cheaper hosting with the same 1-Click Install that Media Temple has.

Upload your WordPress files to the web server

Now that we have hosting we can move on with this installation. Before we can go any further, you need to get the files you downloaded earlier up onto your hosted web server. They're only on your computer right now so you can move them to the web server.

We're going to skip step 2 for now and come back to it once we have our files on the server.

5—min Install Steps
1. Unpack WordPress files
2. Complete config.php
3. Upload files to server
4. Choose a title for your blog and enter a valid email address
5. Install

Start with an FTP client

FTP stands for File Transfer Protocol and it's the easiest way to get files to a remote server—like a web server. Once you log in to the server through the FTP client, you can move files between your local computer and the web server, as if it were just another folder on your computer.

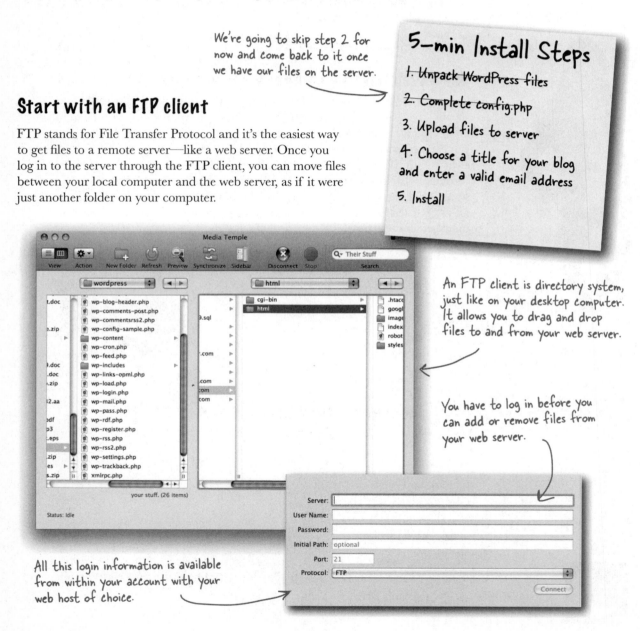

An FTP client is directory system, just like on your desktop computer. It allows you to drag and drop files to and from your web server.

You have to log in before you can add or remove files from your web server.

All this login information is available from within your account with your web host of choice.

FTP client options

There are plenty of free and paid FTP clients out there to choose from.
Here are a few recommendations for both Windows and the Mac.

Transmit (Mac)

http://panic.com/transmit

Smart FTP (Windows)

Free!

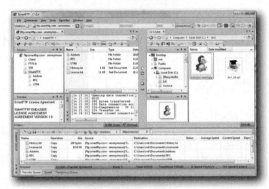

http://www.smartftp.com

Cyberduck

← Free!

http://cyberduck.ch

Cute FTP

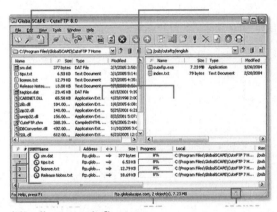

http://www.cuteftp.com

Exercise

Let's take one for a spin. Download and open up one of the above FTP clients, log in to your web server using the credentials supplied by your web host and upload all the files that you downloaded from Wordpress.org. **Hint**: make sure you upload the files to the "public" area on your server (you can find this from your host).

Exercise Solution

Download and open one of the above FTP clients, log in to your web server using the credentials supplied by your web host, and upload all the files that you downloaded from Wordpress.org.

①   **Drag and drop your WordPress files to the server.**
Depending on the FTP client you are using you should be able to drag all the files in the downloaded WordPress folder up to the public directory on your web server (this may vary depending on the host).

On Media Temple the html folder located inside our domain is where we want to drop our files.

Usually, in a split-view FTP client the left side is your local computer and the right side is your web server.

You can drag your files from the desktop or another location on your hard drive directly into the FTP client. This will copy the files to the web server.

WordPress installation step 2: Configuration

You should now be able to browse to your domain (*www.yourblog.com*) and see the screen below. This is the first step in getting a working blog up and running.

Don't worry if you don't have a domain name yet. You can use the temporary URL or IP address that your web host assigned to your site.

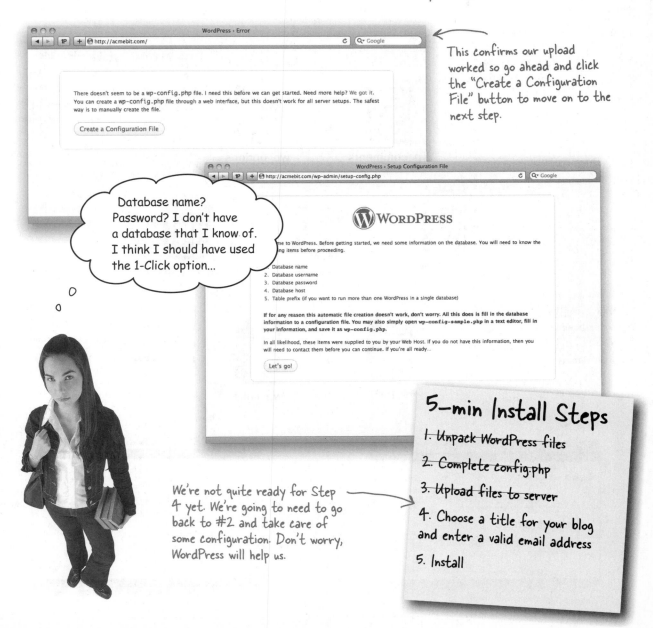

This confirms our upload worked so go ahead and click the "Create a Configuration File" button to move on to the next step.

Database name? Password? I don't have a database that I know of. I think I should have used the 1-Click option...

5-min Install Steps

1. Unpack WordPress files
2. Complete config.php
3. Upload files to server
4. Choose a title for your blog and enter a valid email address
5. Install

We're not quite ready for Step 4 yet. We're going to need to go back to #2 and take care of some configuration. Don't worry, WordPress will help us.

WordPress stores all your stuff in a database

Every time we add content to WordPress, whether it's a new post, page, theme, or comment, we are creating data that has to be stored somewhere. We can't store this on our local computer because it has to be available to the Internet and WordPress 24/7. So, WordPress uses database software called MySQL, a free, open source (just like WordPress) database that is very popular among web-based applications. Because of its popularity, MySQL is already installed on almost every web host so you shouldn't have to worry about it not being available.

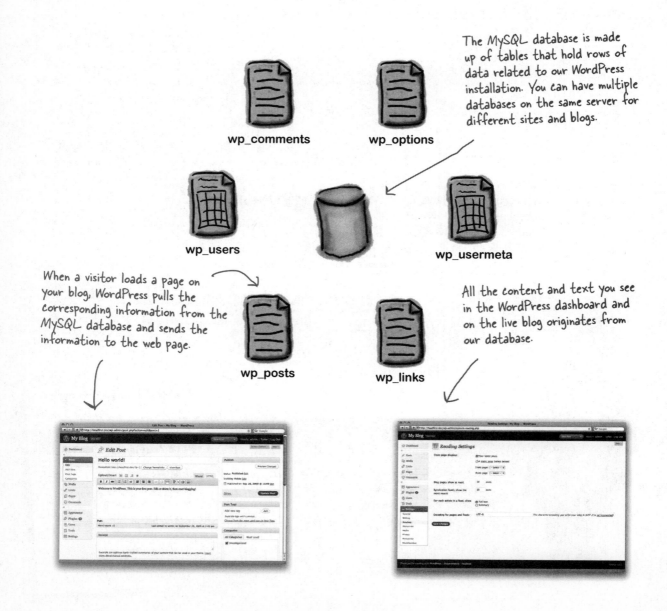

The MySQL database is made up of tables that hold rows of data related to our WordPress installation. You can have multiple databases on the same server for different sites and blogs.

wp_comments

wp_options

wp_users

wp_usermeta

When a visitor loads a page on your blog, WordPress pulls the corresponding information from the MySQL database and sends the information to the web page.

All the content and text you see in the WordPress dashboard and on the live blog originates from our database.

wp_posts

wp_links

Create a new database from your hosting panel

Don't be intimidated by MySQL. For the most part you'll have limited interaction with it and the installation process is the only time you need to mess with settings. To start, we need to log into our hosting panel and get the database set up. On Media Temple, that looks like this:

Media Temple Control Panel

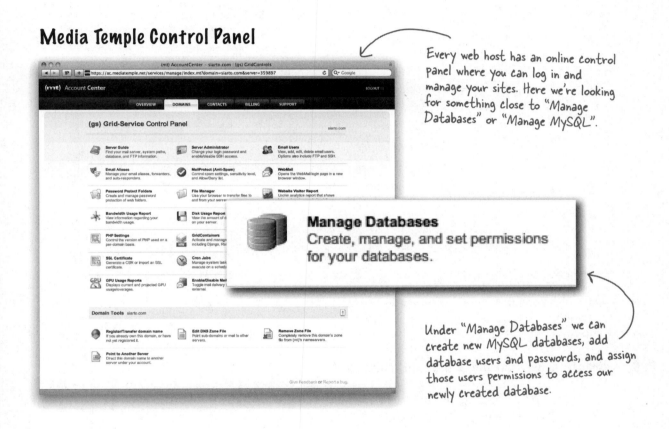

Every web host has an online control panel where you can log in and manage your sites. Here we're looking for something close to "Manage Databases" or "Manage MySQL".

Under "Manage Databases" we can create new MySQL databases, add database users and passwords, and assign those users permissions to access our newly created database.

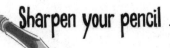 **Sharpen your pencil**

Log into your hosting panel (in our case, Media Temple) and locate the MySQL or Database options. Within that menu, add a new database called *acme*. You will also need to create a database user and grant them full access to the *acme* database.

Sharpen your pencil
Solution

Log into your hosting panel (in our case, Media Temple) and locate the MySQL or Database options. Within that menu, add a new database called *acme*.

① **Create a new database for WordPress.**

Using the "add new database" functionality, create a new database to hold the Acme WordPress data. In Media Temple, they give us an automatic prefix.

Manage Databases
Create, manage, and set permissions for your databases.

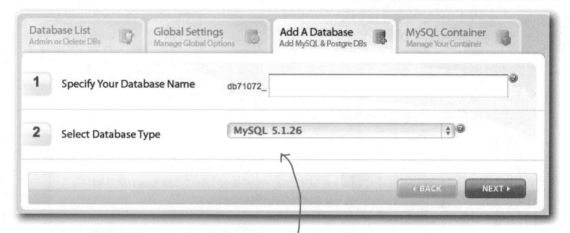

There might be other options for database type—make sure you choose some variation of MySQL.

② **Create a new database user and password.**

We need a username and password to access our database. It's a good idea to create a single user that only has access to a single database. This way we keep all our data secure and avoid confusion with multiple users and passwords.

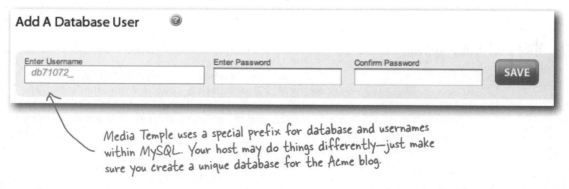

Media Temple uses a special prefix for database and usernames within MySQL. Your host may do things differently—just make sure you create a unique database for the Acme blog.

③ Grant permissions to the new user.

The last thing we have to do is give our new database user the appropriate permission to access the acme database.

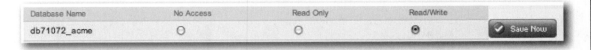

Database Name	No Access	Read Only	Read/Write	
db71072_acme	○	○	◉	✓ Save Now

Clicking on "Admin" will take you to the phpMyAdmin login screen.

④ Take your new database for a spin.

Just to make sure everything is up and running, choose "admin" and enter the username and password you just created. If the login is successful, you should see your database name in the left column.

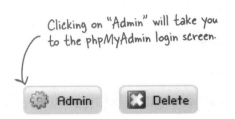

If you click on your database you'll be taken to another detail screen. We don't have tables yet, but after the install this will be full of them.

You shouldn't ever have to come in here to do anything after the install is done. This is more of a "raw" data view—like looking under the hood of WordPress.

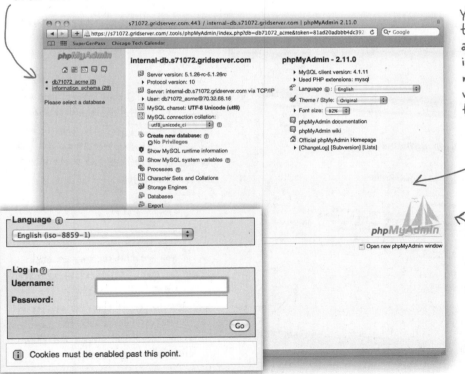

This is called PHPMyAdmin—we use it to see a graphical representation of our MySQL database.

Almost there...

Now that we have our database name, username and password, we're ready to procede with the installation. The next screen has us filling in the database connection information so WordPress can build all the tables it needs.

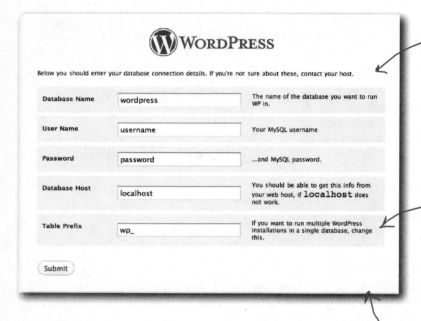

Fill out the fields using the database information we created earlier. Make sure you include any prefixes that your hosting provider appended to users and database names.

You can leave the table prefix at the default "wp_". This is used to prevent table naming collisions if you only have one database to use.

When you click "Submit" WordPress will attempt to create the configuration file (step #2). There is a good chance this won't work and WordPress will just give you text to copy and paste into the configuration file.

If you see this screen—log back in to your FTP client and create a file called config.php in the same folder as the rest of the WordPress files. Paste the text from the install screen and then click "Run the Install."

Every blog needs a title

OK, it's been a little longer than 5 minutes, but we're just about done. The final step is to provide WordPress with a blog title—we're using "Acme Bit Blog" for this project—a username and password for the administrative user (which you'll use to log in to your dashboard), and an email address. Click "Install WordPress" and you should be greeted with a success message. If something went wrong, WordPress will try and help you fix it.

Give your blog a title and choose a username and password for the main account.

Information needed

Please provide the following information. Don't worry, you can always change these settings later.

Blog Title	Acme Bit Blog
User Name	acmeadmin
Password, twice A password will be automatically generated for you if you leave this blank.	●●●●●●●●●●●●●●●
	●●●●●●●●●●●●●●●
	Strong
	Hint: The password should be at least seven characters long. To make it stronger, use upper and lower case letters, numbers and symbols like ! " ? $ % ^ &).
Your E-mail	hello@acmebit.com
	Double-check your email address before continuing.

☑ Allow my blog to appear in search engines like Google and Technorati.

(Install WordPress)

Hint: don't use 'admin' for the username. It's the default and it can leave your site prone to hacking attacks.

Once you click "Install WordPress" you'll be greeted with a success message prompting you to log in with your new username.

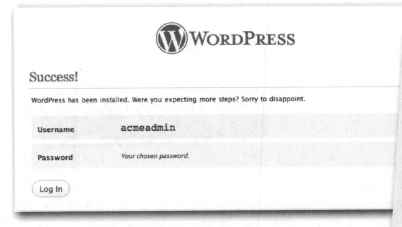

(W) WORDPRESS

Success!

WordPress has been installed. Were you expecting more steps? Sorry to disappoint.

Username	acmeadmin
Password	*Your chosen password.*

(Log In)

5-min Install Steps
1. Unpack WordPress files
2. Complete config.php
3. Upload files to server
4. Choose a title for your blog and enter a valid email address
5. Install

Pilot your blog with the WordPress dashboard

The WordPress dashboard is the starting point for managing your blog and all its content. From here you can add posts, manage users, change options and install plug-ins—all things we'll be doing in the coming chapters. You can even automatically update WordPress when new versions of the software become available. This page will change over time as you add to the site.

Log in to the WordPress admin dashboard with the same username and password you just created.

Clicking the blog title at the top of the dashboard will take you out to your blog home page. Take a look.

WordPress Dashboard Up Close

The main Dashboard navigation takes you back to the home dashboard page and will also alert you when you have software updates.

The top navigation group deals with content on your site. Here you'll find options to create new posts, add links, and upload media.

The bottom navigation group includes links to help you manage your site's configuration. You can add users, change the look and feel, and install plug-ins.

there are no Dumb Questions

Q: What operating system does WordPress run on?

A: WordPress doesn't run on an operating system like you would expect of standard desktop software. Instead it runs on a "platform"—a collection of server and database software. This collection of software usually runs on a Linux operating systems, but Mac and Windows can also be used. It's recommended that you run WordPress in a LAMP (Linux, Apache, MySQL, PHP) environment, a common platform on most webhosts.

Q: Media Temple is expensive. Do you have any other recommendations for hosting providers?

A: If you don't want to make the monthly commitment to Media Temple, there are lots of other options out there. Dreamhost (*http://dreamhost.com*) gives you massive amounts of space and bandwidth at a very inexpensive rate. There are also free options but you may have very little control over your server and software. Just remember to select a host that supports WordPress.

Q: Can't I just run WordPress on my home computer?

A: Actually, you can! We don't recommend you host WordPress on your computer but you can set up a development environment on your local machine so you don't have to set up your site live on the Internet. There's too many steps to list here, but check out the appendix for more info.

Create your first blog post

Your friend Jay has sent over the first post he wants up on the site. Now that the installation is complete we're ready to start adding content to our blog. (soon you'll be able to set Jay up to post on his own, but for now we'll get things started for him).

This text and image can be downloaded from http://www.headfirstlabs.com/WordPress.

Everything you need to write your first post can be found in the Posts menu from the dashboard.

Our Bits are Better

At Acme, all we know are bits. We've been going to great lengths to bring the best talent in the bit industry to our team and that shows in our product. Check out the new features of our 16, 32 and 64-bit models:

• Handmade in Chicago, IL
• Painstakingly built to industry-leading standards
• Available in custom 128 and 256-bit sizes

The copy for the first blog post. We need to get this up ASAP.

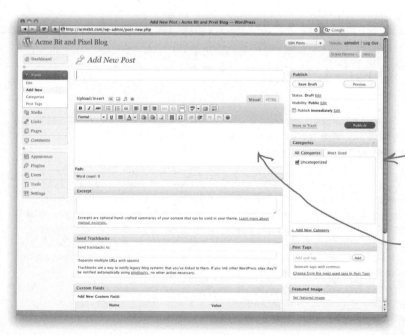

Add a new post from the menu and spend a few minutes playing around with the page. Don't worry about messing anything up, we can always remove this "test" post.

There are two "editors" inside of WordPress: Visual and HTML (or the "Markup" editor). The Visual editor is the default—it's where you create the content for your post, and looks a lot like most word processing software. Take a look at the HTML editor as well—what do you notice are the main differences between the two options?

WHAT'S MY PURPOSE?

Match each new post page element to its function within WordPress.

I allow you to add HTML tags to your pages and posts.

I can help you organize content and information within your site. I'm also a snapshot of the contents of a post.

I'm in the Visual Editor and help you modify the way text looks.

Adding content to me displays alternate text or a teaser on the home page of the blog.

I can help you organize posts into large "buckets" and give you the ability to customize your site based on my content.

WHAT'S MY PURPOSE? SOLUTION

Match each new post page element to its function within WordPress.

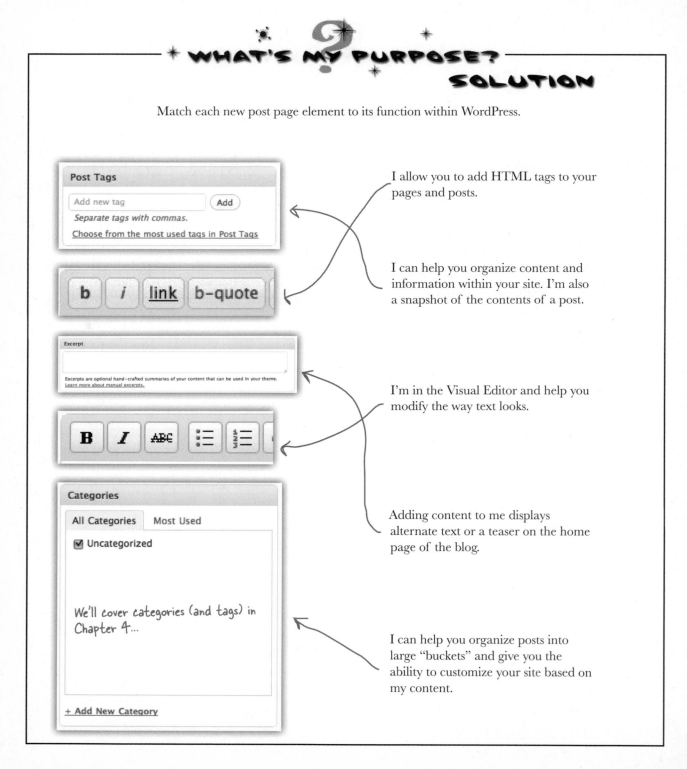

I allow you to add HTML tags to your pages and posts.

I can help you organize content and information within your site. I'm also a snapshot of the contents of a post.

I'm in the Visual Editor and help you modify the way text looks.

Adding content to me displays alternate text or a teaser on the home page of the blog.

I can help you organize posts into large "buckets" and give you the ability to customize your site based on my content.

Use both editors when creating new posts

WordPress has two text editing modes: Visual and Markup. The visual editor will be immediatly familiar to anyone who's used a word processor or services like Google Docs. The markup (or HTML) Editor is different in that it allows you to edit the raw HTML that makes up your post. This comes in handy when you need to do something to your text that's not supported in the visual editor, and it can also be used to add IDs and classes to our HTML tags..

Ed note: "Head First HTML with CSS and xHTML" is a great way to learn all about HTML!

Visual Editor

Wordpress Editors

Permalink: http://acmebit.com/?p=3 (Change Permalinks)

Upload/Insert 🖼 🖼 ♫ ✱   Visual | HTML

| B | *I* | ABC | ☰ | ☷ | ❝ | ☰ | ☰ | ☰ | ☰ | 🔗 | 🎨 ▾ | ▣ | ▦ |

Wordpress Editors

Each editor mode has different pros and cons. Play with both and see which one you like best.

Path: p » span

Word count: 20   Draft saved at 4:03:13 am.

- Also known as a "WYSIWYG" editor (What You See Is What You Get)—it mimics the behavior of an advanced text editor or word processor.

- In this mode you can highlight text, apply styles and see the results immediately—as they'd look on the live site.

Markup Editor

Wordpress Editors

Permalink: http://acmebit.com/?p=3 (Change Permalinks)

Upload/Insert 🖼 🖼 ♫ ✱   Visual | HTML

| b | *i* | link | b-quote | del | ins | img | ul | ol | li | code | more | lookup | close tags |

`<strong>Wordpress Editors</strong>`

`<span style="color: #000000;">Each editor mode has different pros and cons. Play with both and see which one you like best.</span>`

Word count: 20   Draft saved at 4:03:13 am.

- The markup editor gives you more control over what the final HTML of your post will look like. You'll notice paragraphs and some words are surrounded by tags in <> brackets.

- You can highlight and apply styles (just like the visual editor) but the result is a new HTML tag, not the visual style itself. You'll have to click back to the Visual Editor or Preview the post to see the results.

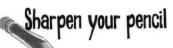

Sharpen your pencil

Add the post content that Jay sent over and give the bulleted list a class of "features."

Hint: Classes are special HTML attributes that help us identify elements in CSS and Javascript. They can also add semantic meaning to container and parent elements like <div> and <span>. Check out *http://w3schools.com/html* for more help.

Sharpen your pencil Solution

Add the post content that Jay sent over and give the bulleted list a class of "features."

Most of the text entry for this post is pretty straightforward. We can create a new list by highlighting the last 3 paragraphs and clicking the bulleted list button.

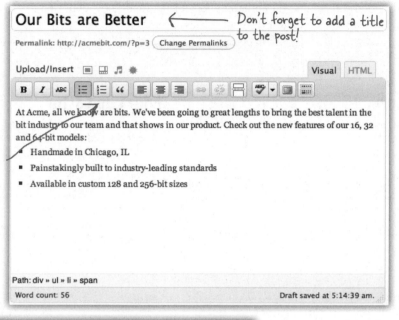

Don't forget to add a title to the post!

Our Bits are Better

Permalink: http://acmebit.com/?p=3 (Change Permalinks)

Upload/Insert

Visual | HTML

At Acme, all we know are bits. We've been going to great lengths to bring the best talent in the bit industry to our team and that shows in our product. Check out the new features of our 16, 32 and 64-bit models:

- Handmade in Chicago, IL
- Painstakingly built to industry-leading standards
- Available in custom 128 and 256-bit sizes

Path: div » ul » li » span

Word count: 56   Draft saved at 5:14:39 am.

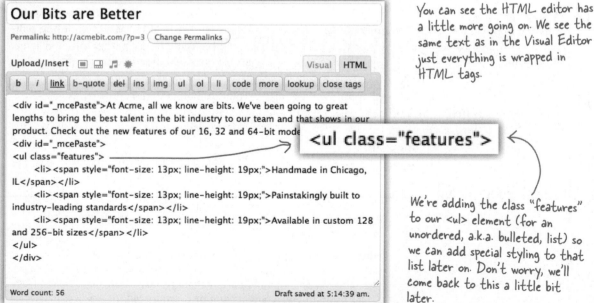

Our Bits are Better

Permalink: http://acmebit.com/?p=3 (Change Permalinks)

Upload/Insert

Visual | **HTML**

b | i | link | b-quote | del | ins | img | ul | ol | li | code | more | lookup | close tags

```
<div id="_mcePaste">At Acme, all we know are bits. We've been going to great
lengths to bring the best talent in the bit industry to our team and that shows in our
product. Check out the new features of our 16, 32 and 64-bit mode
<div id="_mcePaste">
<ul class="features">
     <li><span style="font-size: 13px; line-height: 19px;">Handmade in Chicago,
IL</span></li>
     <li><span style="font-size: 13px; line-height: 19px;">Painstakingly built to
industry-leading standards</span></li>
     <li><span style="font-size: 13px; line-height: 19px;">Available in custom 128
and 256-bit sizes</span></li>
</ul>
</div>
```

Word count: 56   Draft saved at 5:14:39 am.

You can see the HTML editor has a little more going on. We see the same text as in the Visual Editor just everything is wrapped in HTML tags.

<ul class="features">

We're adding the class "features" to our <ul> element (for an unordered, a.k.a. bulleted, list) so we can add special styling to that list later on. Don't worry, we'll come back to this a little bit later.

Use Preview to check your post before you publish

You don't have to commit to publishing your first post just yet. WordPress allows us to save and preview posts before we publish. The "Preview" button opens a new window with a special web address (or URL) that shows the content of your post as it would look on the live blog.

The Publish pane allows you to preview, schedule, and publish posts.

Publish

Save Draft	Preview

Status: **Draft** Edit

Visibility: **Public** Edit

📅 Publish **immediately** Edit

Move to Trash · Publish

The "preview=true" tells WordPress to show this post in preview mode. This content won't become publicly available until you publish from within the WordPress dashboard.

When you're ready, click Publish and check out your first post. Don't worry if something looks wrong, you can always "un-publish" your post and remove it from the blog.

http://acmebit.com/?p=3&preview=true

http://acmebit.com/?p=3&preview=true

Acme Bit Blog

Just another WordPress site

About

← Hello world!

Our Bits are Better

Posted by acmeadmin on April 7, 2010 | Edit

At Acme, all we know are bits. We've been going to great lengths to bring the best talent in the bit industry to our team and that shows in our product. Check out the new features of our 16, 32 and 64-bit models:

- Handmade in Chicago, IL.
- Painstakingly built to industry-leading standards
- Available in custom 128 and 256-bit sizes

This entry was posted in Uncategorized. Bookmark the permalink. Follow any comments here with the RSS feed for this post. Edit

Search

Search

Recent Posts
- Hello world!

Recent Comments
- Mr WordPress on Hello world!

Archives
- April 2010

Categories
- Uncategorized

Meta
- Site Admin
- Log out

Your first post is now live!

That was pretty easy! But hmmm, there is another post we didn't even create on the Acme Bit blog. Where did that come from?

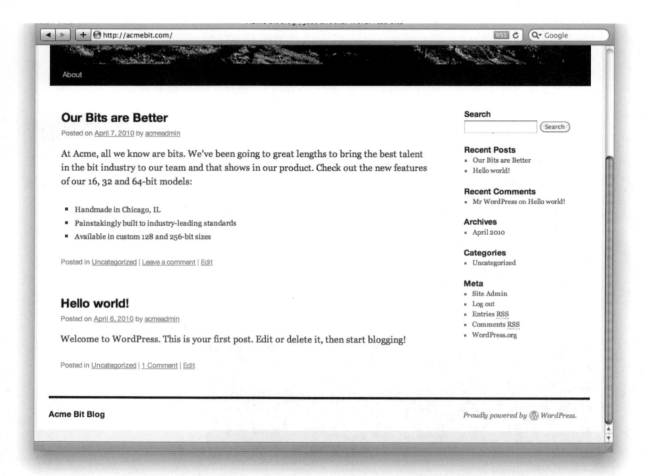

Remove or replace sample posts before you go live

By default, WordPress comes with a sample post and a sample comment to show you how things will show up on your blog. We want to remove these before the site goes live so we don't have placeholder content on display to the world.

Here's the post title, and name of the person who wrote it.

WordPress automatically associates your post with the date you published it.

We'll cover categories, permalinks, and RSS in the coming chapters...

WordPress handles comments for you—unless you disable them, anyone can comment on any of your posts.

Let's remove this sample post now, so only our Acme Bit posts show up on the blog:

1 **Remove a comment from the dashboard.**
You can moderate and delete comments right from the dashboard. Find the "Recent Comments" section and click Trash to remove the sample comment.

2 **Use the Post menu to edit and remove unwanted posts.**
From the list of posts (Posts > Edit) you can select and remove any post you want—just like a comment on the dashboard.

Comments are a staple of just about any blog. We're not going to cover them in too much detail here, but you can learn a bit more about managing them in the appendix.

If you remove a post from the blog, WordPress automatically deletes all the comments associated with that post.

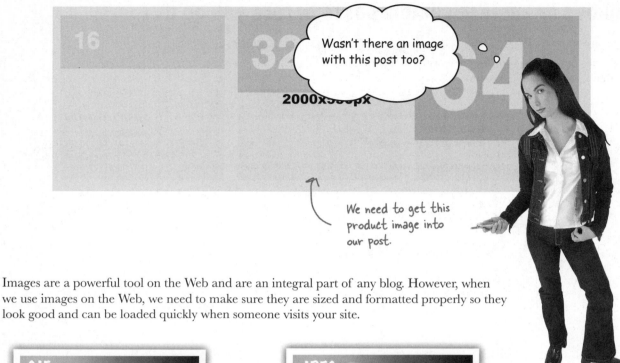

We need to get this product image into our post.

Images are a powerful tool on the Web and are an integral part of any blog. However, when we use images on the Web, we need to make sure they are sized and formatted properly so they look good and can be loaded quickly when someone visits your site.

GIF and PNG8 are smaller file formats perfect for icons and non-photographic images. They also have a limited color palette (256 colors).

JPEG and PNG24 reproduce photographic images much better than GIF but with slightly larger file sizes. That means they'll take longer to load.

PNG-24 allows you to do transparent backgrounds (not available in JPEG) but this is not supported by Internet Explorer 6 (which a lot of people still use).

You don't need Photoshop to edit an image

Although Photoshop is by far the most popular image editing program—it's not the cheapest and it can be overkill if all you need to do is resize and prepare images for the Web. Here are some free alternatives for simple image editing.

GIMP

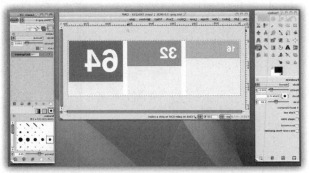

GIMP is a free image editor that runs on multiple operating systems and is the open source alternative to Photoshop. **http://www.gimp.org/**

Picnik

Picnik is an online image editor that runs completely in the browser. It only does the basics but sometimes that's all you need. **http://picnik.com**

Paint.NET

Paint.NET is a good Photoshop alternative if you're running Windows. **http://www.getpaint.net**

Exercise

The image that Jay gave you is too big to fit into the post properly. Download bits.png from *www.headfirstlab.com/WordPress*, and then use Picnik to resize the image and export it as a high-quality PNG-24.

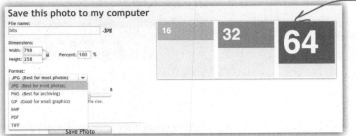

Go to http://picnik.com and upload the image to their site. Just like with WordPress, all the editing is done in your favorite web browser.

Exercise Solution

The image that Jay gave you is too big to fit into the post properly. Download the image from *www.headfirstlab.com/WordPress*, and then use Picnik to resize the image and export it as a high-quality PNG-24.

1

Upload bits.png to Picnik.

Once you've grabbed it off the Head First Labs site for this book, upload bits.png to Picnik so you can resize and save for use on your blog. You don't have to create an account to use Picnik—just upload, edit, and save.

2

Click on Save and Share to export photo.

Since all we need is basic editing we can skip right to the "Save and Share" section and adjust the pixel width to something 500 pixels or less. After that, save as a PNG and you're good to go.

That's the max size your header image can be. We'll learn more about this when we start customizing our site's look and feel.

3

Save to your computer.

Once the export is done, you'll be prompted to select a download location on your local computer. Save it somewhere on your machine and you're ready to use it in WordPress.

Add an image using the media library

There are two different ways to get your images into WordPress, and both ways end up putting your images in the same place. You can add an image to the media gallery from within a post, or you can add new images outside the post in the Media Library editor and then select them when you are creating a post.

You can always add images and other media from within a post.

In-post upload

You can upload images to a post directly from either editor when creating a post. A dialog box will pop up and prompt you to select a file to upload.

Media Library

If you want to upload media for use in a post later on, select "Media" then "Add New" from the Dashboard navigation. Images can then be chosen from the library and added to a new post.

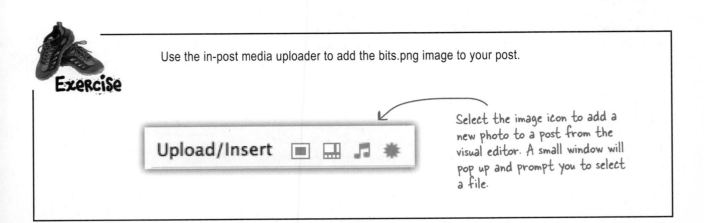

Use the in-post media uploader to add the bits.png image to your post.

Exercise

Upload/Insert

Select the image icon to add a new photo to a post from the visual editor. A small window will pop up and prompt you to select a file.

Uh-oh...

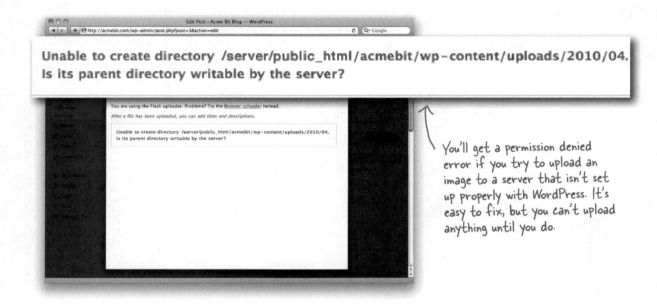

Unable to create directory /server/public_html/acmebit/wp-content/uploads/2010/04. Is its parent directory writable by the server?

You'll get a permission denied error if you try to upload an image to a server that isn't set up properly with WordPress. It's easy to fix, but you can't upload anything until you do.

Prepare to upload

Depending on your web host and their support for WordPress, you may be greeted with a permissions-related error when you try to upload an image or other media file to a post. This happens when the code that runs WordPress does not have permission to create or write to folders on your server. This is pretty easy to fix, but first a little background on what's going on under the hood.

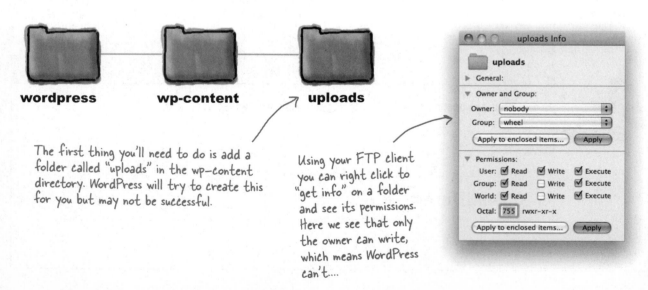

The first thing you'll need to do is add a folder called "uploads" in the wp-content directory. WordPress will try to create this for you but may not be successful.

Using your FTP client you can right click to "get info" on a folder and see its permissions. Here we see that only the owner can write, which means WordPress can't....

Update group permissions to get image uploads working

① **Launch your FTP client.**
You'll need some way to access folders on your server—log in to your FTP server and navigate to the main WordPress directory.

② **Right click and "Get Info".**
Create the folder "uploads" within the wp-content directory then right click and select "Get Info." A dialog box similar to the one on the right should appear.

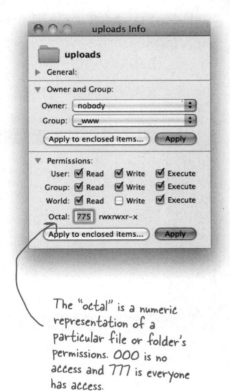

③ **Update group user permissions.**
There are two options you need to change: 1. Change the group user to whatever the web server runs as (usually www, apache, or nobody) and 2. Give the group "write" permissions. You should end up with the numbers 775 in the "octal" window.

You may need to consult your web host to figure out what user the web server runs as. Any host that supports WordPress should support file uploads.

The "octal" is a numeric representation of a particular file or folder's permissions. 000 is no access and 777 is everyone has access.

Watch it!

Beware of 777 or "all access" permissions

You might be tempted to just set your permissions to 777 in lieu of setting a new group user and permission setting. This is a bad habbit to get in to, because 777 permissions on a shared server can leave your files open to malicious users. Be carefull!

> Permissions:
> User: ☑ Read ☑ Write ☑ Execute
> Group: ☑ Read ☑ Write ☑ Execute
> World: ☑ Read ☑ Write ☑ Execute
> Octal: 777 rwxrwxrwx

Let's try uploading that image again now...

The image that Jay gave you is too big to fit into the post properly. Download bits.png from *www. headfirstlab.com/WordPress*, and then use Picnik to resize the image and export it as a high-quality PNG-24.

1 **Re-upload your bits.png image.**
Once your directory permissions have been fixed, you should be able to upload media within WordPress. A thumbnail will appear on the left and should be a cropped or smaller version of the file from your desktop.

If the upload is successful, you should see a new dialog box with your image in it and some options to add content and adjust the dimensions of the image.

2 **Set the image size.**
WordPress will try to slightly scale down your image by default. Since we've already prepped our image for the Web, select the "full size" radio button so we get our full 500 pixel width image. Finally, click "Insert into Post" to add the image to the post.

All WordPress does is just display an image at a smaller size—it doesn't actually resize the pixels like Photoshop or Picnik would.

③ Preview in the visual editor.
After you add the image it should appear in the visual editor as an image and in the HTML editor as an <img> tag.

Once the image is in your post you can manipulate just like any other post element.

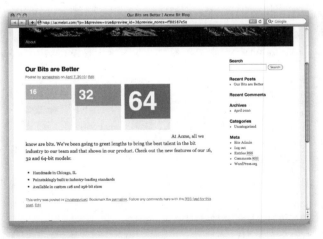

④ Preview in the browser.
Before you publish, make sure you test it in your favorite browser.

If we leave the placement that WordPress gives us, our image pushes the post text to the right...

Hrm. The image is making the text below it display weird.

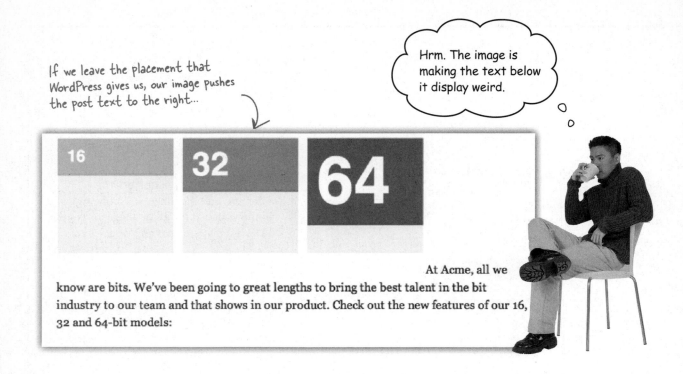

At Acme, all we know are bits. We've been going to great lengths to bring the best talent in the bit industry to our team and that shows in our product. Check out the new features of our 16, 32 and 64-bit models:

Adjusting images within the post editor

Don't worry, you're not stuck with the layout that WordPress gives you when you first upload your media to the post. You can click the image itself to bring back the image editing options and you can also switch to the markup view and make direct changes to the image tag.

Edit your post to move the text down a line

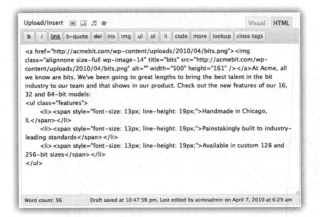

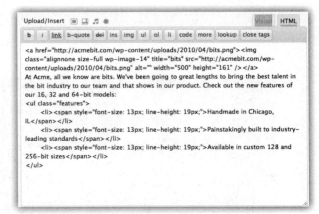

In the HTML Editor you'll notice that the image tag is in the same paragraph as the main post content. This is what's causing the image not to be placed properly when viewed in the browser.

All we need to do is put a "hard" return after the image tag which will create a new paragraph for the main content. Hit enter just after the </a> tag to move the content to the next line. This will make the text and image wrap properly on the page.

You can also add a "hard" return in the Visual Editor. It simply adds a return like you just did above in the HTML editor.

Our post should be nicely formatted now.

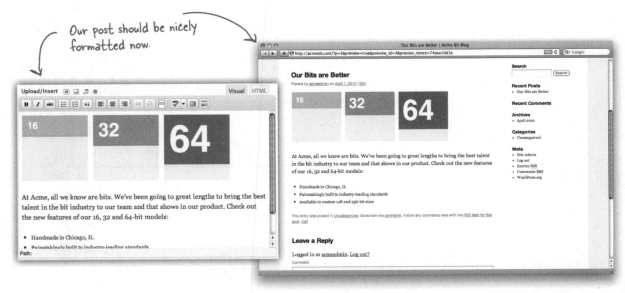

Welcome to the Bit Blog

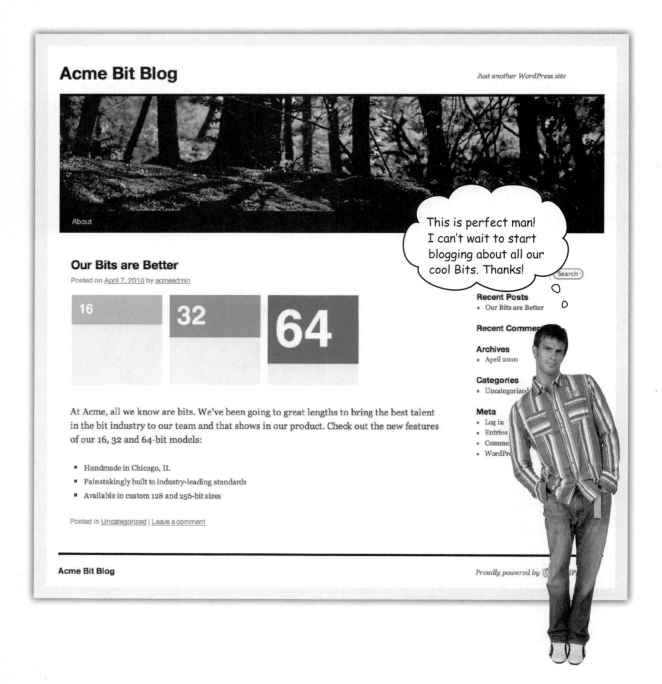

Your WordPress Toolbox

You've got Chapter 1 under your belt and now you've added a basic blog and your first post to your toolbox. Next up, making your blog looks more like, well, *your* blog.

BULLET POINTS

- WordPress must be installed and hosted on a web server. You can find of list of preferred hosting companies at *http://wordpress.org/hosting/*.

- Use an FTP client to upload WordPress to your web server.

- WordPress uses a MySQL database to store all the post, page and comment data for your site.

- WordPress has two editor states, one for editing HTML and the other for editing content like in a word processor.

- Use JPEG and PNG24 for images and and GIF and PNG8 for icons and other visual elements that display properly with a limited color palette.

- Depending on your server you may have to adjust upload folder permissions so that WordPress can save your images on the server.

- Never leave directories with open permissions (777). This allows any user on the system full read and write access to anything in that folder. Yikes!

- Preview your posts before you publish to make sure the text formattng and images look correct.

2 changing your blog's look and feel

A question of style

How can I stand out in this crowd?

You've finally got your own blog. But it looks so…generic.

Time to make it your own. WordPress comes preloaded with lots of **themes** you can apply to your blog, but we're going to go one step further and make our own *custom* theme. Along the way, you'll learn some basic **HTML** and **CSS** to really make your blog look exactly how you want. We'll also delve into CSS **rules**, which allow you to *quickly* change how your blog looks, and take advantage of WordPress **widgets** to easily add sidebar content to the blog.

A tale of two sites

Now that you've got the Acme Bit blog up and running, Jay is hoping to make it look more like the company's regular website...

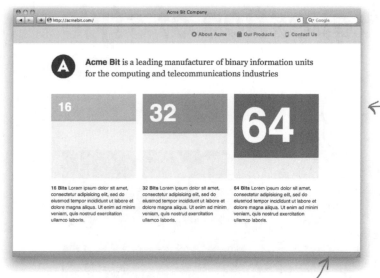

The current Acme Bit website is built with HTML and CSS. We should be able to use some of that work to get our blog looking more like it, because WordPress uses HTML and CSS to create its pages too...

We need to make our blog (below) look like the current company home page.

Nice work on the blog! But it's kinda confusing that it doesn't look like our main site...

The default WordPress blog design isn't too far off from the Acme site's design: it has a large horizontal banner up top, and text down below.

The Acme Bit Company home page

The Acme Bit Company website is a really simple site with only three pages that cover the basic information about their main product: Bits. Even though the site isn't a blog, it's based on the same stuff as our WordPress blog: HTML and CSS. We can definitely use that to our advantage. Let's start by visually comparing the main site with the blog, to see what they have in common, and what is different across the two sites.

Check out http://acmebit.com

 **BRAIN POWER**

Study the Acme Bit Company home page and browse around the site. Start thinking about design elements—images, fonts, colors, etc.—that we will need to duplicate on the blog to make it feel like it was designed and built to accompany the main site.

Identify design elements from Acme's home page that will need to be used on the new blog. What might have to change on the current Acme blog? We've already found one to help get you started.

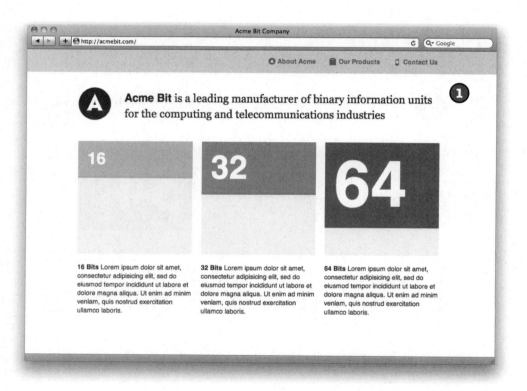

1 **The page widths are the same**

but we'll need to make some

adjustments with the background,

since the site has an all-white

background and the blog doesn't.

Exercise Solution

Identify design elements from Acme's home page that will need to be created on the new blog. What might have to change on the current Acme blog? We've already found one to help get you started.

Consistent navigation will help people navigate between the Acme blog and the main site.

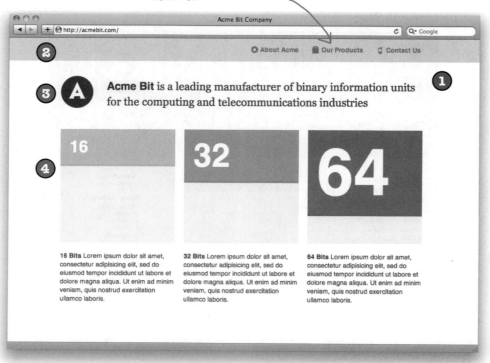

① The page widths are the same but we'll need to make some adjustments with the background, since the site has an all-white background and the blog doesn't.

② We are going to need to add this grey navigation bar at the top of the blog. We want to keep the links the same so we don't confuse visitors.

We'll make the blog 2 columns: one main column for the blog content and a smaller second column for the sidebar.

3 **We'll want to put the Acme Bit logo somewhere, and we need to make the header (top) images the same.**

4 **The content on the blog will be our posts in reverse chronological order, plus a right-hand column, or sidebar, for related links and content.**

There is already a ton of HTML and CSS used in the default WordPress style—we're not going to let that go to waste.

This might seem like a daunting task, but once you dive into HTML and CSS you'll see how easy this is to do.

Both of our sites are actually very similar and share design elements. This means that we should be able to use a lot of the Acme Bit Company website HTML and CSS to get the design transferred over to the blog. We'll use the default WordPress **theme** as a template to create our own Acme Bits theme.

Anatomy of a WordPress theme

We're going to change the way our blog looks by using what WordPress calls "themes." A theme is a collection of PHP/HTML and CSS files (more on these in a minute) that specify how your web page will look. WordPress users can change the entire style of their site by simply installing and activating a new theme. And better yet, you can make your own themes to make your WordPress blog look exactly how you want it to.

A theme tells WordPress how and where to display your content and images

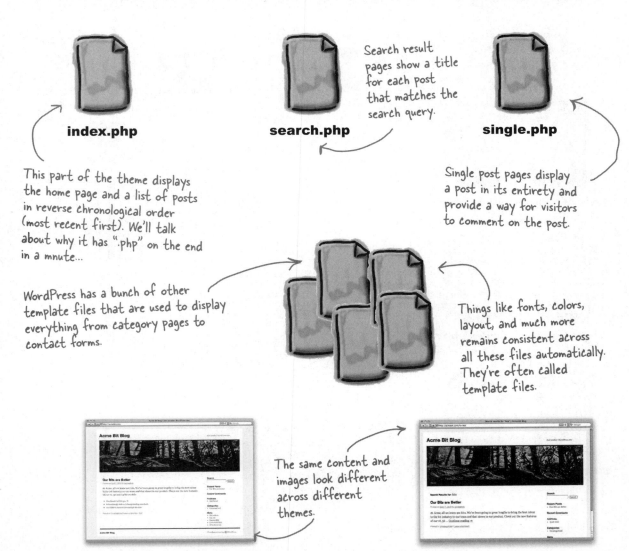

index.php

search.php

Search result pages show a title for each post that matches the search query.

single.php

This part of the theme displays the home page and a list of posts in reverse chronological order (most recent first). We'll talk about why it has ".php" on the end in a mnute...

Single post pages display a post in its entirety and provide a way for visitors to comment on the post.

WordPress has a bunch of other template files that are used to display everything from category pages to contact forms.

Things like fonts, colors, layout, and much more remains consistent across all these files automatically. They're often called template files.

The same content and images look different across different themes.

WordPress themes are a collection of template files...

Each template file in a theme has a specific job. One might display only the sidebar and another might be used to render a comment form. You can also add your own custom template files that can be used for just about anything you want within WordPress.

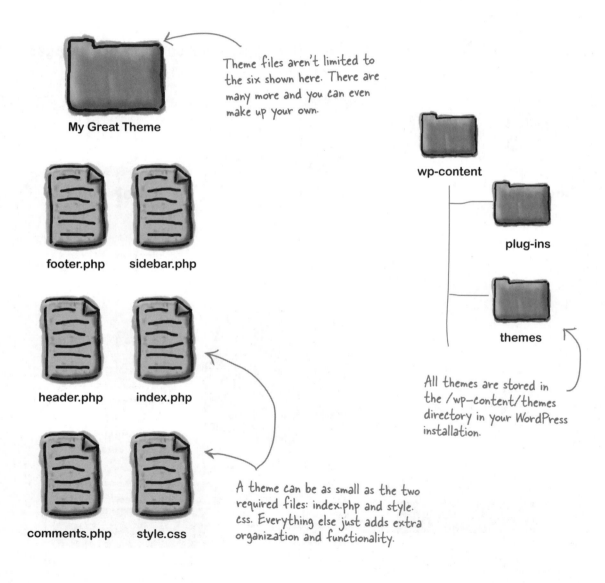

My Great Theme

Theme files aren't limited to the six shown here. There are many more and you can even make up your own.

footer.php   sidebar.php

header.php   index.php

comments.php   style.css

wp-content

plug-ins

themes

All themes are stored in the /wp-content/themes directory in your WordPress installation.

A theme can be as small as the two required files: index.php and style.css. Everything else just adds extra organization and functionality.

... all working in concert

Think of your WordPress theme as an orchestra conductor: there's a ton of instruments that each have their own role, tone, and notes to play, but they all need to combine together to make something that sounds wonderful.

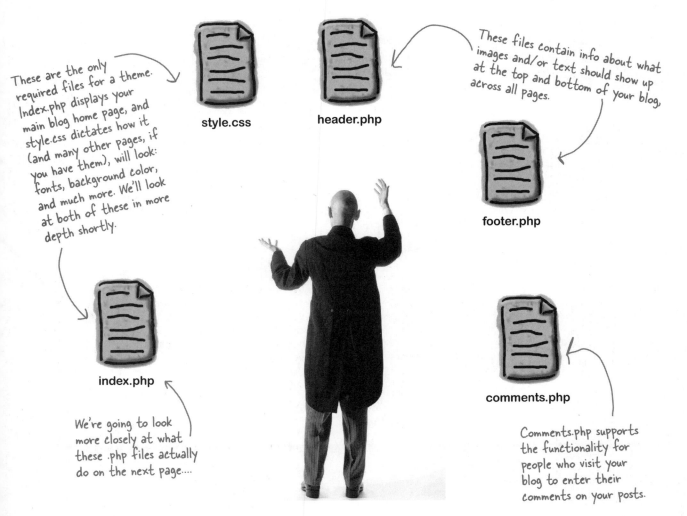

These are the only required files for a theme. Index.php displays your main blog home page, and style.css dictates how it (and many other pages, if you have them), will look: fonts, background color, and much more. We'll look at both of these in more depth shortly.

style.css

header.php

These files contain info about what images and/or text should show up at the top and bottom of your blog, across all pages.

footer.php

index.php

We're going to look more closely at what these .php files actually do on the next page....

comments.php

Comments.php supports the functionality for people who visit your blog to enter their comments on your posts.

PHP is the logic behind your theme

Because your blog is essentially a big collection of lots of little different files, something has to pull that all together to create one page when someone types in your blog's URL. And that thing is PHP. To continue our performing arts metaphor for a minute, PHP is a scripting language, and the "scripting" part refers to the fact that PHP essentially designates what is "said" or "done" by the HTML for your blog. Said slightly differently, PHP is code (not very human-readable) that works together with MySQL (your database) to generate an output (the actual HTML for your browser). Let's take a closer look.

This is a snippet of the PHP from the file that displays an individual blog post (single.php) Anything between the <?php and <?> tags is PHP script—everything else is plain old HTML.

PHP code

This bit of PHP code asks the database for the URL of the post currently being viewed.

```
<h2 class="entry-title"><a href="<?php the_permalink(); ?>" title="<?php printf(
esc_attr__( 'Permalink to %s', 'twentyten' ), the_title_attribute( 'echo=0' ) ); ?>"
rel="bookmark"><?php the_title(); ?></a></h2>

<div class="entry-meta">

        <?php

                printf( __( '<span class="meta-prep meta-prep-author">Posted on </span><a
href="%1$s" title="%2$s" rel="bookmark"><span class="entry-date">%3$s</span></a> <span
class="meta-sep"> by </span> <span class="author vcard"><a class="url fn n" href="%4$s"
title="%5$s">%6$s</a></span>', 'twentyten' ), get_permalink(), esc_attr( get_the_time()
), get_the_date(), get_author_posts_url( get_the_author_meta( 'ID' ) ), sprintf( esc_
attr__( 'View All posts by %s', 'twentyten' ), get_the_author() ), get_the_author());

        ?>

</div><!-- .entry-meta -->
```

And this gets the title for the post.

The author of the post is specified here...

...and the exact time it was posted here.

Here's the date it was posted....

This is what our page looks like if we use the "view source" feature in our web browser It is the actual HTML page sent to your visitor's browser when they type in a URL for your blog. The same PHP has been replaced with content.

HTML output

Here's the actual blog post URL.

```
<h2 class="entry-title"><a href="http://acmebit.com/2010/04/07/our-bits-are-better/"
title="Permalink to Our Bits are Better" rel="bookmark">Our Bits are Better</a></h2>

<div class="entry-meta">

        <span class="meta-prep meta-prep-author">Posted on </span><a href="http://acmebit.
com/2010/04/07/our-bits-are-better/" title="6:29 am" rel="bookmark"><span class="entry-
date">April 7, 2010</span></a> <span class="meta-sep"> by </span> <span class="author
vcard"><a class="url fn n" href="http://acmebit.com/author/acmeadmin/" title="View all
posts by acmeadmin">acmeadmin</a></span>

</div><!-- .entry-meta -->
```

And the title for the post.

All the author, date/time, and other info from the PHP code is now filled in here with actual content from your WordPress database.

So is that why so many of the theme's template files end with .php?

Always use the .php extension for WordPress theme files

Excluding stylesheets, JavaScript, and images, all template files in WordPress should be saved as .php files—even if they only contain HTML. It's OK to have a PHP file that doesn't actually contain any PHP code. These files are just interpreted by the web server as HTML and sent along to the browser.

The extension of a file includes the characters after the dot (.) in the filename. These extensions help the web server figure out what to do with the file.

This file has an .html extension and can only contain HTML markup. PHP code would not work in here.

index.php

index.html

In order for our theme to function properly, all template files must have a .php extension. We can still put HTML inside of them, we just can't use an .html extension.

We're not going to make you write your own PHP.

PHP is a powerful web scripting language that is used all over the Web to build interactive applications (WordPress included). It's also way beyond the scope of this book, so we're not going to cover it here. We'll use some PHP, but it will be code already written for other themes.

Match the WordPress template file with its theme function.

functions.php

Displays a full blog post with title, meta data and a comment form. If the post has comments, those are displayed as well.

single.php

Displays a "page not found" message and can potentially direct the visitor to an alternate page for the one they may have been looking for.

404.php

Displays the top of the .html file for all other theme files. Contains page titles and calls to other resources like stylesheets and JavaScript.

header.php

Doesn't directly display content from WordPress but adds new functionality that can be used by other template files.

page.php

Displays "static content" in WordPress—that is, any content that's not a post.

WHO DOES WHAT? SOLUTION

Match the WordPress template file with its theme function.

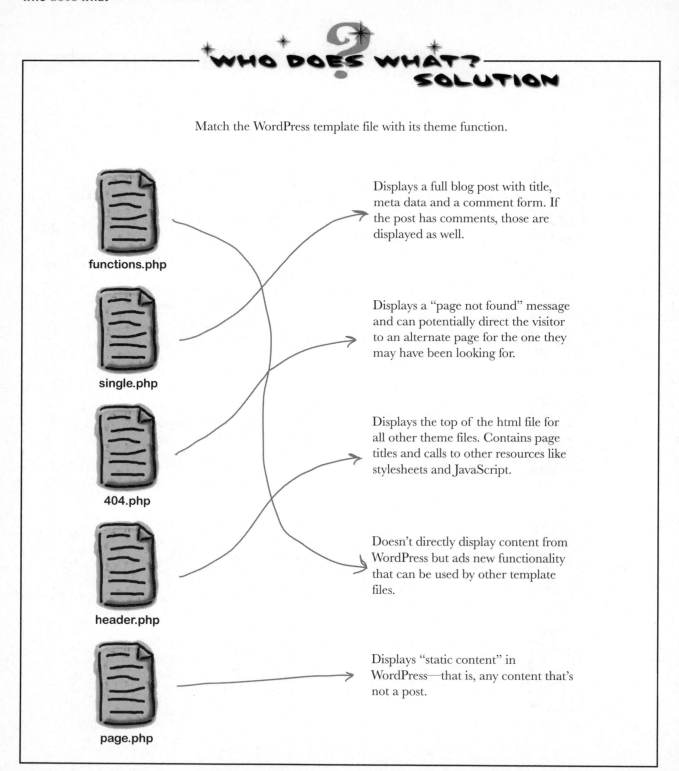

functions.php

single.php

404.php

header.php

page.php

Displays a full blog post with title, meta data and a comment form. If the post has comments, those are displayed as well.

Displays a "page not found" message and can potentially direct the visitor to an alternate page for the one they may have been looking for.

Displays the top of the html file for all other theme files. Contains page titles and calls to other resources like stylesheets and JavaScript.

Doesn't directly display content from WordPress but ads new functionality that can be used by other template files.

Displays "static content" in WordPress—that is, any content that's not a post.

Template Files Up Close

WordPress theme files are a collection of HTML, text, and special template tags that tell WordPress what to display in a particular area of the blog. Remember, even though they contain HTML, all template files in WordPress are saved as PHP. Let's take a closer look at a sample template file:

```php
<?php
/**
 * The main template file
 *
 * @package WordPress
 * @subpackage Twenty Ten
 * @since 3.0.0
 */
?>
<?php get_header(); ?>
        <div id="container">
                <div id="content">
                <?php
                /* Run the loop to output the posts.
                 * If you want to overload this in a child
theme then include a file
                 * called loop-index.php and that will be
used instead.
                 */
                get_template_part( 'loop', 'index' );
                ?>
                </div><!-- #content -->
        </div><!-- #container -->
<?php get_sidebar(); ?>
<?php get_footer(); ?>
```

This is a PHP comment block at the top. The sever ignores this stuff but it helps us stay organized.

The get_header() function displays the contents of header.php.

This is called "The Loop"—within it, most of the WordPress page and post content is displayed.

We can display the sidebar and footer just like we displayed the header.

Create a new theme

Before we can start changing the way the blog looks, we should copy the current theme so we can modify it to look like the Acme Bit site. That way if we mess anything up or don't like the results, we can always just go back and use the original theme again. We're going to need to jump back in our FTP client to do this.

1 Navigate to the themes folder.
Connect to your web server using FTP and in the wp-content folder, you'll find a directory called "themes." Inside is the default "twentyten" theme that got installed when you created your blog. We're going to copy it and modify it to make our own custom theme.

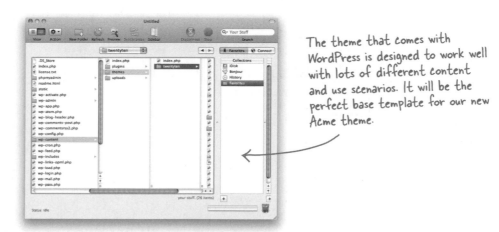

The theme that comes with WordPress is designed to work well with lots of different content and use scenarios. It will be the perfect base template for our new Acme theme.

2 Copy "twentyten".
Duplicate the twentyten theme and all its files and then rename the folder to "acme" or something similar.

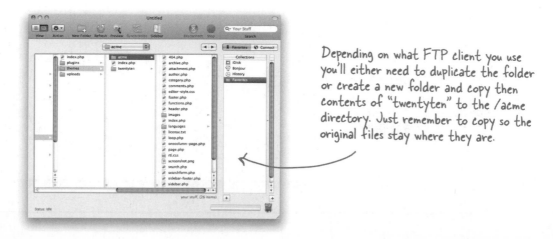

Depending on what FTP client you use you'll either need to duplicate the folder or create a new folder and copy then contents of "twentyten" to the /acme directory. Just remember to copy so the original files stay where they are.

3 **Check your files.**

Navigate to the /acme directory in your FTP client and make sure all the files are there. It should look identical to the "twentyten" theme.

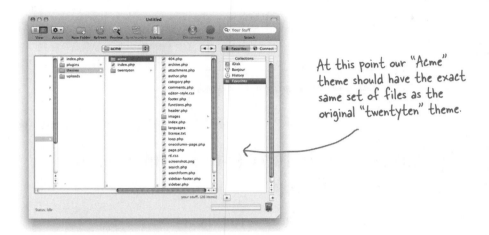

At this point our "Acme" theme should have the exact same set of files as the original "twentyten" theme.

4 **Activate the "acme" theme.**

Once everything is in order, head over to the Appearance section of your WordPress dashboard and activate the new theme. The image thumbnail and text should be the same, but don't worry, we're going to change all that a little later.

We now basically have two of the same themes in WordPress. As we modify Acme, we'll update the thubmnail and text to reflect the new theme.

These two themes still look exactly the same. How are we going to make this look like the Acme site?

Stylesheets dictate the look and feel of pages in WordPress

Cascading Style Sheets (CSS) are the standard way in which you apply "styles"—fonts, colors, background images, etc—to web pages. Using rules and special selectors (which we'll explain in a minute) that reference HTML elements within a WordPress page, you can have a ton of control over how your pages look in a browser.

In order for CSS to work its magic, we need to tell our template files where they can find the stylesheet. This bit of markup goes in the <head> element, which can be found in the header.php template.

```
<head>

    ...

    <link rel="stylesheet" type="text/css" media="all" href="<?php bloginfo(
'stylesheet_url' ); ?>" />

    ...

</head>
```

Because the header.php template file gets used all over our theme, the styles rules we use can be used by any page on our site. Cool!

header.php

Rules do a lot of work for you

A CSS rule describes what something should look like, such as the color or font of text, or where things line up on the page. The really cool thing about rules, though, is that they're reusable. You can assign a color and a font to a paragraph (a <p> element in HTML) and then any other page that uses a paragraph element in your site will inherit those rules. It also means that if you want to change the font across your entire blog, you just update the CSS rule for the <p> element, and voila! Your new font is automatically updated everywhere on your site.

```
#header {
        background: #ddd;
        height: 50px;
}
#nav ul {
        float: right;
        margin: 17px 0 0 0;
}
```

These rules describe how our navigation will look. Our header background is grey (#ddd is "hexadecimal", a mathematical notation for colors) and since the the navigation is within the header, it too will have a grey background.

This is a selector, which we mentioned earlier. It comes before the curly bracket (that's the { symbol) and it determines which HTML elements the style will be applied to. In this case, that's the h2 (second header) element.

```
#mast h2 {
        float: left;
        font-family: Georgia, serif;
        font-weight: normal;
        font-size: 2.4em;
        line-height: 1.4em;
        width: 700px;
}
```

These navigation icons are actually background images. We can use HTML classes to make each item in the navigation list display a different background image.

Our masthead CSS rule is focused mostly on typography— these are the font rules. We also use a "float" element, which helps us position our text next to the logo.

Sharpen your pencil

Let's give this CSS thing a try—it's not as hard as it may look. Open up the style.css file in our newly copied Acme WordPress theme and change the background color and font for the whole site. **Hint:** Look for the "Fonts" and "Global Elements" sections in the CSS file.

Use these websites to help you with this exercise.

http://www.w3schools.com/css/css_text.asp

http://www.w3schools.com/css/css_background.asp

Sharpen your pencil Solution

Let's give this CSS thing a try—it's not as hard as it may look. Open up the style.css file in our newly copied Acme WordPress theme and change the background color and font for the whole site. **Hint:** Look for the "Fonts" and "Global Elements" sections in the CSS file.

This is the original blog with the copied "twentyten" theme.

The main content fonts are declared in this rule. It's a big list of selectors, but it covers much of the typography for the site.

```
h3#comments-title,
h3#reply-title,
...
.reply,
.widget_search label,
.widget-title
{
        font-family: Georgia;

}
```

To change the font on the blog, we just have to pick a new one. In this case we went with Georgia, which is one of our web-safe fonts. (Ed note: you can find out lots more on web-safe fonts in Head First Web Design...)

Changing the background color is even easier. In the body selector, all we have to do is add a different hexadecimal color to the background rule. Here, #ff3a15 makes the whole background orange.

```
/* Main global 'theme' and typographic
styles   */
body {
        background: #ff3a15;

}
```

You can look up hexadecimal values easily online at sites like this: http://html-color-codes.com/

WordPress uses stylesheets two different ways

As we just saw, the main role of style.css in a WordPress theme is to tell your web browser how to display your blog. Colors, fonts, images, layout—all those settings are specified in the CSS file. However, WordPress also uses style.css to store more "meta" information about the theme, like the author, version and a description of the theme itself.

The main role of CSS in WordPress is to tell our web browser how to display our pages—the "look and feel."

1 **Style and presentation of pages**

```
body {
        font-size: 62.5%; /* Resets 1em to 10px */
        font-family: 'Lucida Grande', Verdana, Arial, Sans-Serif;
        background: #d5d6d7 url('images/kubrickbgcolor.jpg');
        color: #333;
        text-align: center;
}
```

WordPress uses a comment block at the top of style.css to tell the dashboard (and other services) details about the theme. Comments come between the slash and asterisk characters, /* like this */. They are ignored by browsers but WordPress can use them to display information about the current theme.

2 **Theme information and description**

```
/*
Theme Name: Twenty Ten
Theme URI: http://wordpress.org/
Description: The 2010 default theme for WordPress.
Author: the WordPress team
Versi
Tags:
threa
edito
*/
```

Twenty Ten 0.7 by the WordPress team

The 2010 default theme for WordPress.

All of this theme's files are located in `/themes/acme` .

Tags: black, blue, white, two-columns, fixed-width, custo
sticky-post, translation-ready, microformats, rtl-language

Sharpen your pencil

Check out the CSS from the main Acme site below and identify elements that we need to use in our new blog theme. Look back at the exercise on page 63 and try to find the corresponding CSS rules for those design elements. Remember, the selectors (the word before the opening curly bracket) correspond to an element within the HTML in the main Acme site.

We know we are going to need some style rules for what is called the "body" or main content area of the blog—especially fonts and colors. What other rules make the Acme site look how it does?

```css
body {
        margin: 0px;
        padding: 0px;
        font-family: "Helvetica", Arial,
sans-serif;
        line-height: 1;
        font-size: 62.5%;
        background: #fff;
        color: #424242;
}

.wrap {
        width: 800px;
        margin: 0 auto;
}

.replace {
        background-image: url(../images/
sprite.png);
        background-repeat: no-repeat;
        display: block;
        text-indent: -9000px;
}
```

```css
a:link {
        color: #424242;
        text-decoration: none;
}

p, ul, ol, li {
        font-size: 1.2em;
        margin: 0;
        padding: 0;
}

ul {
        list-style-type: none;
}

#header {
        background: #ddd;
        height: 50px;
}
```

```
#nav ul {
        float: right;
        margin: 17px 0 0 0;
}

#nav ul li {
        float: left;
        margin-left: 15px;
}

#nav ul li a {
        color: #777;
        padding: 5px 15px 5px 20px;
        font-weight: bold;
}

#nav ul li a.active {
}

.about {
        background: url(../images/sprite.png)
no-repeat 0 -128px;
}

.products {
        background: url(../images/sprite.png)
no-repeat 0 -76px;
}
```

```
.contact {
        background: url(../images/sprite.png)
no-repeat 0 -102px;
}

#mast {
        margin-top: 20px;
        height: 130px;
}

#mast h1 {
        float: left;
        width: 100px;
}

#mast h2 {
        float: left;
        font-family: Georgia, serif;
        font-weight: normal;
        font-size: 2.4em;
        line-height: 1.4em;
        width: 700px;
}
```

Sharpen your pencil
Solution

Check out the CSS from the main Acme site below and identify elements that we need to use in the blog theme. Look back at the exercise on page 63 and try to find the corresponding CSS rules for those design elements. Remember, the selectors (the word before the opening curly bracket) correspond to an element within the HTML in the main Acme site.

This is a really important rule—it will set the foundation for the rest of the Acme blog style rules.

The a:link rule specifies the color of hyperlinks, while the p, ul, ol, li rules dictate the size of the font used in paragraphs and bulleted or numbered lists.

```css
body {
        margin: 0px;
        padding: 0px;
        font-family: "Helvetica", Arial,
sans-serif;
        line-height: 1;
        font-size: 62.5%;
        background: #fff;
        color: #424242;
}

.wrap {
        width: 800px;
        margin: 0 auto;
}

.replace {
        background-image: url(../images/
sprite.png);
        background-repeat: no-repeat;
        display: block;
        text-indent: -9000px;
}
```

The .wrap rule is what keeps our site centered in the page. Can't leave this out.

```css
a:link {
        color: #424242;
        text-decoration: none;
}

p, ul, ol, li {
        font-size: 1.2em;
        margin: 0;
        padding: 0;
}

ul {
        list-style-type: none;
}

#header {
        background: #ddd;
        height: 50px;
}
```

.replace is a rule that uses a technique called Text Replacement. It "replaces" text with an image, in the event that you need to display something in an unusual font that browsers might not be able to display. It's not something we'd plan to use very often.

We will reuse most of the navigation rules from the main
Acme site, as we'll be replacing the entire header of the
blog with this same navigation.

```css
#nav ul {
        float: right;
        margin: 17px 0 0 0;
}

#nav ul li {
        float: left;
        margin-left: 15px;
}

#nav ul li a {
        color: #777;
        padding: 5px 15px 5px 20px;
        font-weight: bold;
}

#nav ul li a.active {
}

.about {
        background: url(../images/sprite.png)
no-repeat 0 -128px;
}

.products {
        background: url(../images/sprite.png)
no-repeat 0 -76px;
}
```

```css
.contact {
        background: url(../images/sprite.png)
no-repeat 0 -102px;
}

#mast {
        margin-top: 20px;
        height: 130px;
}

#mast h1 {
        float: left;
        width: 100px;
}

#mast h2 {
        float: left;
        font-family: Georgia, serif;
        font-weight: normal;
        font-size: 2.4em;
        line-height: 1.4em;
        width: 700px;
}
```

The mast shows the main text and logo header at
the top of the Acme home page. We should hang on
to this rule as a reference so we can reuse it for
our own header on the blog as well.

Stylesheets identify elements in your HTML

Just because you have a rule in a stylesheet doesn't mean that you have the corresponding elements in your HTML files. In order for CSS to work, both the HTML and the stylesheet have to be referencing the same thing.

> So all we really have to do is just copy these rules over to the new theme? And we're good to go?

```
#mast h2 {
        float: left;
        font-family: Georgia, serif;
        font-weight: normal;
        font-size: 2.4em;
        line-height: 1.4em;
        width: 700px;
}
```

The #mast selector in the CSS matches the "mast" attribute in the HTML file below.

In CSS, ID's are referenced with # signs (#header) and classes are referenced with dots (.) (.header).

```
<div id="mast" class="wrap">
        <h1><a class="replace" title="Acme Pixel Company" href="#">Acme Pixel Company</a></h1>
        <h2><strong>Acme Bit</strong> is a leading manufacturer of binary information units for the computing and telecommunications industries</h2>
</div>
```

Will simply copying and pasting the CSS rules from the main Acme website to the blog just work? What aspects of the blog might differ enough from the site such that you might need to further modify your new theme?

Putting it all together

Now that we know what CSS rules we need, let's get our Acme blog theme looking just like the main site.

Ready Bake Code

Do this!

Download "Acmestyle.css" from *www.headfirstlabs.com/wordpress*, listed under the Chapter 2 files.

1 **Copy the original Acme site CSS to the new WordPress theme CSS file.**
Copy and paste the CSS from the main Acme site into the style.css of your new Acme WordPress theme. Be sure to paste it just below the RESET portion of the style rules (look for the "reset" comment block) —we want to keep those for consistency.

```css
body {
        margin: 0px;
        padding: 0px;
        font-family: "Helvetica", Arial, sans-serif;
        line-height: 1;
        font-size: 62.5%;
        background: #fff;
        color: #424242;
}

.wrap {
        width: 940px;
        margin: 0 auto;
}

.replace {
        background-image: url(../images/sprite.png);
        background-repeat: no-repeat;
        display: block;
        text-indent: -9000px;
}

...
```

style.css

Clean out some unnecessary CSS rules.

There are a few rules in the Acme site stylesheet that will cause problems with our blog layout. We need to strip those out so that our blog pages render correctly.

Ready Bake Code

```css
#header {

        margin-top: 20px;

        padding: 30px 0 0 0;

}

#site-title {

        float: left;

        margin: 0 0 18px 0;

        width: 700px;

        font-size: 30px;

        line-height: 36px;

}

#site-title a {

        color: #000;

        font-weight: bold;

        text-decoration: none;

}

#site-description {

        clear: right;

        float: right;

        font-style: italic;

        margin: 14px 0 18px 0;

        width: 220px;

}
/* This is the custom header image */

#branding img {

        clear: both;

        border-top: 4px solid #000;

        display: block;

}
```

These are the rules that define the way the original header and masthead look. If we don't remove this code, they will conflict with the new rules we added earlier. And, because they are lower in the file, they will oerride any rule with the same class or ID.

```css
/* Main global 'theme' and typographic
styles   */

body {

        background: #f1f1f1;

}

body, input, textarea {

        color: #666;

        font-size: 12px;

        line-height: 18px;

}
```

Use the "find" or "search" feature in your text editor to locate these rules and remove them. Don't worry if you mess up and delete the wrong rules—we copied the original theme so you can just go back to the "twenntyten" folder and re-copy the original style.css.

② **Clean up the header.php markup.**

Just as we had to get rid of unused CSS rules—we need to do the same for our markup. Replace <div id="wrapper" class="hfeed"> and everything below it with the code below. (Make sure you're in header. php and not index.php in the acme theme.w)

Ready Bake Code

```
<div id="header-acme">

        <div id="nav" class="wrap">

                <ul>

                        <li><a class="about" title="About Acme" href="#">About Acme</a></
li>

                        <li><a class="products active" title="About Acme" href="#">Our
Products</a></li>

                        <li><a class="contact" title="About Acme" href="#">Contact Us</
a></li>

                </ul>

        </div>

</div>

<div id="mast" class="wrap">

        <h1><a class="replace" title="Acme Pixel Company" href="#">Acme Pixel Company</
a></h1>

        <h2><strong>Acme Bit</strong> is a leading manufacturer of binary information
units for the computing and telecommunications industries</h2>

</div>

<div id="main">
```

We put a rule in our CSS file for the navigation, and we need the corresponding elements here in the HTML.

This shows the company information in the masthead at the top of the blog.

header.php

✏️ **Sharpen your pencil**

Everything is looking good so far, but we need a footer for our site. Below is some content for the footer—insert it into footer.php and create some simple style rules to get it looking presentable.

Acme Bit Company - Handmade bits for the technology industry

Home | About | Products | Contact Us ←

A small title and some navigation links are all we really need for the Acme footer.

Sharpen your pencil
Solution

Everything is looking good so far, but we need a footer for our site. Below is some content for the footer—insert it into footer.php and build some simple style rules to get it looking presentable.

Acme Bit Blog

About Acme | Our Products | Contact Us

This is how the left side of our footer will look once we get some markup in the proper place.

You need to modify footer.php, more specifically, the site-info div within the footer.

Just two paragraphs (using the <p> element) is all we need to hold the blog title and the navigation links.

```
<div id="site-info">
        <p><a href="<?php echo home_url( '/' ) ?>" title="<?php echo esc_attr( get_
bloginfo( 'name', 'display' ) ); ?>" rel="home"><?php bloginfo( 'name' ); ?></a></p>

        <p><a title="About Acme" href="#">About Acme</a> | <a title="About Acme"
href="#">Our Products</a> | <a title="About Acme" href="#">Contact Us</a></p>

</div>
```

footer.php

Finally, we need to add the nav links from the top of the page to the footer. We don't need to copy the whole list structure, just the links. We can put them in a <p> tag right below the blog title.

Test Drive

Be sure to save header.php and footer.php, and then reload the Acme Bit blog in your browser. Let's see how our new style is shaping up...

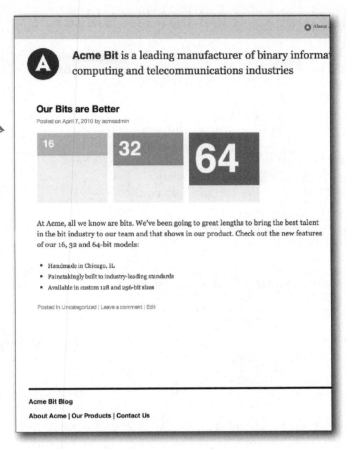

Now our Acme Bit blog is starting to look like the main site!

there are no Dumb Questions

Q: Does CSS only work with WordPress?

A: Nope, CSS is a web standard and is the primary presentation language on the Web. Almost every modern website utilizes it in some way and future releases promise even more styling power and effects.

Q: Why would I use a class instead on an ID in HTML?

A: HTML has two ways of identifying elements: classes and IDs. The main difference is that classes are reusable, meaning you can have more than one element on a given page with that identical class name. IDs, on the other hand, must be unique and therefore can only show up once on a page. So, use IDs for specific naming and styling needs and classes for elements that you plan to reuse throughout your page.

Q: Do I always have to make my own themes? That's a lot of work!

A: While building your own themes is often fun and rewarding—it's also a lot of work and requires a fairly deep knowledge of WordPress. If you just want a different look than the default—check out *http://wordpress.org/extend/themes/*. This is the main source to find thousands of free themes that you can use for you blog.

Everything looks good but the sidebars

The Acme Bit Blog is coming together nicely and we're almost ready to show it to Jay. Before we can do that, we need to clean up our sidebar a little. Because the main Acme site didn't have a sidebar, there wasn't any CSS for it. But we want to keep it in the blog—it's a very standard and expected design element for most blogs. So we'll need to modify the new CSS to make the current sidebar match the look and feel of the site.

The new theme for the Acme blog looks great but the sidebar—it has the searchbox and some links on the top right— is a bit small compared to everything else on the page. We want to make it larger and remove some links that don't need to be there.

We don't need the "meta" links (we don't want people knowing where our login screen is!) and some quick CSS should make the sidebar fit better into the overall design.

Update your sidebar content with widgets

Widgets are like drag-and-drop design elements that you can easily add to your blog. Aside from being a funny word, widgets are an easy way to customize content and the look and feel of your site without touching any HTML or CSS.

The widgets section is located within the Appearance menu in the WordPress dashboard. Here you'll find options for sidebar and footer content widgets too.

Each widget area and the widgets it contains correspond with an identical sidebar on the blog. This sidebar will show up wherever sidebar.php is called in the template files.

All widget elements are drag and drop—so move them around all you want.

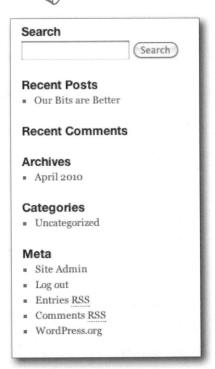

Drag and drop widgets where you want them

Adding and removing widgets from the different sidebar areas is as easy as dragging and dropping them into the appropriate place. You can add as many or as few widgets as you want and you're in complete control over order and custom title options.

1 **Find the Widget settings in the Appearance menu.**
Because widgets are theme-dependent, they are grouped with other theme options.

2 **Add elements to your sidebar.**
Drag elements from the widget pool on the left to the sidebar container on the right.

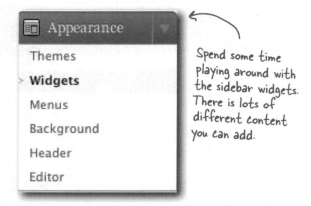

Spend some time playing around with the sidebar widgets. There is lots of different content you can add.

3 **Add header and widget details.**
Each sidebar widget has its own set of files for customizing the look of the element.

Exercise

Update the content and links in your sidebar, and then add the content chunk (below) about Acme Bit above it. You should be able to do all this without modifying any of the theme files.

1 **Remove the "meta" and "recent comments" sections from the main sidebar.**

We don't need to show the meta information (login, etc...) to the world. Let's get rid of that and the recent comment area—we don't have any right now but we can easily add this back in later if we want!

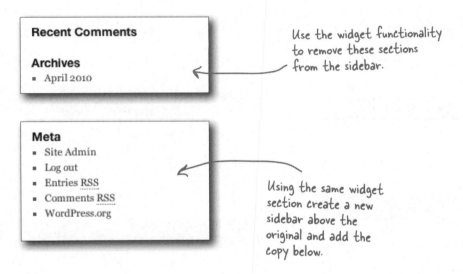

Recent Comments

Archives
- April 2010

Use the widget functionality to remove these sections from the sidebar.

Meta
- Site Admin
- Log out
- Entries RSS
- Comments RSS
- WordPress.org

Using the same widget section create a new sidebar above the original and add the copy below.

2 **Add the "About" copy above the main sidebar on the home page.**

Add the text to the right to a new sidebar above the original. That means you might have to move some things around in your widgets settings. Remember, you shouldn't need to change any template files, markup, or CSS.

The Acme Bit Company has been building quality bits for the computing industry since 2009. We are a family company that works and supports our local community-donating millions of bits a year to local and regional charities. Have a look at our products and you'll see firsthand why we are the only name is high-quality bits.

Exercise Solution

Update the content and links in your sidebar, then add the content chunk (below) about Acme Bit above it. You should be able to do all of this without modifying any of the theme files.

① **Move the main widgets down to the Secondary Widget Area.**
After you remove the the recent comments and meta widgets, place the remaining widgets in the "Second Widget Area" by dragging them below the first. Then, drag and drop the "Text" widget to the "Primary Widget Area."

The primary and secondary widget areas display the sidebar in the same order you see in the dashboard. Since we can't move the widget areas around, we need to move the widget elements down instead.

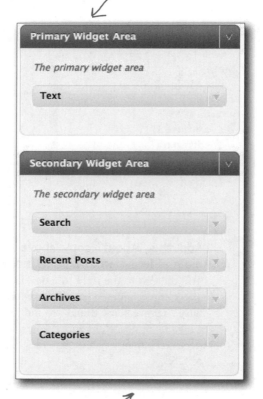

Don't forget to remove any unwanted widgets.

② **Add the sidebar copy to the the Text Widget.**
Copy and paste the About copy into the text box of the "Primary Widget Area."

By clicking the down arrow in the Text widget you can enter a title and block of text that will appear in the sidebar. We won't include a title here, just the text.

Once you save and navigate back out to the home page, you should see the new two-section sidebar.

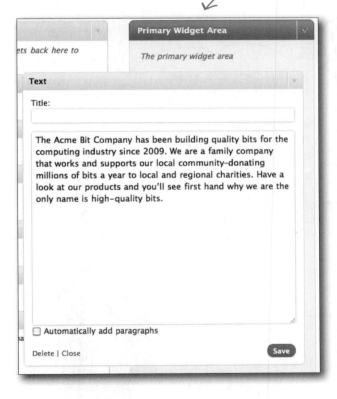

Primary Widget Area

ts back here to

The primary widget area

Text

Title:

The Acme Bit Company has been building quality bits for the computing industry since 2009. We are a family company that works and supports our local community–donating millions of bits a year to local and regional charities. Have a look at our products and you'll see first hand why we are the only name is high-quality bits.

☐ Automatically add paragraphs

Delete | Close   **Save**

The Acme Bit Company has been building quality bits for the computing industry since 2009. We are a family company that works and supports our local community–donating millions of bits a year to local and regional charities. Have a look at our products and you'll see first hand why we are the only name is high-quality bits.

Search

[   ] (Search)

Recent Posts
- Our Bits are Better

Archives
- April 2010

Categories
- Uncategorized

Test Drive

Now that we have the new widgets in place—let's take the Acme Blog for a spin.

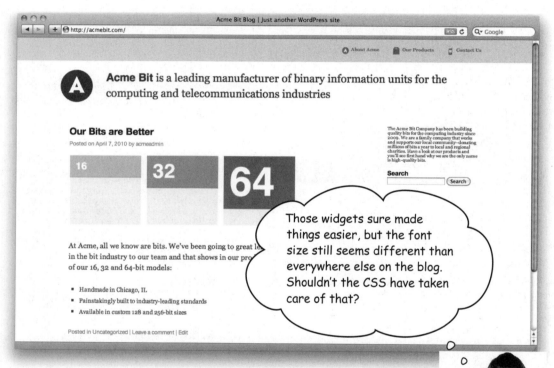

Brain Power

Why might the sidebar font not be fitting in with the style of the rest of the blog?

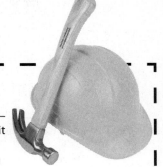

SIDEBAR CONSTRUCTION

The new theme and content are in place but the original Acme site didn't have a sidebar—so it didn't have any CSS related to sidebars. We need to write some custom CSS to make it really fit in with the new theme.

The Acme Bit Company has been building quality bits for the computing industry since 2009. We are a family company that works and supports our local community—donating millions of bits a year to local and regional charities. Have a look at our products and you'll see first hand why we are the only name is high-quality bits.

Search

[   ] Search

Recent Posts
- Our Bits are Better

Archives
- April 2010

Categories
- Uncategorized

The main issue with the sidebar is the font size—it seems smaller than the rest of the blog.

The copy is also a bit mushed together, it could be spaced out a bit more. Look at the CSS rules below to help you come up with a solution.

Use the CSS attributes below to add some style to the new sidebar. Check out http://www.w3schools.com/css/css_reference.asp to learn more about what these properties do.

Look for this rule in the style. css file and make some changes to improve the look of the sidebar.

`#main .widget-area ul`

`font-size`

`line-height`

`background`

`padding`

SIDEBAR CONSTRUCTION SOLUTION

The new theme and content are in place but the original Acme site didn't have a sidebar—so it didn't have any CSS related to sidebards. We need to write some custom CSS to make it really fit in with the new theme.

We need to increase the font size to match the typography on the rest of the site.

Search

[   ] (Search)

Recent Posts
- Our Bits are Better

Archives
- April 2010

Categories
- Uncategorized

```
#main .widget-area ul {
        margin-left: 0;
        padding: 0 20px 0 0;
        font-size: 1.4em;
        line-height: 1.4em;
}

#main .widget-area ul ul {
        border: none;
        margin-left: 1.3em;
        font-size: 1em;
        padding: 0;
}
```

Our new style.css already has a #main .widget-area ul rule for the bullets, so all we need to do is add a few rules to make the font size and line height a bit bigger.

The Acme Bit Company has been building quality bits for the computing industry since 2009. We are a family company that works and supports our local community—donating millions of bits a year to local and regional charities. Have a look at our products and you'll see first hand why we are the only name is high-quality bits.

```
.textwidget {
        background: #eee;
        padding: 10px;
}
```

Adding a background color and some padding (or space around all of the text block) will make the About text easier to read.

These CSS additions should made our sidebar a little more presentable—once we get some more posts on the site, it will look even better.

One theme to rule them all

You've just created your own custom theme for the Acme Bit blog, and it looks just like the main site! Time to let Jay take it for a spin...

We added new CSS and HTML that added the Acme header and masthead.

We also brought the navigation over so that our visitors could find their way back to the main Acme site.

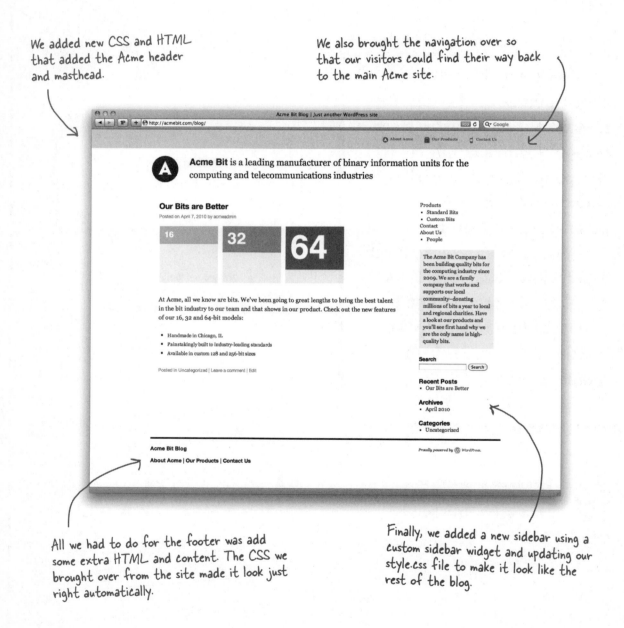

All we had to do for the footer was add some extra HTML and content. The CSS we brought over from the site made it look just right automatically.

Finally, we added a new sidebar using a custom sidebar widget and updating our style.css file to make it look like the rest of the blog.

Your WordPress Toolbox

You've got Chapter 2 under your belt and now you've added themes to your tool box. Next up, moving beyond the blog to see how WordPress can help you manage a whole website.

BULLET POINTS

- WordPress uses PHP, HTML, and CSS to get content to the visitor through their browser

- HTML is the language of the Web and is used to "markup" content with meaningful tags which then get interpreted by a web browser.

- CSS or Cascading Style Sheets are used to add a presentation layer to HTML and allow you to change the look and feel of plain old HTML.

- For every rule in CSS, there needs to be a corresponding element (like a <p> tag) in the HTML.

- WordPress themes allow you to change the style of your site without changing any of your content directly.

- Sidebar widgets allow you to dynamically add and remove content from your blog sidebar. Some themes support more than one sidebar widget.

- You can download 1000s of free WordPress themes from the Theme Directory: *http://wordpress.org/extend/themes/*.

3 content management with wordpress

Beyond the blog

Gentlemen, we have a lot of stuff. How are we going to keep track of it all?

You're starting to outgrow the blog.

Maybe your business is growing, maybe you need more control of what shows up where on your blog, and *when*. Luckily, WordPress handles a lot more than just chronological blog posts. We'll start to tap into its **content management system** capabilities by creating **static pages** like on a regular website, adding **navigation** for the new pages, and changing the home page of your new site so it isn't your blog. Get ready to build a full-fledged **website** practically without writing a single line of HTML or CSS.

I hate to ask again—but now I need to update our main site. Some consultant built it for us years ago and I have no idea how to make changes on it!

Jay has written three posts in the last few days and has caught on quick to blogging with WordPress.

Our Bits are Better
Posted on April 7, 2010 by acmeadmin

| 16 | 32 | |

At Acme, all we know are bits. We'
in the bit industry to our team and
of our 16, 32 and 64-bit models:

- Handmade in
- Painstakingly
- Available in c

Posted in Uncatego

The Anatomy of a Qubit
Posted on June 3, 2010 by acmeadmin

Here at Acme Bit, we focus primarily on classic bits–the basic unit of computer information. Over the past year we have been experimenting with a *different* kind of bit, a quantum bit or "qubit." Qubits have many of the same characteristics as bits in that they can be in two different states, on or off. However, they have an extra state called a superposition which is special to quantum bits and represents a linear of 0 and 1.

We're still looking at practical applications for our customers, but the future definitely is

The Duality of the Bit
Posted on June 3, 2010 by acmeadmin

No matter what size bit you have, 16, 32 or 64 each comes with only 2 discreet states: on or off. Now you may be thinking, "that's not a lot of options, how is that going to help my business?" Well the truth is, you only really need 2 states. Think of all the information that can be represented that way: on/off, 1/2, hot/cold, up/down, white/black. The possibilities are endless.

So don't get hung up on your lack of options–embrace simplicity and wonderful duality of the bit.

Posted in Uncategorized | Leave a comment | Edit

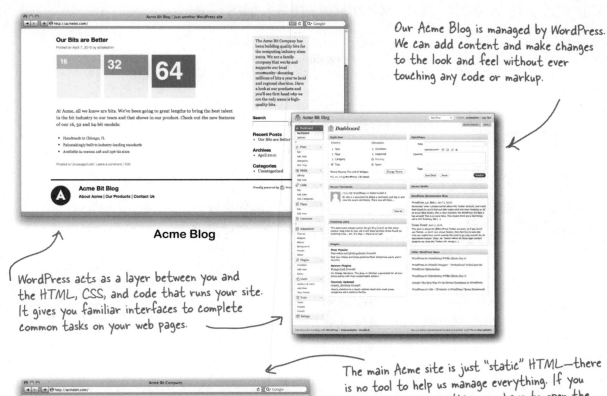

Acme Blog

Our Acme Blog is managed by WordPress. We can add content and make changes to the look and feel without ever touching any code or markup.

WordPress acts as a layer between you and the HTML, CSS, and code that runs your site. It gives you familiar interfaces to complete common tasks on your web pages.

The main Acme site is just "static" HTML—there is no tool to help us manage everything. If you want to change something you have to open the file in a text editor and change the HTML, CSS, and content.

Main Acme Site

Not everyone knows HTML—or even wants to. Without WordPress, or some other tool, very few people could make changes to this. What if you're a big company and have 10,000 pages? You can see this website would be difficult to manage by more than a few people, and Jay doesn't have anyone on staff at Acme to help him change his site.

WordPress is a content management system

WordPress can do way more than manage your blog, it's powerful enough to control all the content of typical website. Technically, all blogging platforms are a form of content management system, but WordPress makes it simple to build full-featured websites on top of its posts, pages, and themes.

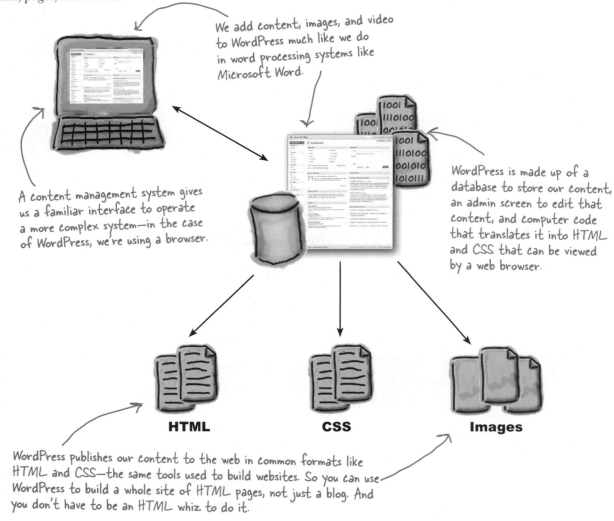

We add content, images, and video to WordPress much like we do in word processing systems like Microsoft Word.

A content management system gives us a familiar interface to operate a more complex system—in the case of WordPress, we're using a browser.

WordPress is made up of a database to store our content, an admin screen to edit that content, and computer code that translates it into HTML and CSS that can be viewed by a web browser.

HTML   **CSS**   **Images**

WordPress publishes our content to the web in common formats like HTML and CSS—the same tools used to build websites. So you can use WordPress to build a whole site of HTML pages, not just a blog. And you don't have to be an HTML whiz to do it.

A content management system allows users to edit websites using forms and word processor-like controls instead of modifying HTML files and code directly.

WordPress has three main management sections

① **Content**
We already know that WordPress can handle a blog post but you can also create pages, add lists of links, and upload media to include in your site.

We're going to focus on pages for now. They will help us get the main Acme site moved into WordPress.

② **Structure and Organization**
WordPress gives us tools like categories and tags to help organize our content. Pages also help us build heirarchical structures within our site.

③ **Look and Feel**
Finally, WordPress gives us built-in themes (and the ability to make our own) so we can make our site look however we want.

OK, so there are a few more "management" sections to WordPress—but they're mostly site settings so we'll ignore those for now.

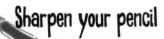

Sharpen your pencil

Take a look at the current Acme site and write down all the pages we'll need to move over to WordPress. You can view the Acme site at *http://acmebit.com*.

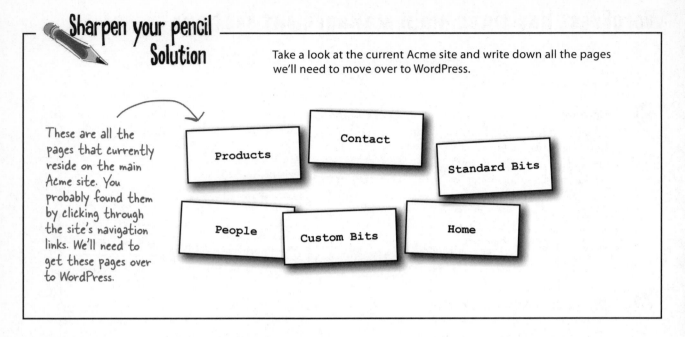

Sharpen your pencil Solution

Take a look at the current Acme site and write down all the pages we'll need to move over to WordPress.

These are all the pages that currently reside on the main Acme site. You probably found them by clicking through the site's navigation links. We'll need to get these pages over to WordPress.

Products

Contact

Standard Bits

People

Custom Bits

Home

WordPress pages are just posts "outside" the blog

WordPress allows you to create a special kind of post called a page. A page does exactly what you might think—it adds a new webpage to your WordPress blog, which then is really turning into more of a website. By default, WordPress ships with an "About" page that you can take a look at to get an idea of how a page looks in your dashboard. You can add as many pages as you like and they can be used to build a whole additional site around your blog.

From the pages navigation in your dashboard, you can edit an existing page (About is there by default) or create a new one—just like a creating a blog post.

Pages are the backbone of your CMS

Without the ability to create pages, WordPress would just be a blogging tool. Pages are obviously important for providing content, but how you name them and where you store them within the WordPress file structure also impacts the organization of your site. Helping you keep track of all that is part of what makes WordPress a true content management system (CMS).

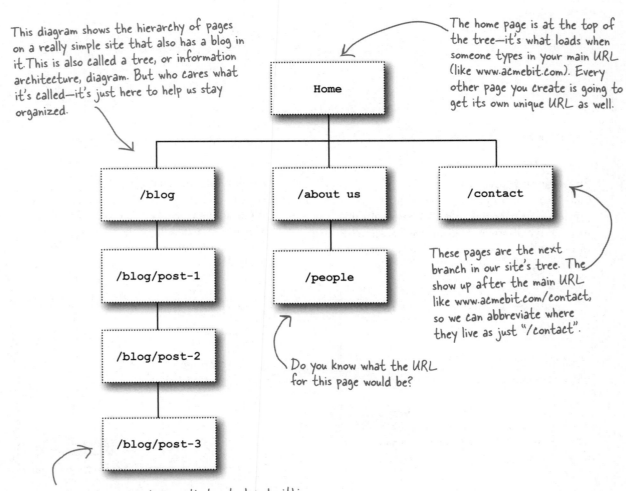

Most of the time you will see "content management system" abbreviated as CMS.

This diagram shows the hierarchy of pages on a really simple site that also has a blog in it. This is also called a tree, or information architecture, diagram. But who cares what it's called—it's just here to help us stay organized.

The home page is at the top of the tree—it's what loads when someone types in your main URL (like www.acmebit.com). Every other page you create is going to get its own unique URL as well.

These pages are the next branch in our site's tree. The show up after the main URL like www.acmebit.com/contact, so we can abbreviate where they live as just "/contact".

Do you know what the URL for this page would be?

Posts are just individual pages that get placed within the context of your blog. All your posts will appear under /blog in your site structure.

Adding a new page is just like adding a new post

① **Select Add New from the Pages menu.**
This will bring up a new empty page that will look just like the "add new post" page.

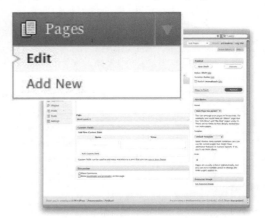

② **Add a title and some content.**
You can use the visual editor or code editor and HTML is allowed in the page (also just like a post).

③ **Preview and save your draft.**
Once your title and content are in place you can preview your page before you publish it for the world to see. If you're not quite ready yet, click "Save Draft" and you can come back later and finish things up.

④ **Publish when you're ready.**
You can add images just like in a blog post, and thanks to the CSS work you did earlier, your page will already inherit the style of your blog. Once you hit Publish, your new page will be available on your site.

WORDPRESS CONSTRUCTION

Use the pages you wrote down in the earlier exercise as a reference and add new pages for each content section of the Acme site.

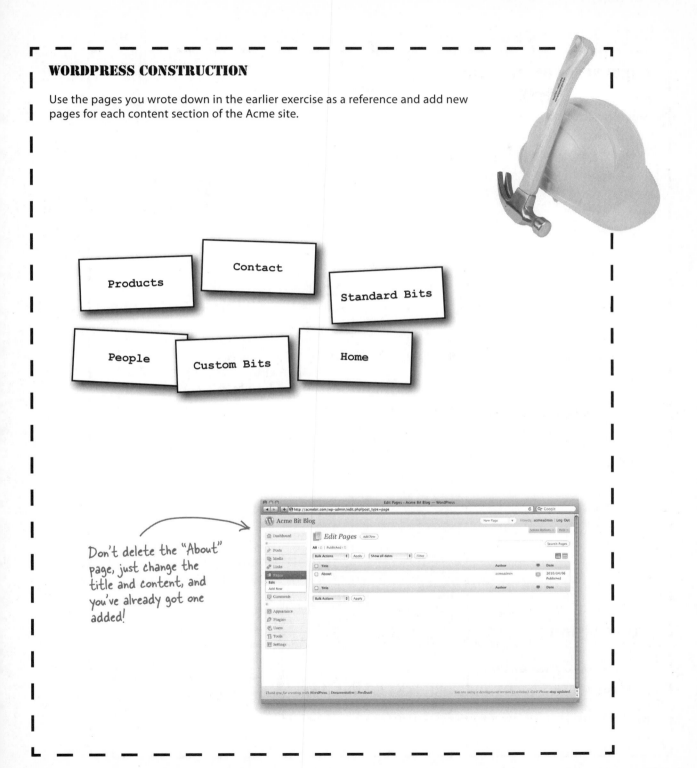

Don't delete the "About" page, just change the title and content, and you've already got one added!

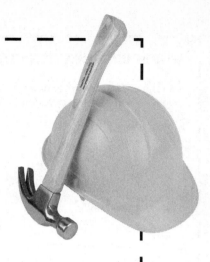

WORDPRESS CONSTRUCTION

Use the pages you wrote down in the earlier exercise as a reference and add new pages for each content section of the Acme site.

Each page should show up in the Pages list and a preview will be available to see what it looks like in the site.

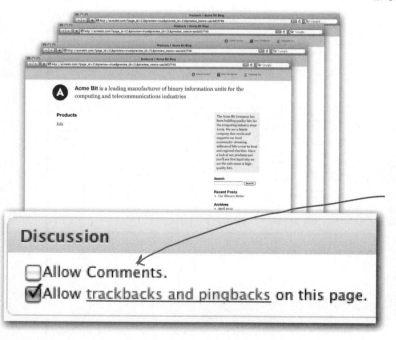

Make sure you disable comments by unchecking the "Allow Comments" at the bottom of the new page form. This way we won't get a comment form on our pages that may confuse people—you only want them commenting on your blog posts.

http://acmebit.com/?pageid=23...

> All of the pages are there but the URLs for each page are showing up with numbers and question marks in them! Weren't they supposed to look like /contact and /about?

That is a pretty ugly link. And it doesn't tell us much about the page, either.

URLs are an important part of the Internet. They are the street addresses of our favorite sites on the Web. Because of this, we want them to be easily memorable. A link with a bunch of question marks an equal signs is tough to remember—our brains don't work that way. We like to see links that have human-readable and speakable parts so we can remember them. These are called "pretty permalinks" because they look and sound nice. They also serve another purpose—they can be like little bits of meta data tucked away inside your link. When you see /products you know exactly what to expect on that page, before a single pixel loads. Pretty, usable URLs make the Internet a happier place.

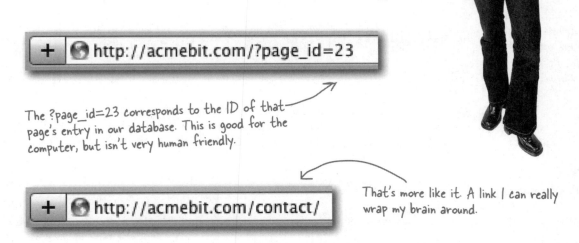

`+ 🌐 http://acmebit.com/?page_id=23`

The ?page_id=23 corresponds to the ID of that page's entry in our database. This is good for the computer, but isn't very human friendly.

`+ 🌐 http://acmebit.com/contact/`

That's more like it. A link I can really wrap my brain around.

Pretty permalinks make life on the Internet easier by giving visitors a readable, memorable link that reflects the content of the page.

Make your URLs manageable with permalinks

By default, WordPress creates links for your posts and pages using syntax that ends with something like this: ?p=xxx . The "xxx" part is the number of that page in your database. You can change this setting by selecting a new "permalink" structure from a list in WordPress. The "Day and name" option is one that you see on a majority of blogs because it gives you date information along with a title in the URL.

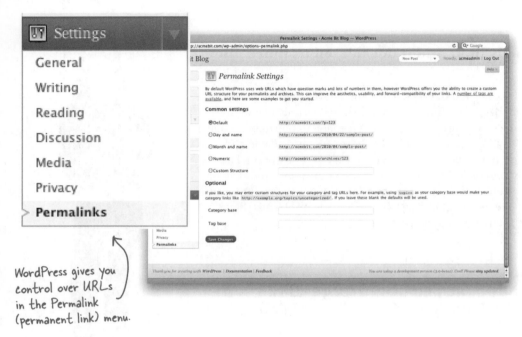

WordPress gives you control over URLs in the Permalink (permanent link) menu.

The default setting will always display posts and pages by their ID in the database. Any of the other settings will trigger "pretty" URLs for pages (/products, /contact) and then the specified URL structure for the posts.

If you want, you can add a custom structure and make up your own permalinks. To learn more about this feature, check out the WordPress Codex: http://codex.wordpress.org/Using_Permalinks#Choosing_your_permalink_structure.

Permalinks are handled by the web server

Most of the work to make your URLs more attractive is done by the server. The web server looks at the incoming URL, like acmebit.com/contact, and compares it to a set of rules it has on file. If the URL matches a rule, say "?p=123 is the same as /contacts", the web server would route the request to serve up the appropriate page based on its database ID. This process is called rewriting and it's usually handled by code called a "rewrite engine." WordPress steps in to automatically change the links on your site to point to the new, more readable URLs.

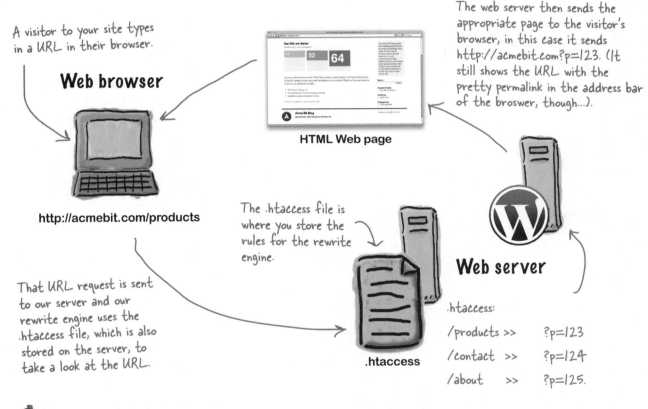

A visitor to your site types in a URL in their browser.

Web browser

http://acmebit.com/products

That URL request is sent to our server and our rewrite engine uses the .htaccess file, which is also stored on the server, to take a look at the URL.

HTML Web page

The web server then sends the appropriate page to the visitor's browser, in this case it sends http://acmebit.com?p=123. (It still shows the URL with the pretty permalink in the address bar of the browser, though...).

The .htaccess file is where you store the rules for the rewrite engine.

Web server

.htaccess

.htaccess:

/products >>   ?p=123

/contact >>   ?p=124

/about   >>   ?p=125.

Exercise

Go into the Permalink menu and modify your settings so that posts and pages can have pretty permalinks. Start with the "Day and name" permalink setting as that is the most common format on blogs. Then go to a browser and navigate to the /contact page at your site's URL.

Page Not Found?

Now that we've selected the permalink structure that we want for the Acme site, we should be able to browse to a page by title (/contact) and see that page in our site. Sometimes, however, the new pretty URL will instead display a Not Found error. These errors occur when the server can't find the file being requested based on the URL. *Depending on your host, your permalinks may or may not work at this point. If they do work, you can skip this next section (or stick around and learn about the .htaccess file).*

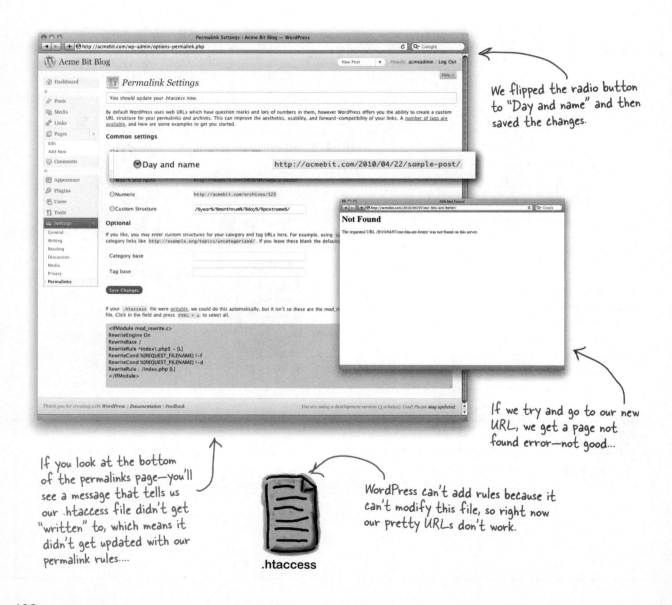

We flipped the radio button to "Day and name" and then saved the changes.

If we try and go to our new URL, we get a page not found error—not good...

If you look at the bottom of the permalinks page—you'll see a message that tells us our .htaccess file didn't get "written" to, which means it didn't get updated with our permalink rules....

.htaccess

WordPress can't add rules because it can't modify this file, so right now our pretty URLs don't work.

Minding your .htaccess file

If WordPress can't write to, or modify, your .htaccess file, it can't make your permalinks pretty. Normally, your .htaccess file is located in the public html directory on your web server— sometimes called the website "root" directory (this is also where WordPress is installed). Some servers may have special rules that allow that file to be located elsewhere (and some servers don't have the file at all). Since WordPress might not be able to add those rules because it can't write to the file, we'll add the rules manually instead.

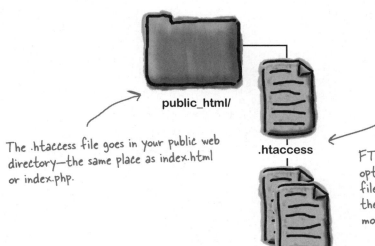

public_html/

The .htaccess filename starts with a dot (.) for security reasons and so they're not accidentally deleted. Because of this, files that start with dot are often "invisible" when viewing your files in your FTP client.

The .htaccess file goes in your public web directory—the same place as index.html or index.php.

.htaccess

FTP clients usually have an option to show or hide invisible files. You only need to have them visible if you need to modify the file.

Other WordPress files...

These 8 lines of code (which you can find in the WordPress permalink menu in your dashboard) will need to go at the top of your .htaccess file. Once they're there, your permalinks should work as expected.

Watch it!

Because most operating systems hide "invisible" files from you, the .htaccess usually doesn't show up on your own computer. Copy it in your FTP client and rename it to htaccess.txt (no dot in front of it). Download the .txt file to modify it on your local machine, and then rename it to .htaccess again when you upload the new version in your FTP client.

```
<IfModule mod_rewrite.c>
RewriteEngine On
RewriteBase /
RewriteRule ^index\.php$ - [L]
RewriteCond %{REQUEST_FILENAME} !-f
RewriteCond %{REQUEST_FILENAME} !-d
RewriteRule . /index.php [L]
</IfModule>
```

Exercise Solution

Go into the Permalink menu and modify your settings so that posts and pages can have pretty permalinks. Start with the "Day and name" permalink setting as that is the most common format on blogs.

① **Create and open your .htaccess file.**
In your FTP client, create a file called .htaccess in the public html folder (if it's not already there). Then open the file in a text editor.

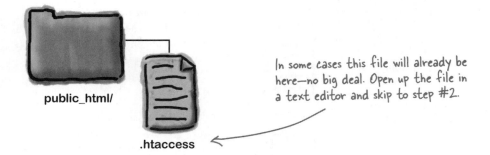

public_html/

.htaccess

In some cases this file will already be here—no big deal. Open up the file in a text editor and skip to step #2.

② **Add our rewrite rules.**
Paste the rules we copied from the WordPress permalink menu into the top of the .htaccess file and save.

```
<IfModule mod_rewrite.c>
RewriteEngine On
RewriteBase /
RewriteRule ^index\.php$ - [L]
RewriteCond %{REQUEST_FILENAME} !-f
RewriteCond %{REQUEST_FILENAME} !-d
RewriteRule . /index.php [L]
</IfModule>
```

Watch it!

If you are having problems getting your permalinks working, head over the WordPress Codex and read their detailed page on Permalinks and URL rewriting: http://codex.wordpress.org/ Using_Permalinks.

Nice work! Now we need to start filling these pages with the content from the main site...

Now you should see our products page when you type /products after your site's URL in your browser.

there are no Dumb Questions

Q: Why doesn't WordPress just call itself a content management system?

A: According to their website, WordPress is a "publishing" system, which is really just another phrase for content management system. The reason their mostly known for blogging software is because that's what WordPress was originally created for and that's where they built their following.

Q: Is there a limit to how many pages and posts I can create?

A: WordPress can handle hundreds of thousands of pages and posts which would only be limited by hard drive space for the database and server power to serve the pages. You'll most likely never reach the limit of WordPress's capabilities, and if you do, congratulations—you're a web rock star!

Q: I don't understand anything inside the .htaccess file. Help!?

A: That's OK, once you add that code to your .htaccess you'll most likely never have to look at that file again. All you need to know is that code is for WordPress and it needs to be in there for your site and pages to work properly with permalinks.

Build your pages with the visual editor

Now that we have our pages added and the permalinks in order, it's time to get the copy from the original Acme site over onto our new WordPress-powered site. To do this we're going to revisit the visual editor that we learned about in Chapter 1, and we'll dig in to see a few more things that it can help us do.

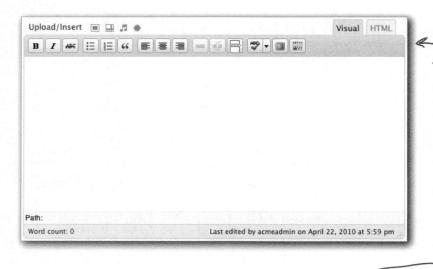

This is the default visual editor which will allow you to compose pages close to how they will look when published on the site. This is often referred to as the "What you see is what you get" or WYSIWYG (sounds like "whizzywig") view.

The "kitchen sink" button will add another row to the visual editor menu giving you more options for modifying the text and paragraphs in your page.

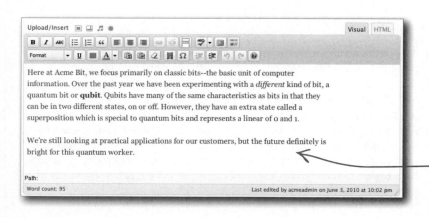

Here at Acme Bit, we focus primarily on classic bits--the basic unit of computer information. Over the past year we have been experimenting with a *different* kind of bit, a quantum bit or **qubit**. Qubits have many of the same characteristics as bits in that they can be in two different states, on or off. However, they have an extra state called a superposition which is special to quantum bits and represents a linear of 0 and 1.

We're still looking at practical applications for our customers, but the future definitely is bright for this quantum worker.

As you can see, when you use the visual editor style is added to your content the same way it would be on the live site. For many people, it's easier to compose pages when you don't have to sort through all the HTML in the code editor.

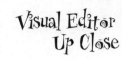

Visual Editor
Up Close

This cluster of options controls links (or <a> elements) and "more" tags inserted into posts. The ABC drop-down selects the post language and the monitor will toggle WordPress into full screen mode.

The kitchen sink button toggles between the default and the expanded visual editor menu.

The expanded menu gives you a style drop-down for automatically applying a style rule (like say, 18pt bold) to a particular section, and more advanced layout buttons like alignment and font color. Your new pages will inherit your blog's style, but sometimes you want something different. Just remember it only applies to the text you're currently working with—it doesn't update your CSS rules for the whole site.

These buttons are used to modify characters and paragraphs within your post or page. If you're familiar with word processing software, these should look familiar.

These buttons help you paste in from other sources. Make sure you use the Microsoft Word button when pasting in from a Word document to ensure that all the special characters display properly.

Finally, the last cluster of buttons on the expanded menu allow you to insert movies and other media as well as special characters like foreign currency symbols and special punctuation. We'll get to some of these options later in the book.

Exercise

Use the visual editor to add content to all the new pages you've created to bring over from the old Acme site (*http://acmebit.com*).

We need to get the content for all these pages into WordPress. Add the content and try to match the formatting as closely as possible using the visual editor.

Pay attention to the old Acme site and make sure you are getting all the content. Remember, you can preview your pages in WordPress before you commit to publishing them to the world.

Use the visual editor to add content to all the new pages you've created to bring over from the old Acme site (*http://acmebit.com*).

About (/about)

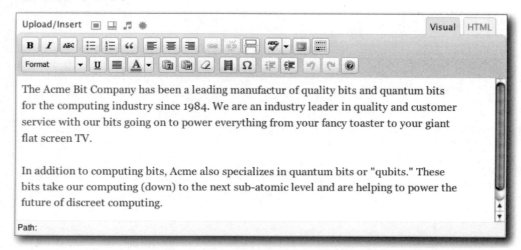

The Acme Bit Company has been a leading manufactur of quality bits and quantum bits for the computing industry since 1984. We are an industry leader in quality and customer service with our bits going on to power everything from your fancy toaster to your giant flat screen TV.

In addition to computing bits, Acme also specializes in quantum bits or "qubits." These bits take our computing (down) to the next sub-atomic level and are helping to power the future of discreet computing.

Path:

Contact (/contact)

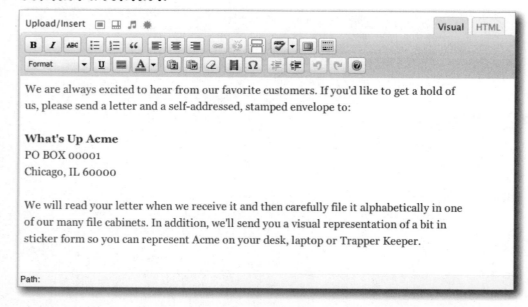

We are always excited to hear from our favorite customers. If you'd like to get a hold of us, please send a letter and a self-addressed, stamped envelope to:

What's Up Acme
PO BOX 00001
Chicago, IL 60000

We will read your letter when we receive it and then carefully file it alphabetically in one of our many file cabinets. In addition, we'll send you a visual representation of a bit in sticker form so you can represent Acme on your desk, laptop or Trapper Keeper.

Path:

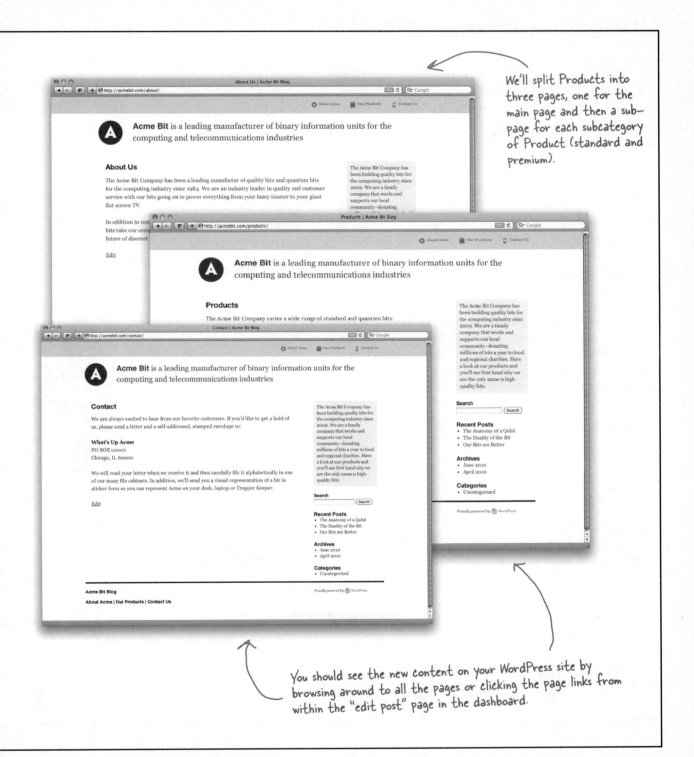

We'll split Products into three pages, one for the main page and then a sub-page for each subcategory of Product (standard and premium).

You should see the new content on your WordPress site by browsing around to all the pages or clicking the page links from within the "edit post" page in the dashboard.

All pages are not created equal

We've created all our new pages, but something's still not quite right. We just have a bunch of pretty URLs, but they aren't organized the way they were on the main Acme site. Creating a hierarchy is an important part of organizing your content. Some pages are what we call "top-level" content, which is like introducing a main subject. The AcmeBit page about Products is a top-level page, but some of the other pages are not.

> Wasn't there something we were supposed to do with that "tree" diagram from earlier? These pages don't have any hierarchy, maybe that has something to do with it?

True. Not all these pages are equivalent.

Creating a hierarchy entails making "nested" pages, or sub-pages out of secondary content. It helps people visiting your site know what to expect, and it will also make our URLs match the site organization. Like we saw earlier in our tree diagram, the top-level page is the parent page, and the sub-page is the child page. This creates a "nested" navigation, and our page URLs should then reflect the parent-child relationship.

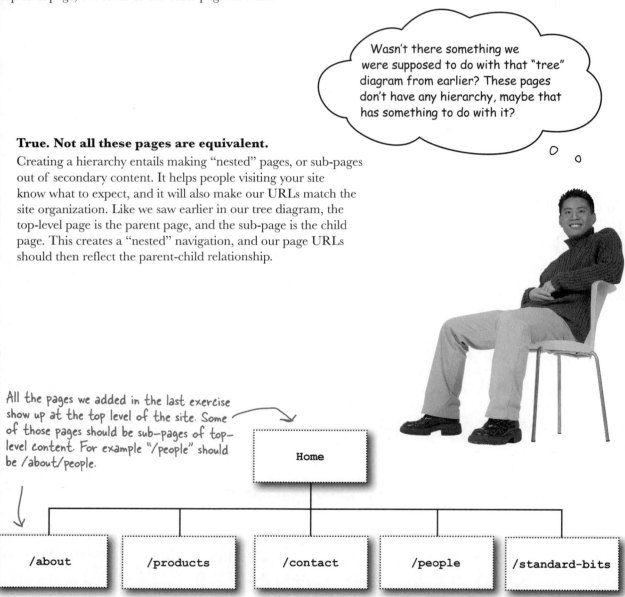

All the pages we added in the last exercise show up at the top level of the site. Some of those pages should be sub-pages of top-level content. For example "/people" should be /about/people.

```
                          Home

  /about    /products    /contact    /people    /standard-bits
```

Tree Diagram Magnets

Place the content magnets in the appropriate spots on the tree diagram. You may need to go back and look at the main Acme Bit site for help.

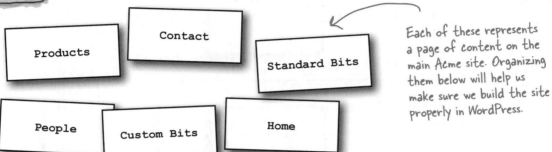

Products

Contact

Standard Bits

People

Custom Bits

Home

Each of these represents a page of content on the main Acme site. Organizing them below will help us make sure we build the site properly in WordPress.

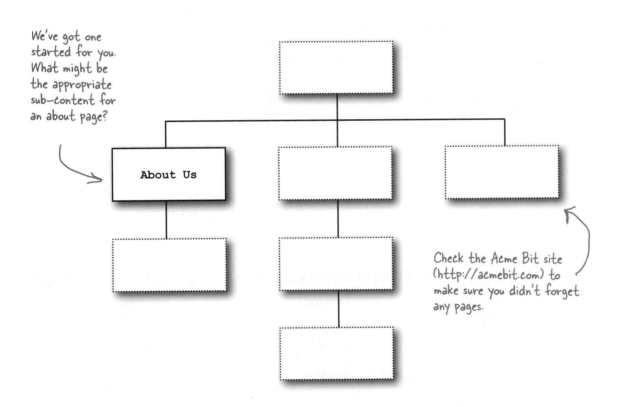

We've got one started for you. What might be the appropriate sub-content for an about page?

About Us

Check the Acme Bit site (http://acmebit.com) to make sure you didn't forget any pages.

Tree Diagram Magnets

Place the content magnets in the appropriate spots on the information architecture diagram. You may need to go back and look at the main Acme Bit site for help.

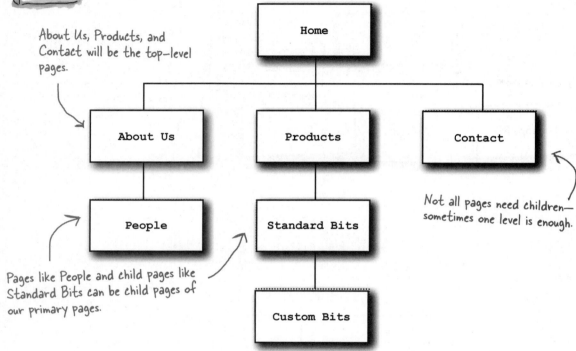

About Us, Products, and Contact will be the top-level pages.

Not all pages need children—sometimes one level is enough.

Pages like People and child pages like Standard Bits can be child pages of our primary pages.

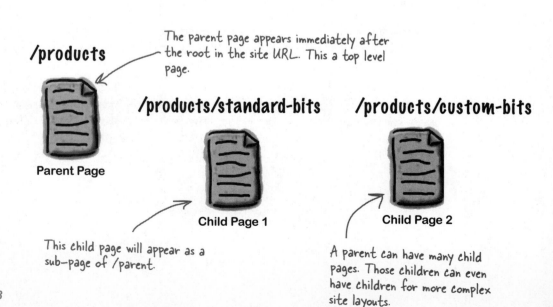

/products

The parent page appears immediately after the root in the site URL. This a top level page.

Parent Page

/products/standard-bits

Child Page 1

This child page will appear as a sub-page of /parent.

/products/custom-bits

Child Page 2

A parent can have many child pages. Those children can even have children for more complex site layouts.

Sharpen your pencil

Now that you've figured out which pages should go where, let's get that set up in WordPress. Look at the options in the page edit screen and build the parent-child relationships for all the pages.

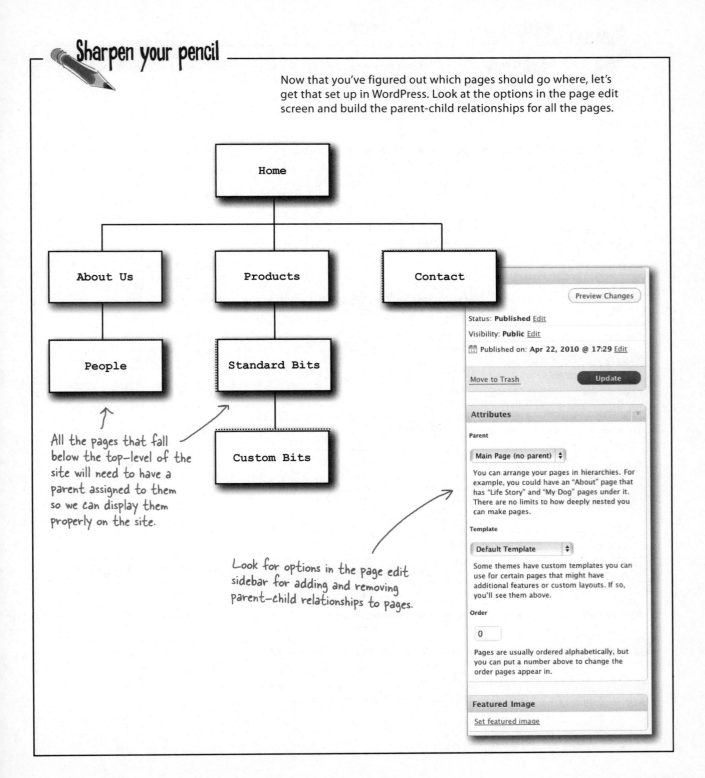

All the pages that fall below the top-level of the site will need to have a parent assigned to them so we can display them properly on the site.

Look for options in the page edit sidebar for adding and removing parent-child relationships to pages.

Sharpen your pencil
Solution

Look at the options in the page edit screen and build the parent-child relationships for all the pages.

1 **Find the Parent option in the Attributes sidebar.**
This drop-down will set the parent for the page you are editing. When you're in the Page list view, the child pages will appear indented.

All of the pages you have added will show up in the drop-down. Any page can be a parent of another page—just not for itself.

You can check your parent-child settings in the list view.

Main Page (no parent)
About Us
People
Contact
✓ Products
Standard Bits

You can arrange your pages in hie~~
example, you could have an "Abo~~
has "Life Story" and "My Dog" pag~~
There are no limits to how deeply ~~
can make pages.

Template

Default Template

Some themes have custom templ~~
use for certain pages that might ~~
additional features or custom lay~~
you'll see them above.

Order

2 **Select another WordPress page to act as the parent.**
Any other page in the system can act as the parent to your current page. After you select a new parent, make sure you save your page. You can make sure the relationship is correct by checking the indents in the page list view.

That's nice that they have parents, but how is that going to make those pages show up on the site? I don't see them in the navigation anywhere...

Build navigation using the WordPress menu system

WordPress has built-in functionality that allows you to build "menus" out of pages (and categories) and then use them in your themes. A menu is basically just a list of links—in this case the links will be for our site's pages that we just created. The great thing about this feature is that is recognizes our parent-child relationships and builds the appropriate nested navigation for us. Take a look at the screen shot below—notice how our child pages appear indented? This gives us extra options to control when and where the sub-page URLs get displayed.

Menus can be created from the Menu page of the Appearance section in your dashboard. You can create as many as you like and use them all over your site or blog.

Exercise

Locate the Menu admin section in your dashboard and build a navigation menu for the Acme site. Use the screenshot above as a guide.

Exercise Solution

Locate the Menu admin section in your dashboard and build a navigation menu for the Acme site.

1 **Select all available pages in the Add Pages sidebar.**
You can bring this selection list up by clicking the "Show All" link below the search field. This will add all the links to the Main Navigation.

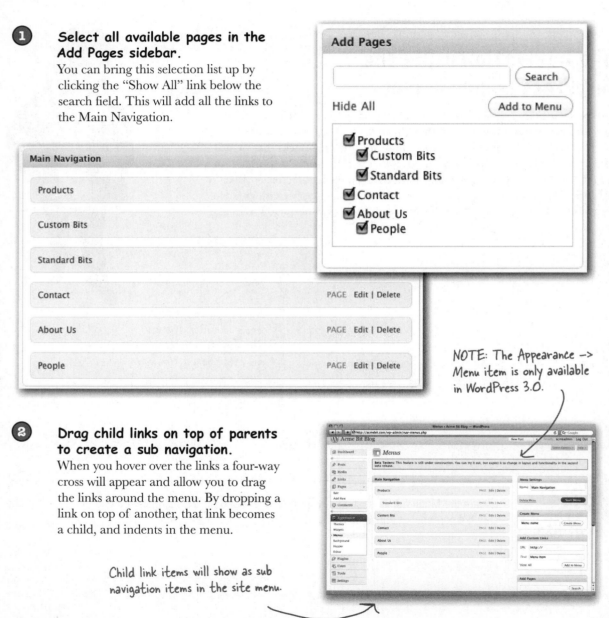

Add Pages

Search

Hide All   Add to Menu

☑ Products
    ☑ Custom Bits
    ☑ Standard Bits
☑ Contact
☑ About Us
    ☑ People

Main Navigation

Products

Custom Bits

Standard Bits

Contact   PAGE Edit | Delete

About Us   PAGE Edit | Delete

People   PAGE Edit | Delete

NOTE: The Appearance –> Menu item is only available in WordPress 3.0.

2 **Drag child links on top of parents to create a sub navigation.**
When you hover over the links a four-way cross will appear and allow you to drag the links around the menu. By dropping a link on top of another, that link becomes a child, and indents in the menu.

Child link items will show as sub navigation items in the site menu.

Modify your theme to enable the navigation menu

Now that we have our menu built, we need to get it onto our site. This feature is not enabled by default in our Acme theme so we need to add a bit of code to our template files so we can see the new navigation we built.

Once you've set all the parent-child elements in the menu it should look something like this. Notice how you can have multiple links set as children. This works great for our Product section that has multiple subsections.

Ready Bake Code

Add this to your sidebar.php template file.

Add just this line to your sidebar.php file in the Acme theme. This will place a navigation list in your sidebar on the pages that use the "sidebar" template.

You can leave everything else in here in the file just as it is.

```php
<div id="primary" class="widget-area">

        <?php wp_nav_menu(); ?>

        <ul class="xoxo">
<?php if ( ! dynamic_sidebar( 'primary-widget-area' ) ) :
// begin primary widget area ?>
        <li id="search" class="widget-container widget_
search">
                <?php get_search_form(); ?>
        </li>
        <li id="archives" class="widget-container">
                <h3 class="widget-title"><?php _e(
'Archives', 'twentyten' ); ?></h3>
                <ul>
                <?php wp_get_archives( 'type=monthly' ); ?>
                </ul>
        </li>
```

sidebar.php

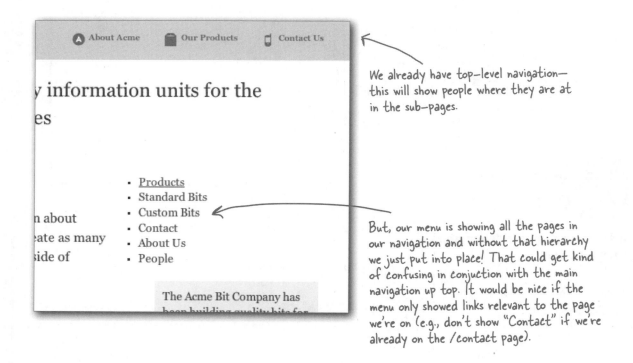

We already have top-level navigation—this will show people where they are at in the sub-pages.

But, our menu is showing all the pages in our navigation and without that hierarchy we just put into place! That could get kind of confusing in conjuction with the main navigation up top. It would be nice if the menu only showed links relevant to the page we're on (e.g., don't show "Contact" if we're already on the /contact page).

Use CSS rules to control what shows up in the menu

Getting our new menu into the page was only the first step. Since we didn't have any code in our theme's template to display the menu—and we just added that—we also didn't have any rules in our CSS file to make it work properly with the rest of the site. Let's create some rules that show and hide the sub-pages based on what page is currently being viewed, so our menu properly reflects the hierarchy we just put into place.

Ready Bake
Code

Update the CSS to make the menu play nice with the rest of the site

```
.menu li {
}

.menu li.current-menu-item {
        display: block;
        font-weight: bold;
}

.menu li.current-menu-item .menu-item-object-
page {
        display: block;
        font-weight: normal;
}

.menu li .submenu li.current-menu-item {
        display: block;
        font-weight: normal;
}
```

Add this to the bottom of your style.css file in the acmebit theme directory.

These CSS rules will make sure that our menu displays links depending on the page that is currently active.

style.css

Products
Standard Bits
▪ Custom Bits
Contact
About Us
▪ People

This is what our menu should look like in the sidebar of our pages.

TEST DRIVE

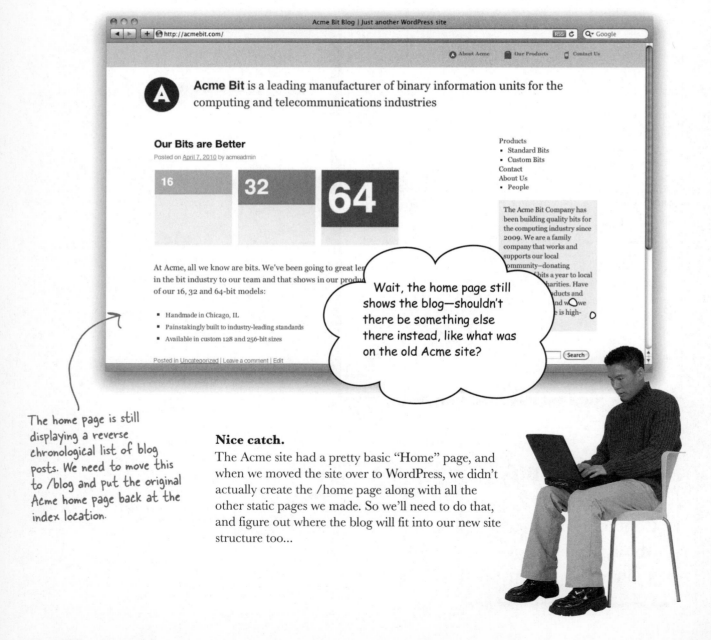

The home page is still displaying a reverse chronological list of blog posts. We need to move this to /blog and put the original Acme home page back at the index location.

Wait, the home page still shows the blog—shouldn't there be something else there instead, like what was on the old Acme site?

Nice catch.

The Acme site had a pretty basic "Home" page, and when we moved the site over to WordPress, we didn't actually create the /home page along with all the other static pages we made. So we'll need to do that, and figure out where the blog will fit into our new site structure too...

WordPress has different home page options

Sometimes you don't want your site's home page to be your blog. If you're just writing a blog this is fine, however, if the blog is just a small part of larger site (like our newly migrated Acme Bit site)—you may want to choose a different page to be the home page.

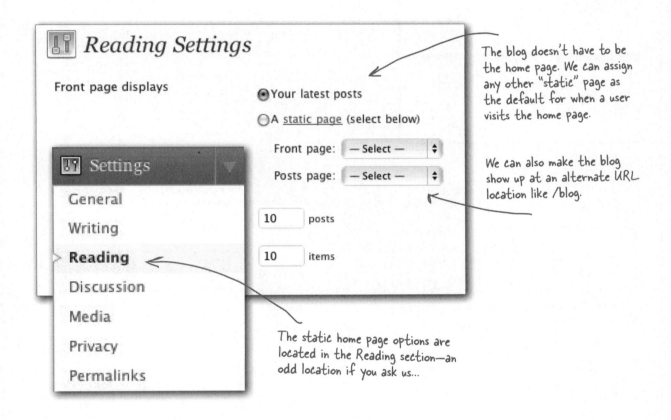

The blog doesn't have to be the home page. We can assign any other "static" page as the default for when a user visits the home page.

We can also make the blog show up at an alternate URL location like /blog.

The static home page options are located in the Reading section—an odd location if you ask us...

Sharpen your pencil

Use this menu and the static page options to make the blog appear at /blog and the original Acme home page (now powered by WordPress) appear as the default page for the site. (**Hint**: you probably have to create a few new static pages to make this work.)

Sharpen your pencil
Solution

Use this menu and the static page options to make the blog appear at /blog and the original Acme home page (now powered by WordPress) appear as the default page for the site. (**Hint**: you probably have to create a few new static pages to make this work.)

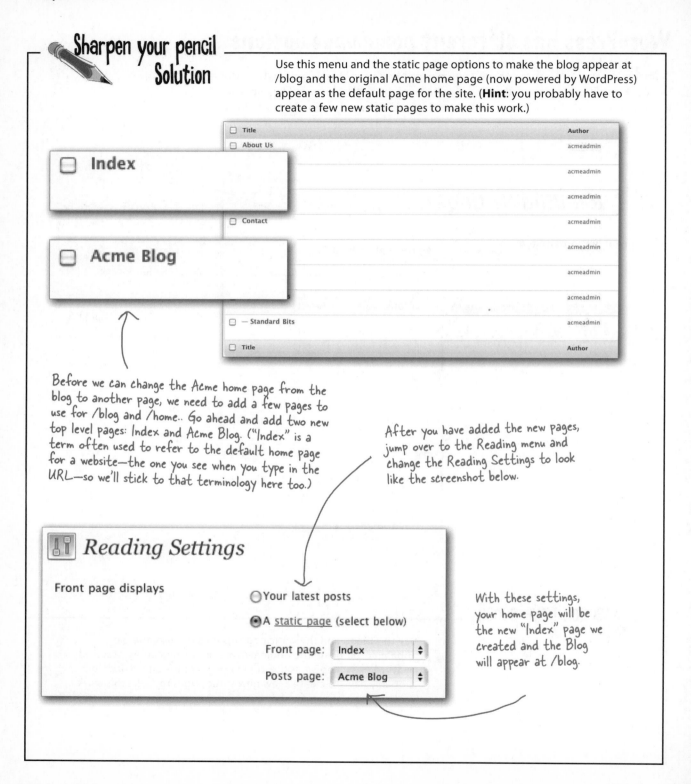

☐ Title	Author
☐ About Us	acmeadmin
	acmeadmin
	acmeadmin
☐ Contact	acmeadmin
	acmeadmin
	acmeadmin
	acmeadmin
☐ — Standard Bits	acmeadmin
☐ Title	Author

☐ **Index**

☐ **Acme Blog**

Before we can change the Acme home page from the blog to another page, we need to add a few pages to use for /blog and /home.. Go ahead and add two new top level pages: Index and Acme Blog. ("Index" is a term often used to refer to the default home page for a website—the one you see when you type in the URL—so we'll stick to that terminology here too.)

After you have added the new pages, jump over to the Reading menu and change the Reading Settings to look like the screenshot below.

Reading Settings

Front page displays

○ Your latest posts

● A static page (select below)

Front page: Index

Posts page: Acme Blog

With these settings, your home page will be the new "Index" page we created and the Blog will appear at /blog.

No more blog... No more home page either?

Like most sites on the Internet, the home page is usually somewhat unique. Maybe it has a rotating image at the top or a slightly different layout then the other pages. This helps anyone visiting your site identify whether they are on the main page or a sub-page of the site; it also helps set the brand and tone of your site. To accommodate this, we need to add a new template file to our theme to hold the special markup and layout for our new Acme home page.

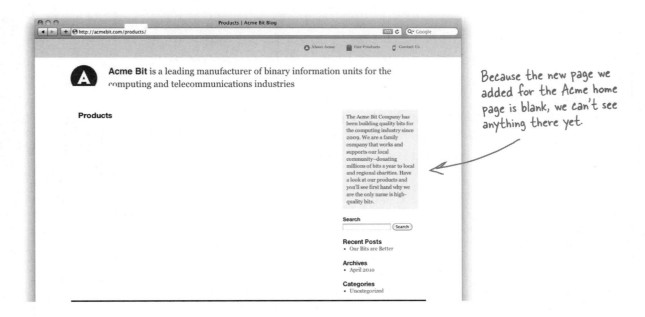

Because the new page we added for the Acme home page is blank, we can't see anything there yet.

The original home page already had its own special style—all we need to do is get this and the associated content into the new home page template file we just added.

Add HTML to your new home page template file

Ready Bake Code

Add this to your file (homepage.php), which you should have saved in the root of your template directory with the rest of your themes.

```php
<?php
/* Template Name: Homepage */
?>
<?php get_header(); ?>
<div id="content" class="wrap">
        <ul id="products">
                <li><p class="bit-16">16</p></li>
                <li class="center"><p class="bit-32">32</p></li>
                <li><p class="bit-64">64</p></li>
        </ul>
        <ul id="descriptions">
                <li><p><strong>16 Bits</strong> Lorem ipsum dolor sit amet,
consectetur adipisicing elit, sed do eiusmod tempor incididunt ut labore et
dolore magna aliqua. Ut enim ad minim veniam, quis nostrud exercitation ullamco
laboris.</p></li>
                <li class="center"><p><strong>32 Bits</strong> Lorem ipsum dolor sit
amet, consectetur adipisicing elit, sed do eiusmod tempor incididunt ut labore et
dolore magna aliqua. Ut enim ad minim veniam, quis nostrud exercitation ullamco
laboris.</p></li>
                <li><p><strong>64 Bits</strong> Lorem ipsum dolor sit amet,
consectetur adipisicing elit, sed do eiusmod tempor incididunt ut labore et
dolore magna aliqua. Ut enim ad mi
laboris.</p></li>
        </ul>
</div>
<?php get_footer(); ?>
```

This comment is important because it tells WordPress to use this file as a template that is available for us to use for our pages and posts.

homepage.php

This code is very similar to the markup that we found in the static Acme site.

Template

Homepage ⇕

Some themes have custom templates you can use for certain pages that might have additional features or custom layouts. If so, you'll see them above.

Make sure "homepage" is selected as the template for the new Index page.

Then add the Acme site style rules to your CSS file

Ready Bake Code

Add these rules to the bottom of your style.css file. They are all lines from the original Acme site css file. Most of them still work as they did on the old site.

```css
#products li {
        background: #eee;
        float: left;
        width: 250px;
        height: 250px;
        list-style-type: none;
}
#descriptions li {
        float: left;
        width: 250px;
        font-size: 1em;
        line-height: 1.6em;
        margin-top: 20px;
        list-style-type: none;
}
#products li p.bit-16 {
        background: #e8ba4a;
        font-weight: bold;
        font-size: 2.5em;
        padding: 20px;
        border-bottom: 5px solid #d7ac44;
        color: #fff;
}
```

```css
#products li p.bit-32 {
        font-weight: bold;
        font-size: 5em;
        background: #e87826;
        padding: 20px;
        border-bottom: 5px solid #d66e22;
        color: #fff;
}
#products li p.bit-64 {
        font-weight: bold;
        font-size: 10em;
        background: #ff3b16;
        padding: 20px;
        border-bottom: 5px solid #ed3314;
        color: #fff}

#products li.center, #descriptions
li.center {
        margin: 0 20px 0 20px;
}

#descriptions li.center {
        margin: 20px 20px 0 20px;
}
```

style.css

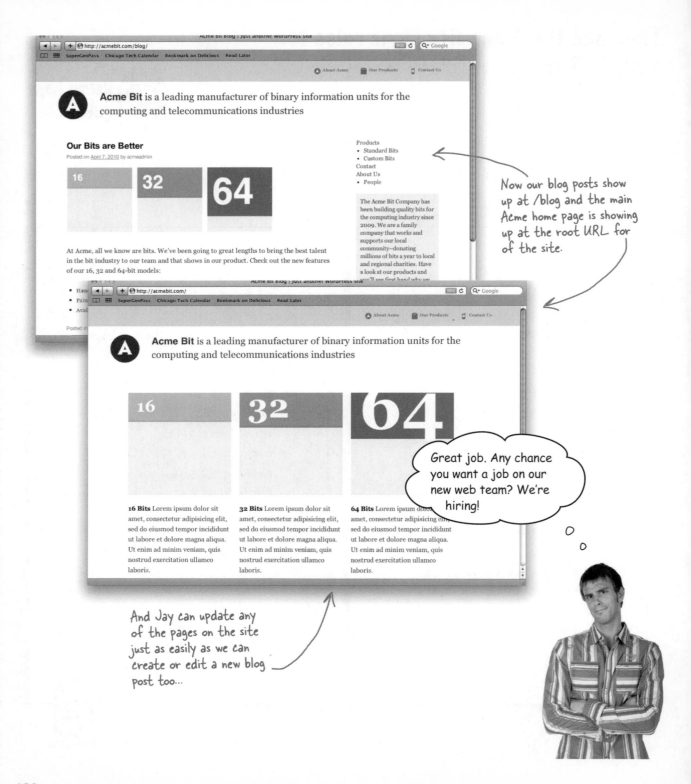

Now our blog posts show up at /blog and the main Acme home page is showing up at the root URL for of the site.

Great job. Any chance you want a job on our new web team? We're hiring!

And Jay can update any of the pages on the site just as easily as we can create or edit a new blog post too...

Your WordPress Toolbox

You've got Chapter 3 under your belt and now you've added managing non-blog content for a website. Next up, letting multiple users post to your blog, and adding categories and tags.

BULLET POINTS

- Although WordPress is billed as a blogging platform, it's perfectly at home in the world of content management systems and can be used to manage all aspects of a website.

- WordPress allows you to add pages which are just like posts but outside the blog.

- Use Pretty Permalinks to change the end of your URLs from /?page=12 to something more user-friendly like /contact.

- The visual editor can be used to style text in post and pages and can even expand to give you more word processor-like functionality.

- Pages can have parents and children which allow you to display the pages on the site in a tree-like hierarchy.

- WordPress 3.0 introduces the concept of menus which will help you build navigation based on pages and posts on your site.

- If you manage a blog and static pages together, you can use the "different first page" feature in WordPress to make your blog appear at a URL other than the home page.

4 users, categories, and tags

Keeping things organized

You want that published when? Let me check our calendar for next spring...

It's time to invite some friends to the party.

Blogging (or managing a WordPress site) doesn't *have* to be a solitary venture. Loads of well-know blogs out there feature multiple user **roles**, from **writers** to **editors** and **administrators**. In this chapter, you'll learn how to get **multiple people** posting on the same blog, manage the **workflow** across all those people, and put **categories** and **tags** to work in organizing your site's content.

You're the new editor of Thanks for Mutton

Thanks for Mutton is an online magazine—OK, a **blog**—that publishes about food and cooking from a uniquely geeky point of view. You've been brought in to bring some organization not only to the site (which runs on WordPress) but also to your group of staff writers and contributors. Let's take a look and see what you've got to work with.

This is the main home page of Thanks for Mutton—notice how the 2 recent posts went live within a few minutes of each other...

You may have noticed these categories on your WordPress blog already. We'll cover them in depth in this chapter, but for now notice that there doesn't seem to be any category other than 'uncategorized.' Doesn't seem too helpful, does it?

	Username	Name	E-mail	Role
☐ ⏻	admin		admin@thanksformutton.com	Administrator

Every staff writer is using the same login to add posts to the blog in WordPress. On top of that, it's the administrator's login, which means writers could have access to lots of sensitive stuff! This can't be good...

There is really no way to tell who wrote what. Some authors added their names to the bottom of the post—others did nothing at all and most of the posts just say 'admin.'

Our readers just care about the writing. We don't have time for categorizing stuff...

We all use the same login because it's easy— you never forget the password!

The TFM staff.

⚛ BRAIN POWER

Now that you've seen what you're dealing with here, take a few minutes to think about how you can get both your writers and the site's content better organized.

WordPress user roles

A "user" in WordPress is any person that has access to your site with a username and password. WordPress allows you to add multiple users and give each of those users a role within the system. For example, we could have a main administrator that controls all aspects of the site and an editor that can only review and publish content but has no access to core WordPress settings. In general, user roles adhere to a heirarchical structure:

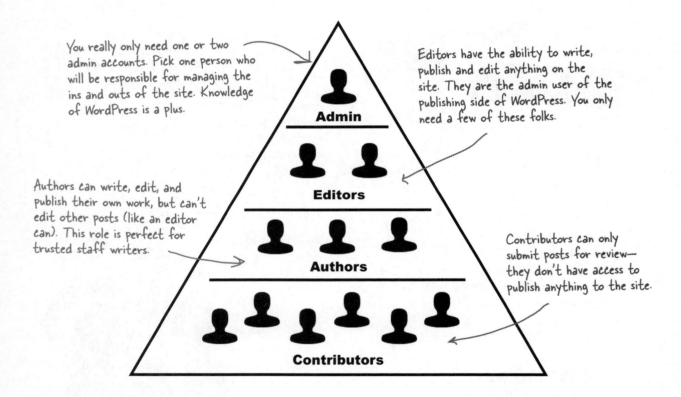

You really only need one or two admin accounts. Pick one person who will be responsible for managing the ins and outs of the site. Knowledge of WordPress is a plus.

Editors have the ability to write, publish and edit anything on the site. They are the admin user of the publishing side of WordPress. You only need a few of these folks.

Authors can write, edit, and publish their own work, but can't edit other posts (like an editor can). This role is perfect for trusted staff writers.

Contributors can only submit posts for review—they don't have access to publish anything to the site.

What are some reasons why there might be a much larger number of Contributors vs. Editors or Administrators?

The anatomy of a WordPress user

You are in control of adding users to your system, but WordPress is also set up to support visitors creating their own accounts too (so they can leave comments, for example). In this chapter, we focus on user accounts that you set up for people to write for your blog. Let's take a look at the options you have for users in your WordPress dashboard.

In your dashboard, each user has a set of attributes that make up his or her "profile" in WordPress. This includes their name, email, and image display settings. We can use these attributes throughout our site to add information to our site's posts and pages, and to control which users have access to specific features.

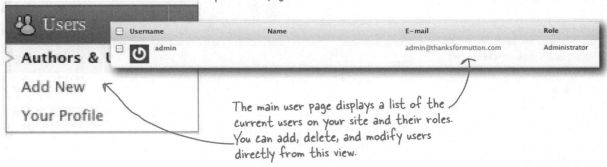

The main user page displays a list of the current users on your site and their roles. You can add, delete, and modify users directly from this view.

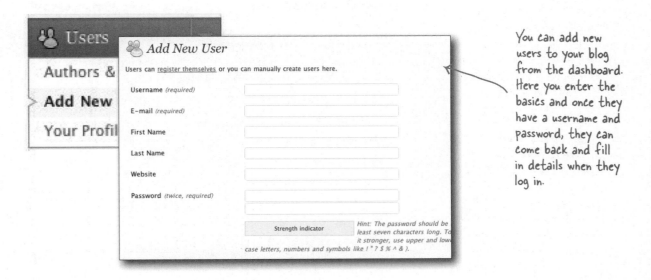

You can add new users to your blog from the dashboard. Here you enter the basics and once they have a username and password, they can come back and fill in details when they log in.

Let's see how the dashboard profile looks from a user's perspective...

A sample user profile

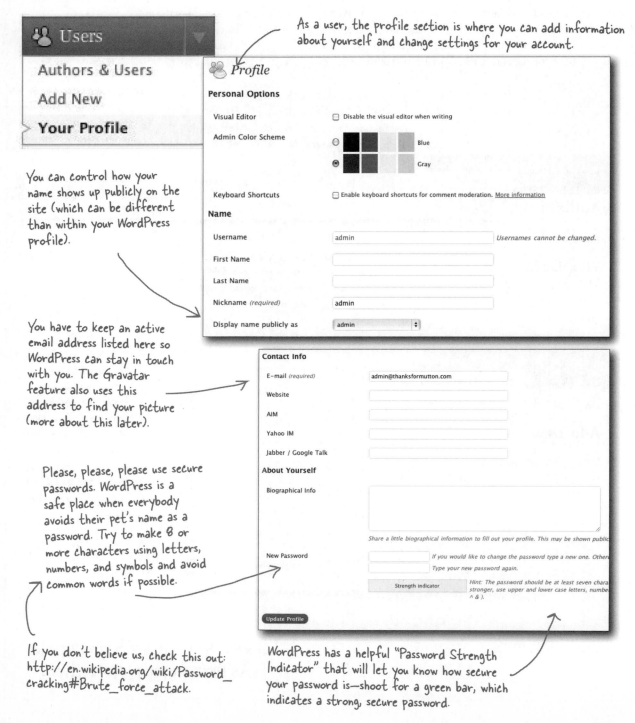

As a user, the profile section is where you can add information about yourself and change settings for your account.

You can control how your name shows up publicly on the site (which can be different than within your WordPress profile).

You have to keep an active email address listed here so WordPress can stay in touch with you. The Gravatar feature also uses this address to find your picture (more about this later).

Please, please, please use secure passwords. WordPress is a safe place when everybody avoids their pet's name as a password. Try to make 8 or more characters using letters, numbers, and symbols and avoid common words if possible.

If you don't believe us, check this out: http://en.wikipedia.org/wiki/Password_cracking#Brute_force_attack.

WordPress has a helpful "Password Strength Indicator" that will let you know how secure your password is—shoot for a green bar, which indicates a strong, secure password.

WHO DOES WHAT?

Match each user role to the permissions it has within WordPress.

👤 Administrator

I can write and edit my own posts but I can't publish—all my posts must be submitted for review.

👤 Editor

I can write and publish my own posts but I can't modify or publish any other user's posts.

👤 Author

I can write and publish my own posts but I also have full access to other users' posts. I can do almost anything in the dashboard related to publishing.

👤 Contributor

I am usually an optional role and have no access to any dashboard features outside of the profile view.

👤 Subscriber

I can do everything inside of WordPress including assigning roles to other users and changing site-wide settings.

Match each user role to the permissions it has within WordPress..

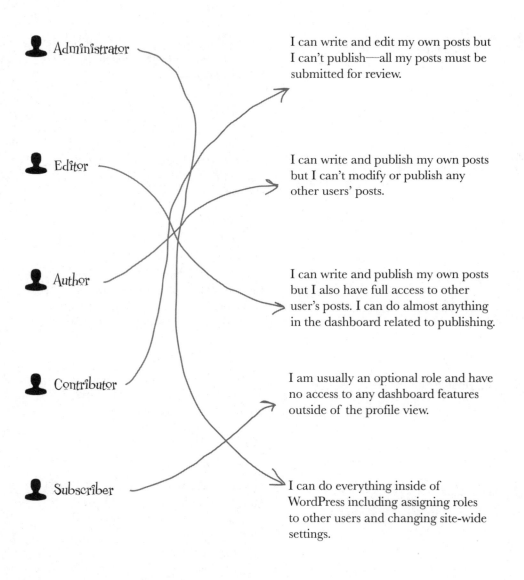

Administrator

Editor

Author

Contributor

Subscriber

I can write and edit my own posts but I can't publish—all my posts must be submitted for review.

I can write and publish my own posts but I can't modify or publish any other users' posts.

I can write and publish my own posts but I also have full access to other user's posts. I can do almost anything in the dashboard related to publishing.

I am usually an optional role and have no access to any dashboard features outside of the profile view.

I can do everything inside of WordPress including assigning roles to other users and changing site-wide settings.

Match users to their appropriate roles

If you set up your blog to have 5 administrators and 20 people that all have access to publish content to the live site whenever they want, you're going to have problems. It may seem a bit foreign at first, but for each user, spend a bit of time thinking about what they are doing on the site, and how much responsibility they should be given. Beyond that, here's a good rule of thumb based on the user hierarchy pyramid: **The higher the role in the system, the fewer users should be assigned to that role.**

Who gets the nice wine glass at your party, and who gets the plastic cup?

Sharpen your pencil

Write down each staff member's role next to their name and then create a user account for them with the appropriate role.

You

You control the site

_____

Ryan

Writes seasonally

_____

Allie

Staff writer

_____

Jeff

Dedicated food reviewer

_____

Staff writer

_____

Dwight

Junior veggie writer

_____

Jerry

Freelance writer

_____

George

Culinary Editor

_____

Sharpen your pencil
Solution

Write down each staff member's role next to their name and then create a user account for them with the appropriate role.

Add New User

Users cannot currently register themselves, but you can manually create users here.

Username *(required)*	allie
E-mail *(required)*	allie@technolligentsia.com
First Name	Allie

Password *(twice, required)*	••••••••••••••
	••••••••••••••
	Strong *Hint: The password upper and lower c...*
Send Password?	☑ Send this password to the new user by email.
Role	Author

Add User

Here you fill out all the required fields for a new user. You can have the users fill in the rest later.

Make sure you are using strong passwords! Safety first.

You are already the administrator—we can leave that alone.

Both these writers can publish themselves because they work for the site.

You
You control the site
Administrator

Ryan
Writes seasonally
Contributor

Allie
Staff writer
Author

Jeff
Dedicated food reviewer
Author

All the contributors write part time for the blog and we don't want to let our junior writer publish quite yet.

Our culinary editor needs to be able to read all the posts and check for technical errors.

Michael
Staff writer
Author

Dwight
Junior veggie writer
Contributor

Jerry
Freelance writer
Contributor

George
Culinary editor
Editor

> Hmm. The roles seem to work but posts are still being published one after the next— sometimes within minutes of one another. Can we do something about that?

Avoid chaos with an editorial workflow

Now that we have a group of users with specific roles for Thanks for Mutton, we can take a quick look at what the editorial workflow might look like. The term "workflow" simply refers to how pages and posts move betwen content producers and editors when some form of review and approval is required— potentially multiple times—before somthing is published. The site has two main content producers: *authors*, who are staff writers with publishing rights, and *contributors*, who are contract or seasonal writers that submit stories for publication.

The author role is perfect for trusted writers on your site and for authors that might have their own section or "column" on the site.

Authors

Authors can publish their own posts but can't edit or publish anyone else's post.

Contributor roles work well for friends or other bloggers to guest post on your site. All their posts have to go through the editor before they go live on the site.

Contributors submit posts to the editor for review and potential publication.

Contributors

Editor

The editor publishes contributor's posts, and reviews the author's posts after they've gone live too.

The editor reviews contributors posts and may request changes before publishing their posts.

Review pending posts from the admin dashboard

Once a post is submitted for review, the editors and administrators need to be able to read it, make changes, and then post it to the site.

① **Submit for Review.**
Contributors submit articles for review by editors. These posts will show "pending" until they've been approved.

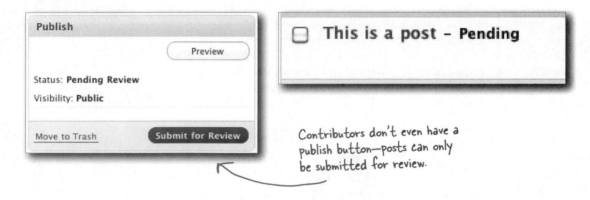

Contributors don't even have a publish button—posts can only be submitted for review.

② **As an editor (or and administrator) you can publish pending posts.**
When an editor sees pending posts, they have the options to read and edit the content before it goes live on the site.

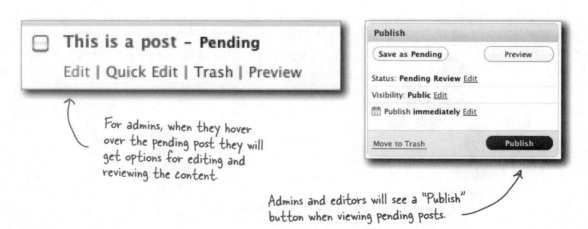

For admins, when they hover over the pending post they will get options for editing and reviewing the content.

Admins and editors will see a "Publish" button when viewing pending posts.

there are no
Dumb Questions

Q: What is the maximum number of users I can have on my site?

A: There is no hard limit on how many users can have accounts on your blog. Odds are you'll never even come close to reaching a number of users that would cause any problems with WordPress.

Q: Can you create your own user roles with special permissions in WordPress?

A: At this time, no. WordPress ships with the six main roles and doesn't give you much else to work with. There are some workarounds if you're comfortable writing PHP and plug-ins—but most people find the current roles to be adequate. For

more information on the WordPress role system, check out *http://codex.wordpress.org/Roles_and_Capabilities*.

Q: Can you have more than one administrator per WordPress install?

A: Yes, WordPress allows you to add other administrators to the system. We recommend you keep these roles to one or two trusted people in your organization.

Things are starting to look more organized...

Each author now has a proper (and correctly named) byline.

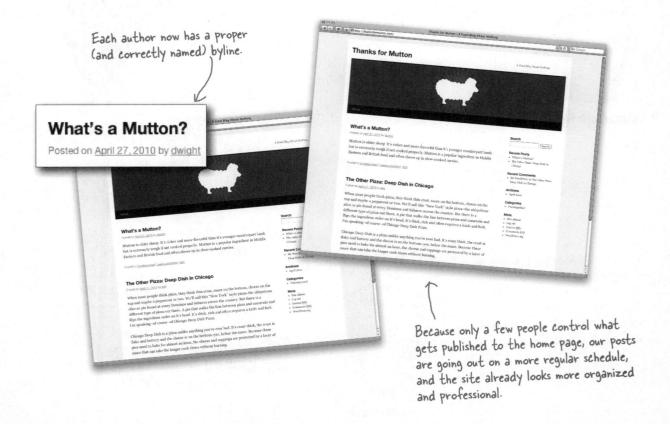

Because only a few people control what gets published to the home page, our posts are going out on a more regular schedule, and the site already looks more organized and professional.

Whew, at least you got all those writers sorted out. But didn't you say something earlier about adding "categories" too?

Categories are big buckets for your content

Categories aren't always required for blogs, but most of the time it helps to have some organizational structure to your posts. Think of categories as broad "buckets" that describe or *hold* your content in WordPress. Once a post is assigned to a category, it can be displayed in WordPress alongside other posts within the same category. They also give visitors a snapshot of what type of content they can expect on your site and help them find other posts they might be interested in.

Each category can contain as many posts as you like.

Restaurant Reviews

Don't use jargon or confusing words when creating categories. Know your audience and pick appropriate terms.

Molecular Gastronomy

Since we're talking to food nerds here, this category is actually appropriate.

It's a good idea to make your categories broad so you don't end up with hundreds of them. This will make your job as an editor easier and your users will definitely appreciate it..

With your content organized by category, users will be able to find posts easier and navigate the site based on their specific interests.

Recipes

Categories help organize your content

When creating categories, think about the big concepts behind particular posts—and even behind the site as a whole. Categories should be very well thought out—almost sacred—so don't just add them on a whim. If you find yourself adding lots of different categories, you're probably not being broad enough. Categories represent the main areas of content of your site, so treat them accordingly.

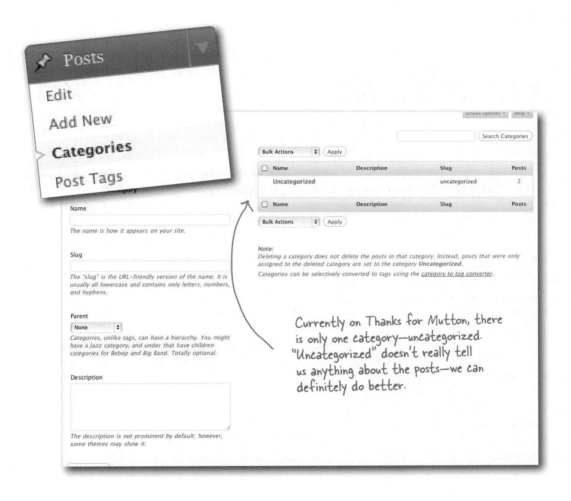

Currently on Thanks for Mutton, there is only one category—uncategorized. "Uncategorized" doesn't really tell us anything about the posts—we can definitely do better.

Content is key when creating category structures

As the editor of *Thanks for Mutton*, you'll want to take some time and think about what you want the site to be about, and what's the best way to organize it before you start adding categories. This way, you can set up a category structure that fits your content well so you're not always scrambling to figure out what bucket a post belongs in, and you (or your authors) are not always creating new categories every time a new post goes up on the site.

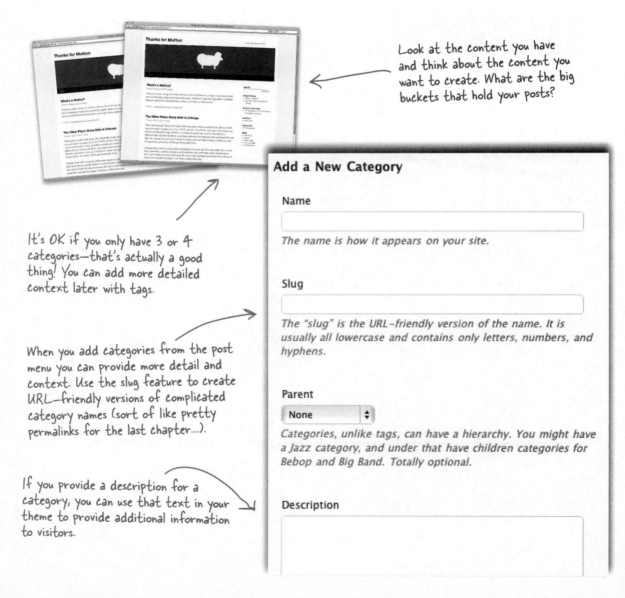

Look at the content you have and think about the content you want to create. What are the big buckets that hold your posts?

It's OK if you only have 3 or 4 categories—that's actually a good thing! You can add more detailed context later with tags.

When you add categories from the post menu you can provide more detail and context. Use the slug feature to create URL—friendly versions of complicated category names (sort of like pretty permalinks for the last chapter...).

If you provide a description for a category, you can use that text in your theme to provide additional information to visitors.

Add a New Category

Name

The name is how it appears on your site.

Slug

The "slug" is the URL–friendly version of the name. It is usually all lowercase and contains only letters, numbers, and hyphens.

Parent

None ⬍

Categories, unlike tags, can have a hierarchy. You might have a Jazz category, and under that have children categories for Bebop and Big Band. Totally optional.

Description

Category Magnets

Use the magnets below to build a category structure for Thanks for Mutton. You don't have to use all the magnets, and remember to think about big, broad bucket for your content.

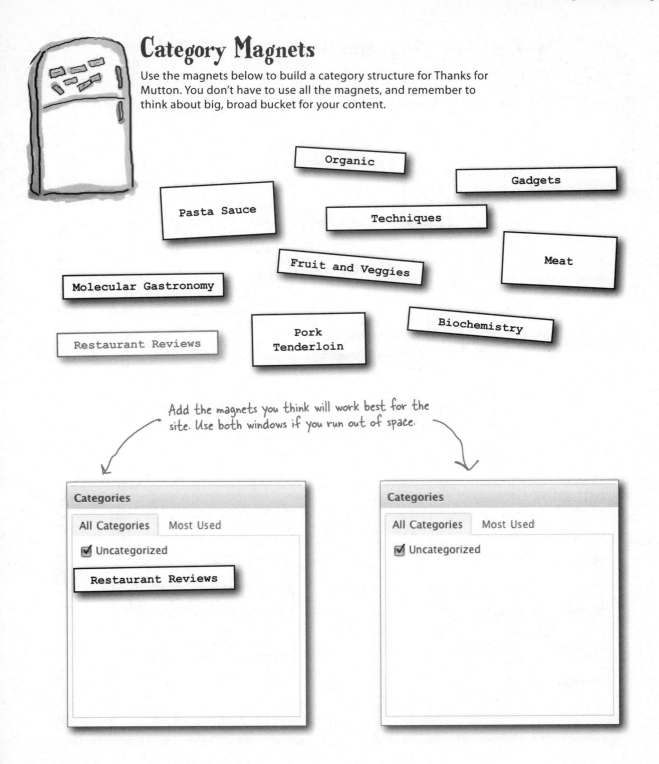

Organic

Gadgets

Pasta Sauce

Techniques

Meat

Fruit and Veggies

Molecular Gastronomy

Biochemistry

Restaurant Reviews

Pork Tenderloin

Add the magnets you think will work best for the site. Use both windows if you run out of space.

Categories

All Categories	Most Used

☑ Uncategorized

Restaurant Reviews

Categories

All Categories	Most Used

☑ Uncategorized

Category Magnets

Use the magnets below to build a category structure for Thanks for Mutton. You don't have to use all the magnets, and remember to think about big, broad bucket for your content.

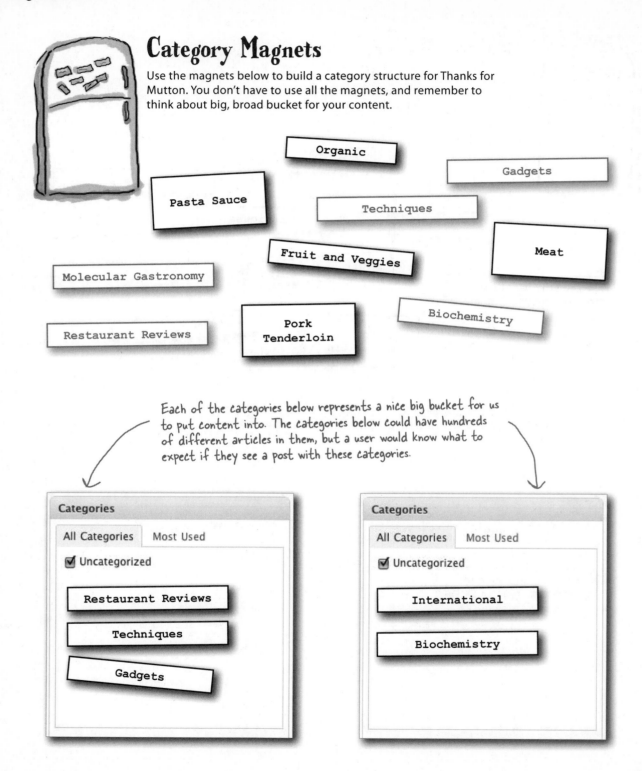

Organic

Gadgets

Pasta Sauce

Techniques

Meat

Molecular Gastronomy

Fruit and Veggies

Restaurant Reviews

Pork Tenderloin

Biochemistry

Each of the categories below represents a nice big bucket for us to put content into. The categories below could have hundreds of different articles in them, but a user would know what to expect if they see a post with these categories.

Categories

All Categories   Most Used

☑ Uncategorized

Restaurant Reviews

Techniques

Gadgets

Categories

All Categories   Most Used

☑ Uncategorized

International

Biochemistry

Leftover categories often make good tags

Don't worry if you have categories left over—that's a good thing! This usually means that the remaining categories are too narrow and might be better used as what are called "tags" within a post. Tags are specific terms that give more detail about the content of the post—a post about sous vide cooking might be in the "Techniques" category and have tags like "sous vide" and "meat." A good rule of thumb is that a post should have a single category and one or more tags. Use tags to add detail once you've placed your post in a larger category bucket.

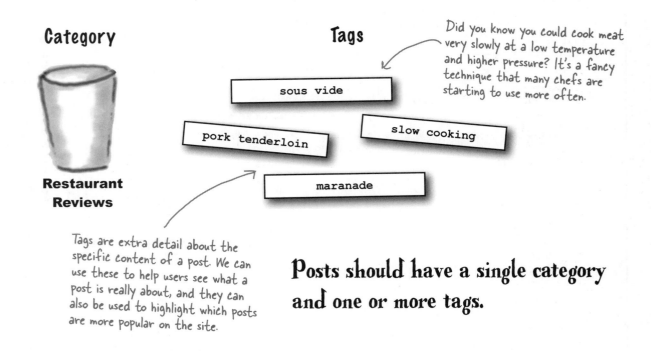

Category

Restaurant Reviews

Tags

sous vide

pork tenderloin

slow cooking

maranade

Did you know you could cook meat very slowly at a low temperature and higher pressure? It's a fancy technique that many chefs are starting to use more often.

Tags are extra detail about the specific content of a post. We can use these to help users see what a post is really about, and they can also be used to highlight which posts are more popular on the site.

Posts should have a single category and one or more tags.

Exercise

Go back into WordPress and add the category structure you built in the Magnets exercise. Then, add specific tags to the posts that have already been published—this will act as a starting point for new posts and authors. **Remember:** look closely at the articles when choosing categories and tags and make them specific to your content.

Exercise Solution

Go back into WordPress and add the category structure you built in the Magnets exercise. Then, add specific tags to the posts that have already been published—this will act as a starting point for new posts and authors. **Remember:** look closely at the articles when choosing categories and tags and make them specific to your content.

You can add and modify all your categories from the category page in the post menu. If you have long category names you can add a shorter 'slug' word or phrase that will show up in the URL for that category.

Popular Categories

Reviews

Add New Category

Name

Restaurant Reviews

The name is how it appears on your site.

Slug

reviews

The "slug" is the URL-friendly version of the name. It is usually all lowercase and contains only letters, numbers, and hyphens.

	Name	Description		Posts
☐	**Biochemistry**			0
☐	**International**			0
☐	**Gadgets**		gadgets	0
☐	**Techniques**		techniques	0
☐	**Restaurant Reviews**		restaurant-reviews	0

Bulk Actions ⬍ (Apply)

1 **Add categories from the post menu.**
You can add categories from within a post or from the category page in the posts menu. Either way, they end up in the same place.

② Assign categories and tags.

Both categories and tags can be added to a post from the new or edit post screens. The sidebar will show all the categories used on your site in addition to a list of the most used tags.

Once you're editing a post, you can select the category you want it to show up in. Remember to try and pick one category that best represents your post.

Like categories, post tags can also be added to your article from the edit page. Here, try and be a little more specific regarding the content of your post.

Once you publish your post, the category and tags will show up in the byline or footer of your post. Visitors can then click on the tags and categories to see the archive and index—showing all posts containing those tags or categories.

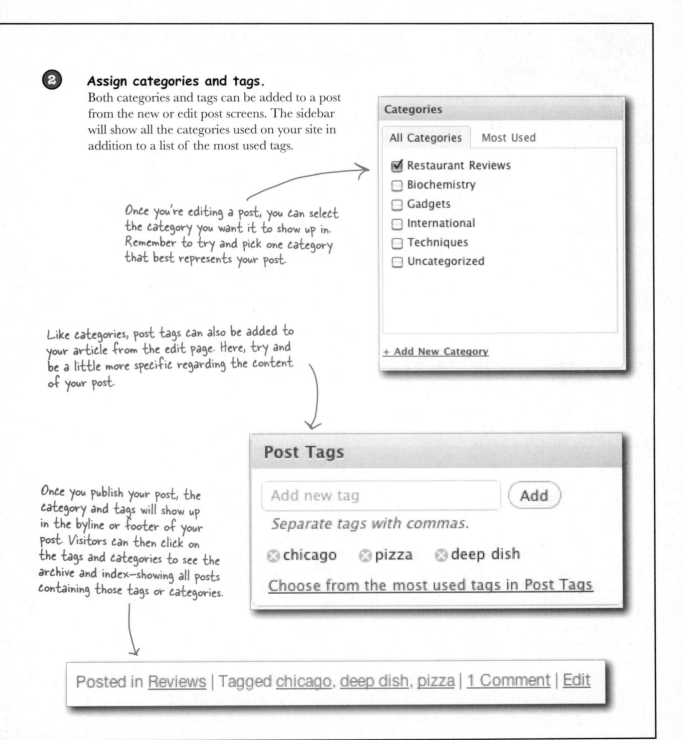

Categories

All Categories | Most Used

☑ Restaurant Reviews
☐ Biochemistry
☐ Gadgets
☐ International
☐ Techniques
☐ Uncategorized

+ Add New Category

Post Tags

Add new tag   (Add)

Separate tags with commas.

⊗ chicago   ⊗ pizza   ⊗ deep dish

Choose from the most used tags in Post Tags

Posted in Reviews | Tagged chicago, deep dish, pizza | 1 Comment | Edit

Fireside Chats

Tonight's talk: **Categories and Tags sound off about who offers the most information to site visitors.**

Categories:

I'd just like to start by saying that I'm the original taxonomy. I was around before tags were even a twinkle in WordPress's eye. In fact, the original tagging structure in WordPress was built on top of the category system.

Tags:

Just because you've been around longer doesn't mean you're better. You are too broad, you give people no in-depth information about an article. Big "buckets." What's that all about?

Oh, come on—broad topics are the only way to go. A site visitor can take one quick look at a category list and know exactly what kind of content is on a site or page. Tags only give me information when I click on a post and scroll all the way to the bottom. Plus, everyone understands *categories*—you always have to explain yourself to people.

Obviously you've never heard of a tag cloud. You can put it right on the home page and it gives you WAY more information then a list of categories. It shows what are the most popular topics on the site. Popular stuff, that's what people want. Plus, it's not enough to say this post is about design—you need to tell them what *kind* of design.

Oh, here we go with the tag cloud argument. You know, if I wanted to I could display myself as a tag cloud. Plus, what year is it—2007? Tag clouds, pssh...

Categories:

Well, if I'm used properly there shouldn't be that many of me. It's kind of hard to make a tag cloud out of 5 categories. Let's just agree that we do different things. You handle the details and I take care of the big picture. You can't have a blog without categories! Can you?...

Agreed... A compromise then. I'll take care of the "big picture" and you can deal with all the little details. I don't want to do that stuff anyway. Oh, you can also keep the tag cloud—I'm old-school like that.

Tags:

Well, why don't you then? I'm sure your users would appreciate it. And don't think my only trick is the tag cloud. I've seen users do pretty cool things with bar graphs and all sorts of other cool visuals based on tags.

Whoa. You sound a little nervous—like you think you may be obsolete. Personally, I think you are useful when used correctly, but most people abuse your power. Have you ever been to a site with hundreds of categories? It's overkill and it just makes you look like you can't focus.

All right, that sounds like a plan to me.

Writers want their pictures next to their posts

Now that we have some organization to Thanks for Mutton, the writers are starting to ask for more features. They'd like to know if you can add their images to posts, and to comments that they make on posts. They've noticed this on other sites and think it would be a good idea to put faces to names on the blog.

Man, we just got our names by our posts not too long ago.

That shouldn't be too hard—especially for our rock star editor.

Look at that! All the writers have an image with their post...

These writers can be a handful sometimes—but images are a good idea and this shouldn't be too hard to get set up.

We have some space on the right-hand side of the post section that would be great for an author picture.

What's a Mutton?

Posted on April 27, 2010 by dwight

Mutton is older sheep. It's richer and more flavorful than it's younger counterpart lamb but is extremely tough if not cooked properly. Mutton is a popular ingredient in Middle Eastern and British food and often shows up in slow-cooked curries.

Posted in Uncategorized | Leave a comment | Edit

Gravatar makes user pictures easy

Gravatar is a service by Automattic—the same folks that maintain WordPress. It stores "avatar," or profile, images tied to an email address on its servers so websites around the Internet can use those images to display the avatar of users logged in to their sites. The idea is that you can upload an image once and use it across any site that supports Gravatar.

Gravatar hosts millions of avatars for users across the Internet. It's a widely supported service used by many social media sites.

You may have noticed this sideways "G" in the dashboard. This is the default from Gravatar—if you "open the image in a new window" you'll see that it's not hosted on our server.

Depending on your WordPress settings and whether or not you have an account with Gravatar, you may see one of the following images. The "mystery man" image on the left is the default for WordPress.

Jeff Siarto

@Mark

That feature was something that I originally considered but I really wanted to

Sarah

Thank you so much for this tut!

I am also interested in what Mark requested, basically being able to define

marlus araujo

Wow! Great plugin example.
Is there a way to filter custom tags?

I've tryed

add_filter('get_post_meta', 'vimeo_code');

but with no success

Gravatar images can show up all over a website, including in the comments area. On our site, commenters must enter an email address and that is used to pull in their Gravatar image.

ExeRcise

Head on over to *gravatar.com* and sign up for an account (if you don't already have one). Once you're all set up, make sure that the email you used for Gravatar matches the email in your WordPress profile.

Exercise Solution

Head on over to *gravatar.com* and sign up for an account (if you don't already have one). Once you're all set up, make sure that the email you used for Gravatar matches the email in your WordPress profile.

① Sign up with your email address.
You have to use an active email address with Gravatar. They will send you a verification to make sure you are who you say you are...

Don't use a phony email address—Gravatar needs the one you use on your favorite sites.

② Upload your image to Gravatar.
Once the account is created you can upload an image, resize it, and link it to your email address within Gravatar.

Choose a file from your hard drive to send to Gravatar. They will let you adjust it in the browser so don't spend too much time editing things.

③ Use your Gravatar email in your WordPress profile.
In order for your avatar image to show up properly in WordPress you need to use the same email address in your profile that you used to set up your Gravatar account.

Gravatar works with your email address

Gravatar works by linking your email address to an avatar image that's stored on the Gravatar servers. When an application or website that uses the Gravatar service wants to display your picture, it sends an encrypted version of your email to Gravatar along with information like file size and type. Gravatar then sends back a picture of your pretty face, auto-magically!

E-mail *(required)*   dreamy@headfirstlabs.com

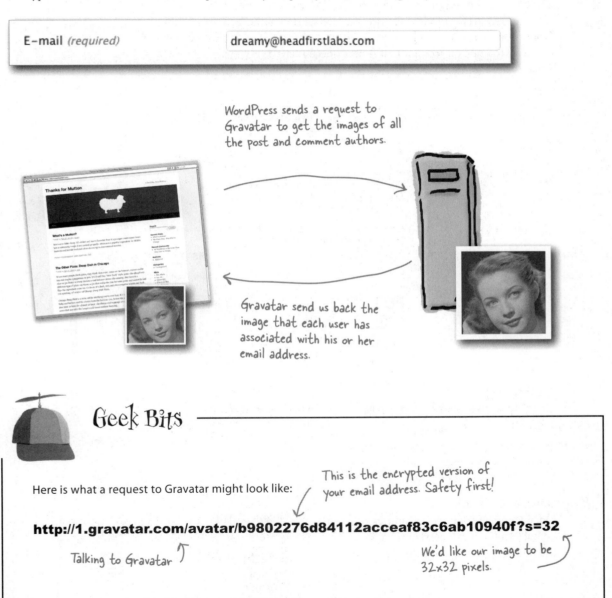

WordPress sends a request to Gravatar to get the images of all the post and comment authors.

Gravatar send us back the image that each user has associated with his or her email address.

Geek Bits

Here is what a request to Gravatar might look like:

This is the encrypted version of your email address. Safety first!

http://1.gravatar.com/avatar/b9802276d84112acceaf83c6ab10940f?s=32

Talking to Gravatar

We'd like our image to be 32x32 pixels.

Gravatar supports WordPress comments out-of-the-box

Gravatar is baked right into WordPress (it helps that they're run by the same company) and only takes a few settings to get it up and running on your blog.

 Check the Gravatar setting in the Discussion menu.
All your options for modifying Gravatar are located at the bottom of the Discussion menu. You can choose to display avatars, what "rating" you'll allow, and how the default icon looks if a user doesn't have Gravatar.

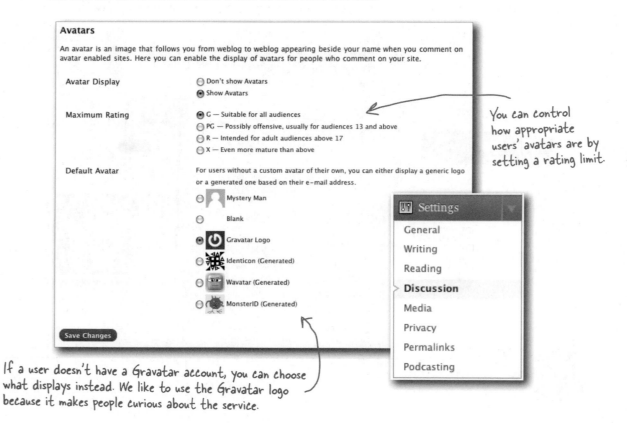

You can control how appropriate users' avatars are by setting a rating limit.

If a user doesn't have a Gravatar account, you can choose what displays instead. We like to use the Gravatar logo because it makes people curious about the service.

 Save and Check
Once you save your avatar settings, go back to the dashboard and see if the new images are showing up.

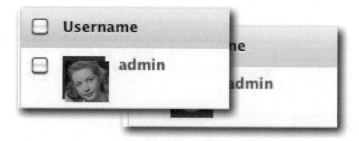

> Looks like these avatars are only showing up in comments. Didn't the writers want them by their posts?

Extending Gravatar's functionality

So it turns out that Gravatar was intended only to support showing images next to comments. To get it working with our author's posts, let's investigate what makes Gravatar work in our comment template and see if we can't use the same code to get avatars showing up in our main post bylines. Often a little detective work like this will help you figure out how to extend certain built-in functionality to other areas of your blog.

functions.php

```php
<?php if ( '' == $comment->comment_type ) : ?>
<li <?php comment_class(); ?> id="li-comment-<?php
comment_ID(); ?>">

        <div id="comment-<?php comment_ID(); ?>">
        <div class="comment-author vcard">

            <?php echo get_avatar( $comment, 40 ); ?>

                <?php printf( __( '<cite class="fn">%s</
cite> <span class="says">says:</span>', 'twentyten' ),
get_comment_author_link() ); ?>
        </div>
        <?php if ( $comment->comment_approved == '0' ) :
?>
        <em><?php _e( 'Your comment is awaiting
moderation.', 'twentyten' ); ?></em>
        <br />
<?php endif; ?>
```

functions.php

This line of code in the functions.php file displays our Gravatar image in comments on post. We need to make this work in another template file so we can display author photos.

BRAIN BARBELL

<?php echo get_avatar($comment, 40); ?>

This is a PHP function that gets our Gravatar image for WordPress. We can give it a size and it will display an image next to the comment. Do you know which file we should add this to in order to get images next to the authors' names on their post?

BRAIN BARBELL SOLUTION

> We need to copy the get_avatar() function into the single. php file because it's the one that controls what shows up in individual blog posts. That way our Gravatar images will display next to the authors' names on the posts and not just their comments.

single.php

```
<div class="entry-meta">
        <span class="meta-prep meta-prep-author"><?php _e( 'Posted by
', 'twentyten' ); ?></span>
        <span class="author vcard"><a class="url fn n" href="<?php
echo get_author_posts_url( get_the_author_meta( 'ID' ) ); ?>"
title="<?php printf( esc_attr__( 'View all posts by %s', 'twentyten'
), get_the_author() ); ?>"><?php the_author(); ?></a></span>
        <span class="meta-sep"><?php _e( ' on ', 'twentyten' ); ?> </
span>
        <a href="<?php the_permalink(); ?>" title="<?php the_time();
?>" rel="bookmark"><span class="entry-date"><?php echo get_the_
date(); ?></span></a>
        <?php edit_post_link( __( 'Edit', 'twentyten' ), "<span
class=\"meta-sep\">|</span>\n\t\t\t\t\t\t<span class=\"edit-link\">",
"</span>\n\t\t\t\t\t\t" ); ?>
</div><!-- .entry-meta -->
<div class="gravatar">
<?php echo get_avatar( get_the_author_meta('user_email'), 40 ); ?>
</div>
<div class="entry-content">
        <?php the_content(); ?>
        <?php wp_link_pages( array( 'before' => '<div class="page-
link">' . __( 'Pages:', 'twentyten' ), 'after' => '</div>' ) ); ?>
</div><!-- .entry-content -->
```

> Let's insert that code right after the closing <div> for "entry meta".

> We need to change the function a bit and give it the author's email address instead of the comment email address (which won't work anyway). Here we'll use get_the_author_meta(), which is a WordPress function for grabbing info about a post author.

single.php

`<?php echo get_avatar( get_the_author_meta("user_email), 40 ); ?>`

Cool! Gravatar is working. But, we need to apply some CSS to this so it shows up at the right-hand side of the post...

What's a Mutton?

Posted on April 27, 2010 by dwight

Mutton is older sheep. It's richer and more flavorful than it's younger counterpart lamb but is extremely tough if not cooked properly. Mutton is a popular ingredient in Middle Eastern and British food and often shows up in slow-cooked curries.

Posted in Uncategorized | Leave a comment | Edit

Ready Bake Code

As you're already starting to figure out, anytime we make a change to our template markup (HTML) we need to make an associated style (CSS) change. Let's add some style rules to make the authors' pictures fit a bit better.

Add this to the bottom of your CSS file. Feel free to experiment with other style rules to get the avatar looking how you want.

```
/* =Gravatar
------------------------------------------------------------ */
.gravatar {
        float: right;
}

.gravatar img {
        border: 2px solid #e3e3e3;
}
```

style.css

Your WordPress Toolbox

You've got Chapter 4 under your belt and now you've added user accounts, categories and tags, and avatar images to your tool box. Next up, adding video to your blog.

BULLET POINTS

- Always create individual accounts for your users. Having everyone log in with the same admin account can cause problems and increases the chance of content going AWOL.

- Assign roles to users based on how much access you want to give them in WordPress.

- A good rule of thumb for permissions is to allow fewer and fewer people access as you get higher into the permission structure.

- Categories help you organize content on your site and act as big "buckets" that group similar posts and pages together.

- An post should have one category and one or more tags.

- Tags are similar to categories but they often focus on more specific content within a post.

- Gravatar is a simple service that allows you to upload a single avatar image to one place and then use it across all your social sites.

5 video and plug-ins

Getting things moving

Just wait until you see this absolutely droll cat video I found online last night...

Video can add a whole other dimension to your blog. For nearly any kind of content, video makes your site more *engaging*, and gives you readers plenty more to comment on and share with their friends. In this chapter, you'll learn how to **host your videos** online and include them (along with other **downloadable files**) in your blog posts. We'll introduce **plug-ins**, which do a lot of heavy lifting (and *coding*) for you, and use **categories** to create a consistent, easy-to-find home for all the videos on your site.

Adding video to Thanks for Mutton

Now that we've got the Thanks for Mutton blog under control and publishing on a schedule, the staff has really started to get creative and wants to add other media to their articles like videos and recipe downloads. Two of the writers have come to you with a cooking video they've made along with some other content that they want to put in a post. But they have no idea how to get it on the site. Do we upload it to the site? What about YouTube or other video sharing sites? On top of that, how do we add more than one piece of media or content to a single post? Let's get to work!

All the major players are publishing cooking videos, we need to get some of ours up so we don't start losing readers to the big guys.

Do we just upload it like an image?

Or we could use YouTube or Vimeo, right? But how do those videos show up on our site?

We already have a bunch of unpublished videos that are just sitting on computers in the TFM offices. We need to help the writers get these up on the site. They also have some "show notes" for the videos, which are text files that include the recipe and other relevant geeky details for each video.

Host your videos outside WordPress

Video hosting sites like Vimeo or YouTube are a great place to host videos for your own site. You can create a free account and start uploading instantly, and then "embed" those videos so they show up in a video player on your blog (more on embedding in a minute). We're going to use Vimeo in all our examples here, but if you're familiar with or prefer YouTube, everything is quite similar across the two sites.

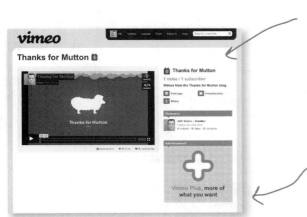

Vimeo accepts a wide variety of video formats, from Quicktime to Windows Media and MPEG (another common video format).

Hosting our videos with Vimeo will leave us more space on our own WordPress server, and it makes it easier to share our videos across other social networking sites.

You can "embed" your videos on your blog without having to upload anything to WordPress. All your video lives on Vimeo's servers and can be accessed from anywhere.

Vimeo server

Let's take a closer look at how video hosting works, and what embedding your video really means...

Hosting with Vimeo

You're probably pretty familiar with the concept of hosting by now. With Vimeo, that means that we upload a video file that we want people to be able to view, and that video file lives on a Vimeo server. Vimeo then provides a URL (on its own site) where people can view, play, and even download the video to their own computer. Hosting with Vimeo saves us space, and they take care of worrying about having enough servers to allow tons of people to watch the videos at the same time.

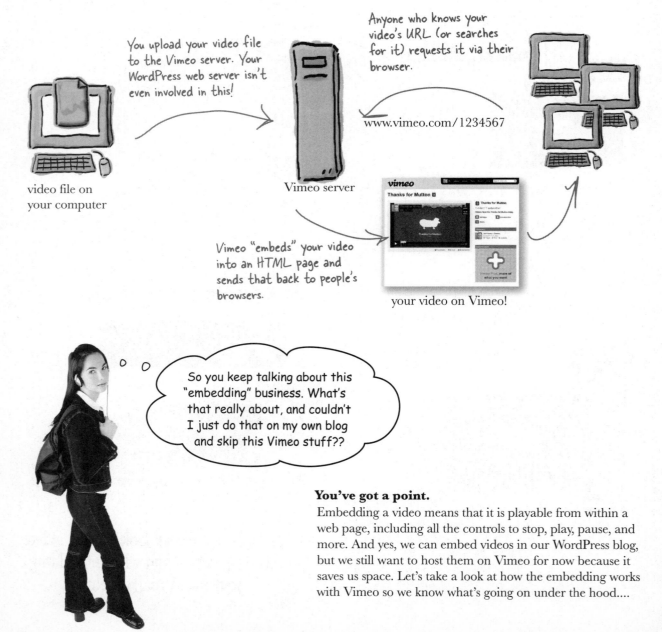

You upload your video file to the Vimeo server. Your WordPress web server isn't even involved in this!

video file on
your computer

Vimeo server

Anyone who knows your video's URL (or searches for it) requests it via their browser.

www.vimeo.com/1234567

Vimeo "embeds" your video into an HTML page and sends that back to people's browsers.

your video on Vimeo!

So you keep talking about this "embedding" business. What's that really about, and couldn't I just do that on my own blog and skip this Vimeo stuff??

You've got a point.

Embedding a video means that it is playable from within a web page, including all the controls to stop, play, pause, and more. And yes, we can embed videos in our WordPress blog, but we still want to host them on Vimeo for now because it saves us space. Let's take a look at how the embedding works with Vimeo so we know what's going on under the hood....

Embedded
video up close

Once you've uploaded your video, if you move your mouse over the right-hand side of the video you'll see an "Embed" link that brings up this screen.

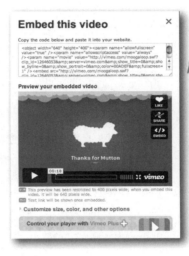

Vimeo shows you code that you can copy and paste into a post on your blog—it's essentially the same code they use to embed your video on their site.

You also get a preview of what it will look like embedded in your site, with Vimeo's play/pause, volume, and full-screen controls, along with options for people to copy the URL, and share it with other people or websites.

This part of the embed code specifies a good size for putting in most blog posts or websites.

And this allows people to click a link on your video and view it in full screen mode. You can disable this by changing the value to "false."

```
<object width="400" height="225"><param name="allowfullscreen"
value="true" />

<param name="allowscriptaccess" value="always" />

<param name="movie" value="http://vimeo.com/moogaloop.swf?clip_
id=1234567&amp;server=vimeo.com&amp;show_title=1&amp;show_
byline=1&amp;show_portrait=0&amp;color=&amp;fullscreen=1" />

<embed src="http://vimeo.com/moogaloop.swf?clip_
id=9822229&amp;server=vimeo.com&amp;show_title=1&amp;show_
byline=1&amp;show_portrait=0&amp;color=&amp;fullscreen=1"
type="application/x-shockwave-flash" allowfullscreen="true"
allowscriptaccess="always" width="400" height="225"></embed>

</object>

<p><a href="http://vimeo.com/1234567">How to Sous Vide Meat</a>
from <a href="http://vimeo.com/TFM">Thanks For Mutton</a> on <a
href="http://vimeo.com">Vimeo</a>.</p>
```

Here Vimeo is declaring to your browser that it is serving up a video (or "movie") and is using Flash (a tool for creating animation on websites) to add the play/pause buttons and other controls.

Lastly, this puts a line under the embedded video that lists its title and your "byline," which is your name linked to your main Vimeo page. You can delete this if you don't want it to show up.

Upload your video to Vimeo

① **Create an account and choose a file to upload.**
When you click "Upload a video" you should see a pop-up dialog box
that allows you to choose a file on your computer's hard drive.

Upload a video ⌐

All this will be replaced with a progress bar to let you know how the upload is going. It shouldn't take too long...

⌐ **Choose a file to upload...**

Problems? Try the basic uploader or our NEW desktop uploader.

The rules to follow

1 Upload ONLY videos you create and have the necessary permissions to upload. more

2 Do Not Upload Videos Intended for Commercial use. more

3 Content restrictions more

Read the full Uploading Guidelines

Learn how to make your videos look great on Vimeo. Read our recommended compression settings.

Still have questions? Watch this tutorial or ask for help.

Using a mobile device?
Upload videos via email:
sisip154@up.vimeo.com

HD **Learn more about HD**
Check out the Vimeo HD FAQ for more info and encoding tips.

② **Don't forget your metadata.**
Once you've selected the file to upload, give it a title, description, and
maybe even a tag or two if you're feeling really *meta*.

Finished uploading! Go to video

Title

Untitled

Description

No HTML please

Remember! If you are a production company, game developer, or you are uploading professional content, please explain your involvement in this description box to help prevent your video from being removed by our moderators.

Tags

Comma separated. Limit to 32 characters each, 20 tags max.

add

You might want to skip this, but you shouldn't. A quick title and description will help other people find and watch your video—and that's the point, right?

③ Now we wait...

Vimeo has to process your video to get it ready to look awesome on the Web—so you have to wait in line. There is a pay option to get bumped to the front, or you can sit back, relax, and enjoy your totally *free* service.

It usually doesn't take this long.

Waiting in line

This video will start converting in approximately **00:29:30**. You can leave this page and we will email you when this video is ready for watching.

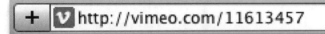

Once you've waited your turn and your video is ready to go, you can find it at the nice short Vimeo URL (which is just vimeo.com + the ID of your video).

You Tube

You can upload and embed videos on YouTube just like you can on Vimeo. If you already have an account with YouTube and already host your videos on their service, feel free to use them instead of Vimeo. If you need help uploading video to YouTube, check out: *http://www.google.com/support/youtube/bin/answer.py?hl=en&answer=57924.*

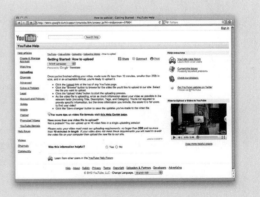

Sharpen your pencil

Upload the Thanks for Mutton video to Vimeo and then copy and paste the HTML code from Vimeo to embed the video on the site. You can download a sample video from the Head First site at *www.headfirstlabs.com/WordPress.*

Sharpen your pencil
Solution

Upload the Thanks for Mutton video to Vimeo and then copy and paste the HTML code from Vimeo to embed the video on the site. You can download a sample video from the Head First site at *www.headfirstlabs.com/WordPress*.

1 **Upload**

Just like in the example, get that video uploaded with a title and a description. Once Vimeo has processed it, we can embed it into our own site.

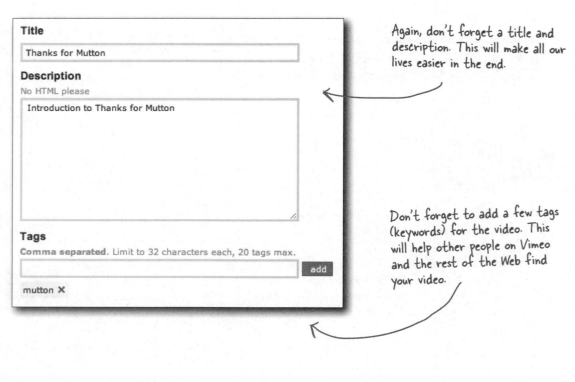

Title

Thanks for Mutton

Description

No HTML please

Introduction to Thanks for Mutton

Tags

Comma separated. Limit to 32 characters each, 20 tags max.

[   ] [add]

mutton ✕

Again, don't forget a title and description. This will make all our lives easier in the end.

Don't forget to add a few tags (keywords) for the video. This will help other people on Vimeo and the rest of the Web find your video.

Don't be discouraged by the wait. It usually goes much faster.

Waiting in line

This video will start converting in approximately **00:29:30**. You can leave this page and we will email you when this video is ready for watching.

Copy the embed code

When you mouse over a video the menu options appear. Select the "embed" button to bring up the code dialog box.

As we saw earlier, the embed code is just HTML that places a video "object" in your blog. Vimeo uses Flash to add the play/pause buttons and other controls. Let's get this copied into our site.

YouTube has a similar interface for embedding videos, with some different customization options like colors and preset sizes.

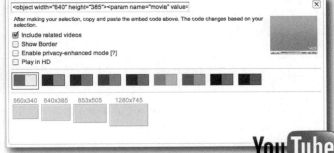

Paste into post

In the HTML view for a new post on Thanks for Mutton, paste the Vimeo code into the post just after the top line of text. Save and refresh the post—you should see your video!

It's important to be in the HTML view when adding this code to your post. If you do it on the Visual side, it won't work right.

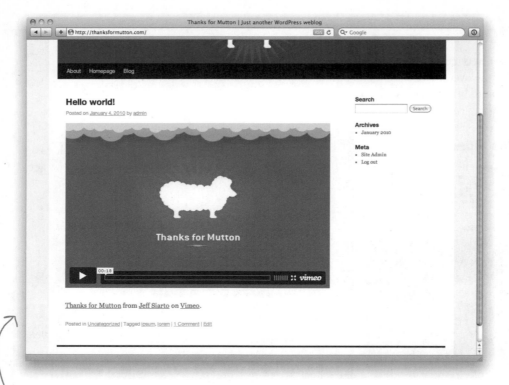

Now you should see your video in the post. Click play, give it a try.

there are no Dumb Questions

Q: Which is better, Vimeo or YouTube?

A: That depends on who you ask. Vimeo is a smaller site and emphasizes higher-quality, non-commercial video. YouTube has a larger user base and much wider audience. Check out both services and see which one works best for you.

Q: What if I don't want people embedding my videos?

A: There are privacy settings that control who can and can't see your video. If you want you can password-protect videos so they can only be seen by a select group. But allowing other people to embed your video means more people will see it, and in most cases that's a good thing!

Q: Can I remove the Vimeo logo from the player?

A: Not with the free version. Vimeo needs to get a little recognition for throwing in the servers and all that storage we're using. To get logo-free embeds, you'll have to purchase the premium service.

Q: Can't I just upload videos to my WordPress server like any other media, and embed them from there?

A: Funny you should ask... We actually do cover that in the next chapter, so stay tuned for more information on that in a few pages.

Plug-ins make working with other web services easier

WordPress itself has a large, but ultimately limited set of features. It does all the basics and way more, but it couldn't possibly do everything everybody needed it to do. So, the WordPress developers built a system where other people could write new features for the platform and then include them in WordPress as "plug-ins."

Each plug-in is a set of files that "talks" to WordPress and adds special functionality.

This plug-in comes with WordPress and helps us manage comment spam.

Akismet

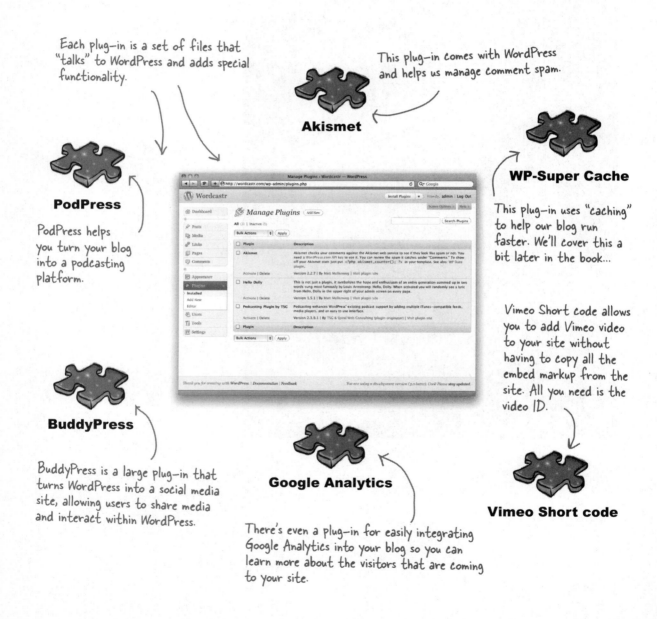

WP-Super Cache

This plug-in uses "caching" to help our blog run faster. We'll cover this a bit later in the book...

PodPress

PodPress helps you turn your blog into a podcasting platform.

Vimeo Short code allows you to add Vimeo video to your site without having to copy all the embed markup from the site. All you need is the video ID.

BuddyPress

BuddyPress is a large plug-in that turns WordPress into a social media site, allowing users to share media and interact within WordPress.

Google Analytics

Vimeo Short code

There's even a plug-in for easily integrating Google Analytics into your blog so you can learn more about the visitors that are coming to your site.

Find a plug-in for almost anything in the Plugin Directory

WordPress is "open source" software, meaning the code that runs the program is free for anyone to use and look at. Projects like WordPress only succeed because of a large group of contributors that donate their time to make the software better. Some of those contributors extend the functionality of WordPress with plug-ins and then add them to the Plugin Directory for others to download. Here you can search for plug-ins that will add extra functionality to your blog and see ratings and reviews of those plug-ins from other WordPress users.

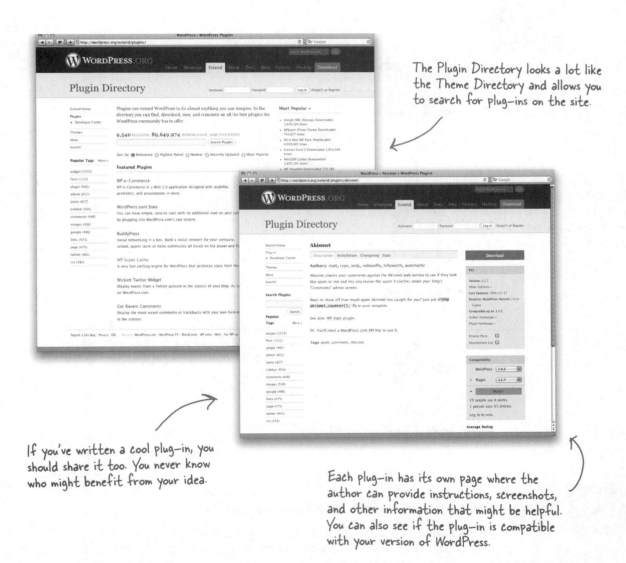

The Plugin Directory looks a lot like the Theme Directory and allows you to search for plug-ins on the site.

If you've written a cool plug-in, you should share it too. You never know who might benefit from your idea.

Each plug-in has its own page where the author can provide instructions, screenshots, and other information that might be helpful. You can also see if the plug-in is compatible with your version of WordPress.

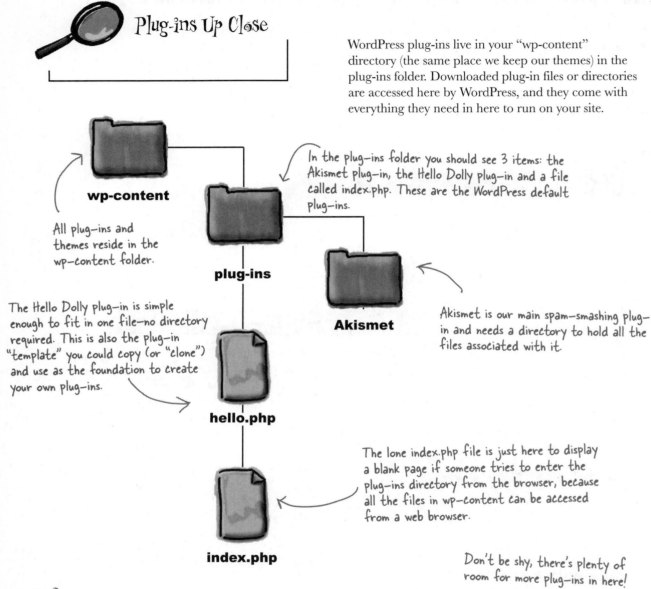

Plug-ins Up Close

WordPress plug-ins live in your "wp-content" directory (the same place we keep our themes) in the plug-ins folder. Downloaded plug-in files or directories are accessed here by WordPress, and they come with everything they need in here to run on your site.

wp-content

All plug-ins and themes reside in the wp-content folder.

In the plug-ins folder you should see 3 items: the Akismet plug-in, the Hello Dolly plug-in and a file called index.php. These are the WordPress default plug-ins.

plug-ins

Akismet

Akismet is our main spam-smashing plug-in and needs a directory to hold all the files associated with it.

The Hello Dolly plug-in is simple enough to fit in one file—no directory required. This is also the plug-in "template" you could copy (or "clone") and use as the foundation to create your own plug-ins.

hello.php

The lone index.php file is just here to display a blank page if someone tries to enter the plug-ins directory from the browser, because all the files in wp-content can be accessed from a web browser.

index.php

Don't be shy, there's plenty of room for more plug-ins in here!

Watch it!

Plug-ins are powerful tools, but don't go crazy!

Try and limit the amount of plug-ins you use to only the essential features you need to run your site. While powerful, plug-ins can cause incompatibility with different versions of WordPress, and can also be a security risk if a plug-in is not used or developed properly.

Browse and install plug-ins from within WordPress

Although you can download plug-in files from the WordPress website, upload them to your /wp-content/ plug-ins directory, and activate them from the admin panel, that's a ton of steps to get a plug-in up and running. An easier way is to use the "Add New" feature within the plug-in menu to browse the directory, and then install and activate your plug-ins directly from WordPress.

Searching for and adding plug-ins from within WordPress is much faster and easier than a manual upload.

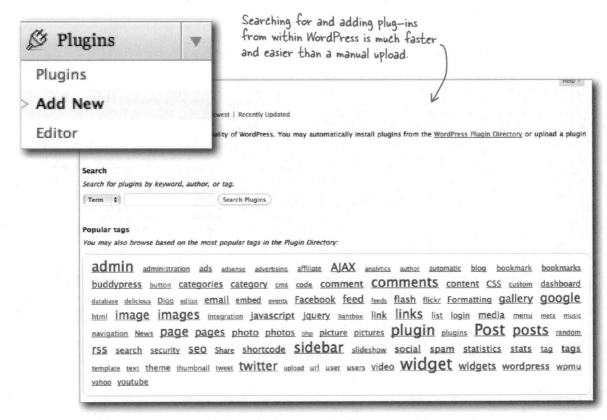

Exercise

Find the WordPress Vimeo plug-in (Vimeo Short code) and install it on the Thanks for Mutton blog. You can use the "Add New" plug-in feature to search the plug-in directory for Vimeo Short code.

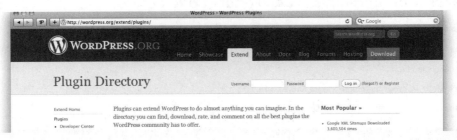

Exercise Solution

Find the WordPress Vimeo plug-in (Vimeo Short code) and install it on the Thanks for Mutton blog. You can use the "Add New" plug-in feature to search the plug-in directory for Vimeo Short code.

1 **Search for Vimeo Short Code**

Using the Add New menu, search the plug-in directory for "Vimeo short code." You should see the plug-in as the top result.

This plug-in will make it much easier to add our Vimeo videos to the blog.

2 **Install**

If the installation goes as planned, you should see a message telling you it was a success and then options for activating or returning to the installer to find new plug-ins.

🔌 Installing Plugin: Vimeo Short Code 1.0

Downloading install package from http://downloads.wordpress.org/plugin/lux-vimeo-shortcode.1.0.zip...

Unpacking the package...

Installing the plugin...

Successfully installed the plugin **Vimeo Short Code 1.0**.

Actions: <u>Activate Plugin</u> | <u>Return to Plugin Installer</u>

③ Activate

Before we can start adding Vimeo videos using this plug-in we need to "activate" the plug-in. This allows it to actually work with WordPress; a plug-in can be installed but deactivated, in which case you can't use it.

When the plug-in is active, it will display with a white background and you should see options to deactivate. It's a good idea to deactivate plug-ins you are no longer using.

④ Use the features in posts and pages

Now that the plug-in is active we can use it to add Vimeo videos quickly to our blog posts and pages.

This plug-in allows us to specify the Vimeo video ID and it fills in all the code for us.

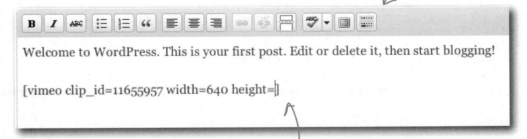

We can even add height and width attributes to make the video fit our own blog's specific layout.

Vimeo short code

Some plug-ins are very complex, and some are quite simple. The more complex plug-ins might have menu options (as with many software programs), and some might just do one simple thing and require very little interaction. The Vimeo plug-in has no menu items, and you can't configure (or change) what it does. The amount of functionality it offers doesn't justify a menu. All you need is the video ID and a height and width value, that's it.

Often the simplest plug-ins offer the most flexibility and control.

Here we have the ability to manipulate the size of our video and place it anywhere in our post or page. That simple feature can be very powerful.

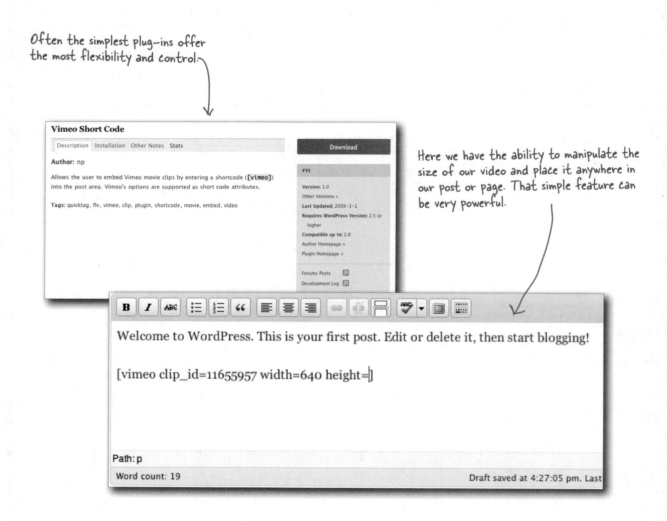

there are no Dumb Questions

Q: Are plug-ins dangerous? I'm basically installing someone else's code that I don't know, right?

A: Yes, you are installing someone else's code—but most plug-ins are vetted by the community and WordPress does some screening of plug-in developers before they allow them to post. Your best bet is to read the user comments on the plug-in and try them out before committing to using them on a production site.

Q: Can I write my own plug-ins?

A: Yes! Writing plug-ins is a great way to become familiar with the inner workings of WordPress. You can use the Hello Dolly plug-in as a template to get started—it's made to be "cloned." Then you can poke around and start figuring out how plug-ins work from the inside out.

Q: Do plug-ins affect the performance of my site?

A: Yes and no—it depends on the function of the plug-in within WordPress. Anytime you add functionality to WordPress, it will need to use resources to make that functionality possible. For example, if a plug-in needs to talk to the MySQL database, that request will (slightly) decrease the performance. It probably won't be noticeable, but all those small performance hits will add up after a while. A good rule of thumb is to always test plug-ins before you use them on your live site and only activate plug-ins you are actually using. Check out Chapter 8 for a ton more detail on how to improve the performance of your WordPress site and keep it running fast and smooth.

Sharpen your pencil

Create your first real video post using the Vimeo Short code plug-in.

If you prefer to use YouTube or already have videos on YouTube, search the plug-in directory for a similar plug-in and embed your YouTube videos in the post.

Sharpen your pencil
Solution

Create your first real video post using the Vimeo Short code plug-in.

1 **Create a new post**

Create a new post and give it a title (you could just rename the test post if you wanted to as well).

Mutton Chops

Permalink: http://thanksformutton.com/2010/01/mutton-chops/

2 **Add the Vimeo Short code**

Now, in the body of the post add our short code along with a width of 640px. Add the height attribute and quotes but leave them blank. Our plug-in will calculate the height automatically.

Upload/Insert

B *I* A̶B̶C̶ ⠿ ⠿ 66 ≡ ≡ ≡ ⧉ ⧉ ⊟ A̶B̶

[vimeo clip_id=12646053 width="640" height=""]

If you leave out the height or the width attribute it will mess up the size of the embedded video. You should either leave them both off (it will use the default size) or use them both as we are.

Once you publish or preview the page, our short code will be replaced with the video wrapped in a Vimeo player.

Well, that seems easy enough, but we still want to give people the ability to download the recipe and our "show notes" about the video.

Add additional content and files to your post

We want to provide the visitors that watch our videos a ZIP file they can download that has additional notes on the video and the recipe associated with the video. Kind of like Thanks for Mutton to go! A ZIP file has the extension ".zip", and is what people call a *compressed* file. It's like taking a bunch of big plastic bags and stuffing them all into one smaller, more compact bag. The resulting file is actually smaller than the sum total of each individual file. That means it takes up less room on our server, and is quicker to download for our visitors. Most computers come with software to help you zip and unzip these files.

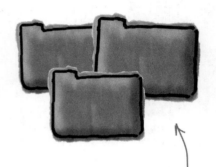

We'll need to add the show notes for the video. This can just be text in our post.

We can add our ZIP file to the media library in WordPress as a link that people can click on to download it.

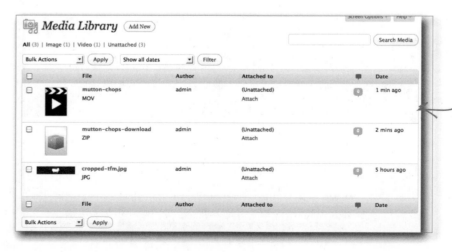

We can upload all kinds of files to the media library, not just images...

Use the media gallery to attach other files

We are not limited to the types of images we upload to the media gallery. We can include ZIP files, PDFs, and other document types for use in our posts and pages.

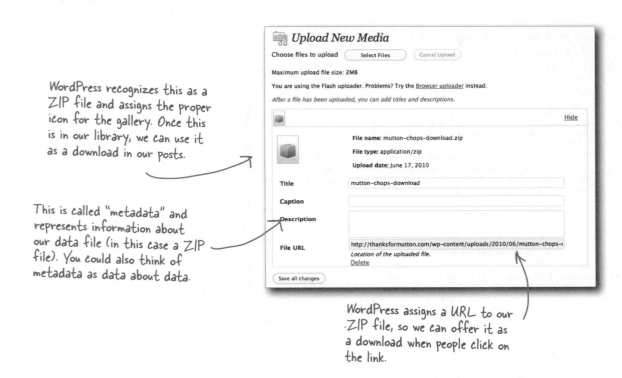

WordPress recognizes this as a ZIP file and assigns the proper icon for the gallery. Once this is in our library, we can use it as a download in our posts.

This is called "metadata" and represents information about our data file (in this case a ZIP file). You could also think of metadata as data about data.

Upload New Media

Choose files to upload [Select Files] [Cancel Upload]

Maximum upload file size: 2MB

You are using the Flash uploader. Problems? Try the Browser uploader instead.

After a file has been uploaded, you can add titles and descriptions.

Hide

File name: mutton-chops-download.zip
File type: application/zip
Upload date: June 17, 2010

Title: mutton-chops-download
Caption:
Description:
File URL: http://thanksformutton.com/wp-content/uploads/2010/06/mutton-chops-
Location of the uploaded file.
Delete

[Save all changes]

WordPress assigns a URL to our .ZIP file, so we can offer it as a download when people click on the link.

Sharpen your pencil

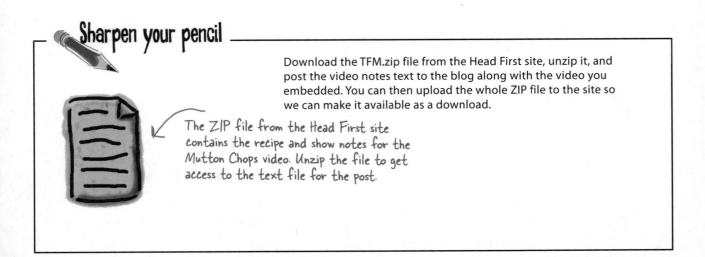

Download the TFM.zip file from the Head First site, unzip it, and post the video notes text to the blog along with the video you embedded. You can then upload the whole ZIP file to the site so we can make it available as a download.

The ZIP file from the Head First site contains the recipe and show notes for the Mutton Chops video. Unzip the file to get access to the text file for the post.

Sharpen your pencil
Solution

Download the TFM.zip file from the Head First site, unzip it, and post the video notes text to the blog along with the video you embedded. You can then upload the whole ZIP file to the site so we can make it available as a download.

① **Add the video notes to the post.**
We can copy these in below the Vimeo short code. This content will display just like in any other post, just below the embedded video.

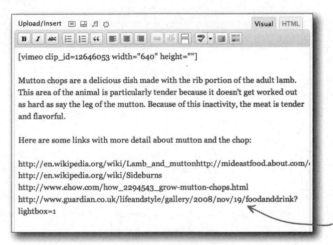

We'll want to put our cursor below the show notes so that when we insert the link to the download, it will display properly in the post.

② **Insert a link to the uploaded .zip file.**
Place your cursor just below the show notes, as and open the "Insert" dialogue. Find the link you uploaded, and insert it into the post.

When you've found the ZIP file you want to include, click "insert into post."

Inserted files show up as links—visitors will need to click them to initiate a download.

Download video and show notes

Posted in Uncategorized | Tagged ipsum, lorem | 1 Comment | Edit

Our video is now playing properly within the blog post, the video notes are there, and our visitors can download a package of the video and recipe. And because we're using the Short code plug-in, it's easy for our writers to add their own videos from here on out.

Yeah, and then it sure would be handy if all our videos were collected in one place on the site...

This is great! We're definitely going to start adding more of these.

Use categories to create a video section

Like we discussed in the last chapter, categories are great way to add context and organization to a site. We can also use them to create an additional navigation structure (with category-specific pretty URLs) for the Thanks for Mutton blog.

 Turn on permalinks.

Before we can use categories in our URLs we need to make sure that pretty permalinks are turned on.

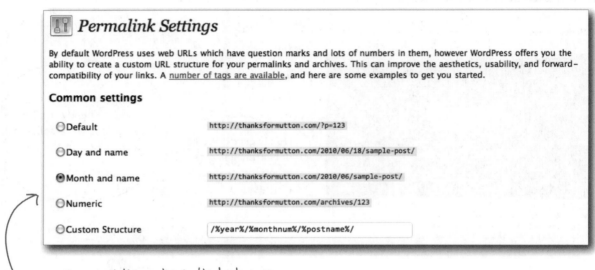

We covered this earlier in the book, so you should be all set. But make sure you are using one of the pretty permalink settings.

 Geek Bits

If you select the "Custom Structure" for your permalinks, you can choose from a variety of tags to make your URLs more meaningful and easier to read and understand. Check out **http://codex.WordPress.org/Using_Permalinks** to see all of the available options.

◯ Custom Structure	/%year%/%monthnum%/%postname%/

2 **Choose one category for videos.**

Because we'd like all of our videos to show up in a single archive, we need to choose a single name for the video category and stick with it. "Video" is the obvious choice, but you could use any term you want.

Name	Description	Slug	Posts
☐ Video		video	0
Uncategorized		uncategorized	1
☐ Name	Description		

3 **Add a category and an excerpt to your post.**

Lastly, assign the "video" category to your post, and add an *excerpt* below the main post entry area.

Categories

| All Categories | Most Used |

☐ Uncategorized
☑ Video

+ **Add New Category**

Remember, only one category. We can use tags later if we want to add extra information about the post.

When we add an excerpt, we can control what text gets displayed about that post on the category index (main) page. It's basically a short summary of what that particular post is all about.

Excerpt

Mutton chops are a delicious dish made with the rib portion of the adult lamb. This area of the animal is particularly tender because it doesn't get worked out as hard as say the leg of the mutton. Because of this inactivity, the meat is tender and flavorful.

Excerpts are optional hand-crafted summaries of your content that can be used in your theme. Learn more about manual excerpts.

thanksformutton.com/categories/video

Now when we add new videos, the video category page will display a title and a short description (excerpt) for each of them.

The home page displays the newest video and its excerpt.

It might be nice if we could hide the excerpt and related content until someone clicked through to the post...

Use the "more" tag to clean up your home page

While the excerpt feature works well for category and tag archive pages, the entire post is still showing up on the home page and that can start to get messy fast. We can use a comment *directive*, which is basically a WordPress command that we wrap in an HTML tag. Wherever we insert the directive, WordPress chops off the post and inserts a link that takes the reader to the full post when they click on it.

<!--more-->   Use this in the HTML editor to set the cut-off point for what displays on the home page.

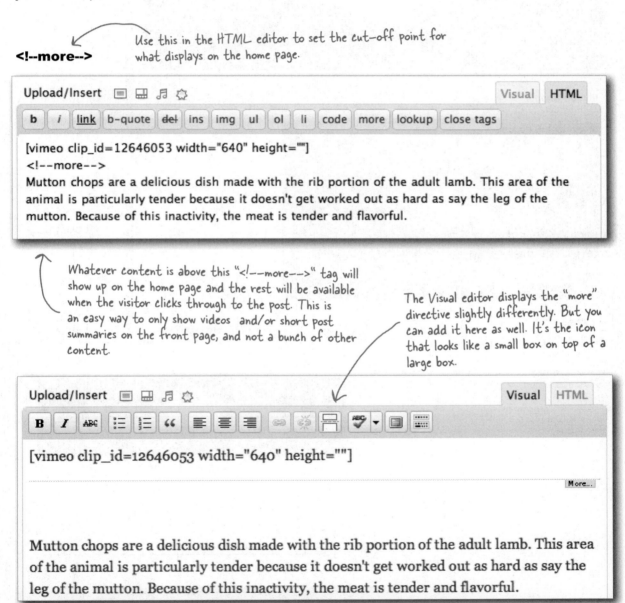

Whatever content is above this "<!--more-->" tag will show up on the home page and the rest will be available when the visitor clicks through to the post. This is an easy way to only show videos and/or short post summaries on the front page, and not a bunch of other content.

The Visual editor displays the "more" directive slightly differently. But you can add it here as well. It's the icon that looks like a small box on top of a large box.

On the home page, only the video shows because our "more" tag was placed right below the Vimeo shortcode.

When the visitor clicks through to the post archive, they will see the remainder of the content below the "more" tag.

You've got Chapter 5 under your belt and now you've added video hosting with Vimeo and plug-ins to your tool box. Next up, podcasting and syndication.

BULLET POINTS

- WordPress can handle many different file types in the media gallery—from ZIP archives to Quicktime video.

- Hosted video services like Vimeo and YouTube are a great place to host your videos, and from there, your videos can be easily embedded into your WordPress site.

- Plug-ins can be used to add extra functionality to WordPress.

- Most plug-ins are free and open source (like WordPress itself) and can be found in the Plugin Directory (*http://WordPress.org/extend/plugins/*)

- You can browse and install plug-ins from within the WordPress dashboard using the Add New plug-in feature.

- Single categories can help organize and separate different types of content on a site.

- Use category index pages to give visitors a listing or archive of a specific type of content.

6 podcasting and syndication

Spreading the word

Say have you heard this new report from Technology Futures? One day we'll all communicate through a series of tubes!

It's time more people knew about your awesome site.

Your blog is humming along, and you've already figured out how to expand WordPress to manage an *entire website*. Now that you've got **video** playing there too, why not *expand* your audience base? In this chapter, we'll discover how to **distribute** videos through Apple's iTunes store as **podcasts**, and how to **syndicate** your content so that a ton more people will find out about your site (and *keep coming back* for **more**).

The Thanks for Mutton podcast

Now that we've got our video up on the Thanks for Mutton site, we need a way to get as many people as possible to see it. A great way to do this is to turn the videos into a *podcast* that viewers can subscribe to and download to take with them on their own devices. You might have thought that podcasts were only for audio—but in fact, video works too and it's a great way to reach a broader audience with your shows. Watch out Food Network!

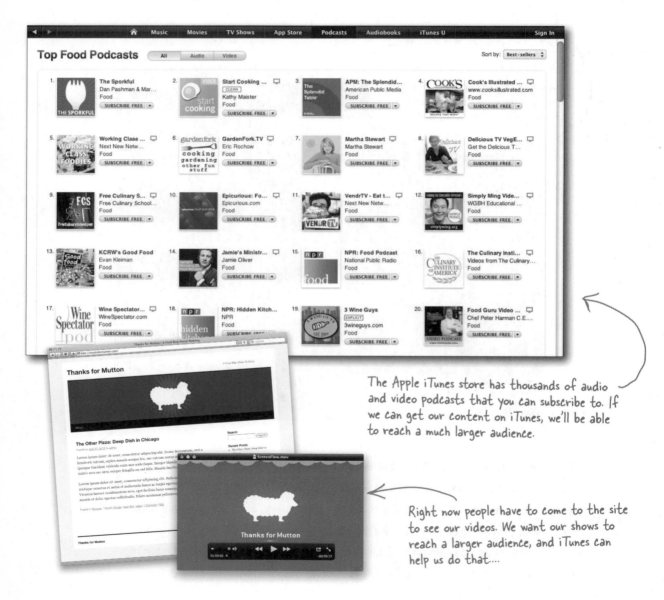

The Apple iTunes store has thousands of audio and video podcasts that you can subscribe to. If we can get our content on iTunes, we'll be able to reach a much larger audience.

Right now people have to come to the site to see our videos. We want our shows to reach a larger audience, and iTunes can help us do that....

WordPress is your hub for content distribution

WordPress is a great platform to host a podcast from. You can upload all different types of media and you can build posts and pages that are a combination of text, images, video, and files. WordPress can also send that content to other sources like news readers and the iTunes Store through a process called web syndication. This means you can use WordPress as your main hub for content distribution—giving you the power to get your content in front of as many people as possible—not just to people who visit your site in a browser..

We create all of our content in WordPress.

WordPress then tells other services about our content using technologies like RSS, which allow WordPress to tell other computers about your content.

Our content can be read in news readers like Google Reader and by other services like the iTunes Store.

RSS Readers

Podcast / iTunes

Other Blogs

Web Browsers

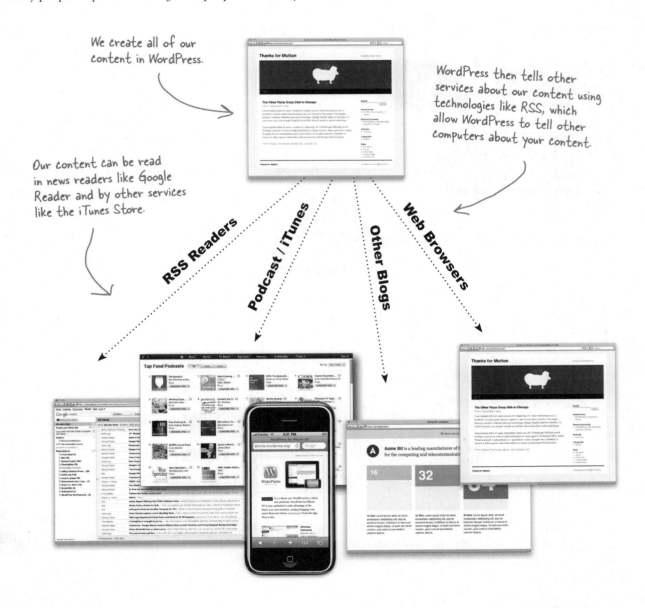

The anatomy of a podcast

A podcast is simply an audio or video program published periodically on the Web. People can typically access it in multiple ways, mostly commonly though it's from a website or downloaded through syndication via applications like iTunes and Google Reader. Regardless of the delivery method, you need two things to "officially" have a podcast: first, you need some media—audio or video will work. Second, you need a way to tell people that you've just "released" a new episode of your podcast.

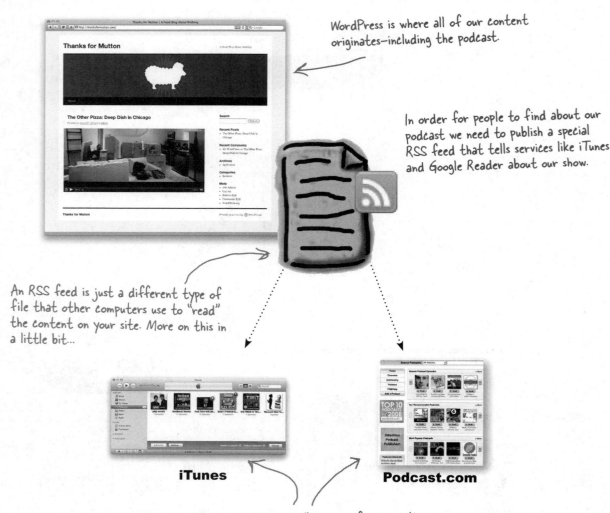

WordPress is where all of our content originates—including the podcast.

In order for people to find about our podcast we need to publish a special RSS feed that tells services like iTunes and Google Reader about our show.

An RSS feed is just a different type of file that other computers use to "read" the content on your site. More on this in a little bit...

iTunes

Podcast.com

Services like iTunes and Podcast.com "subscribe" to your feed and then present your podcast to their audience. When you publish a new podcast episode, it's downloaded automatically onto subscribers' computers.

RSS is one way the Web syndicates content

The way that iTunes knows about new podcasts as they become available is through a handy technology called RSS—or *Real Simple Syndication*. You might use RSS already in tools like Google Reader and NetNewsWire, and it's also used by millions of websites to share and *syndicate* content. If you've ever been asked by websites to subscribe to their feed, what you're really doing is "watching" for changes in their feed file. This file, an XML (Extensible Markup Language) document, gets updated by that site whenever new content is published. Watching the feed means you use some kind of service (like Google Reader or iTunes) that notifies you when a site you subscribe to publishes new content. It's like the digital way of hearing the *thump* of the newspaper when it lands on your front porch.

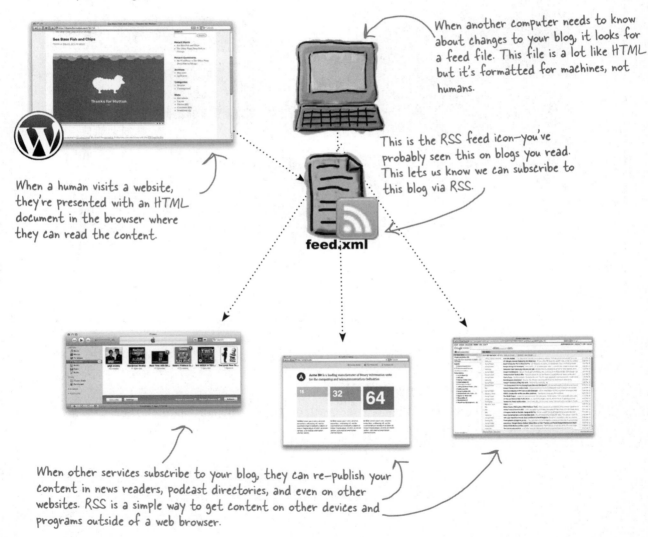

When another computer needs to know about changes to your blog, it looks for a feed file. This file is a lot like HTML but it's formatted for machines, not humans.

This is the RSS feed icon—you've probably seen this on blogs you read. This lets us know we can subscribe to this blog via RSS.

feed.xml

When a human visits a website, they're presented with an HTML document in the browser where they can read the content.

When other services subscribe to your blog, they can re-publish your content in news readers, podcast directories, and even on other websites. RSS is a simple way to get content on other devices and programs outside of a web browser.

The lifecycle of an RSS feed

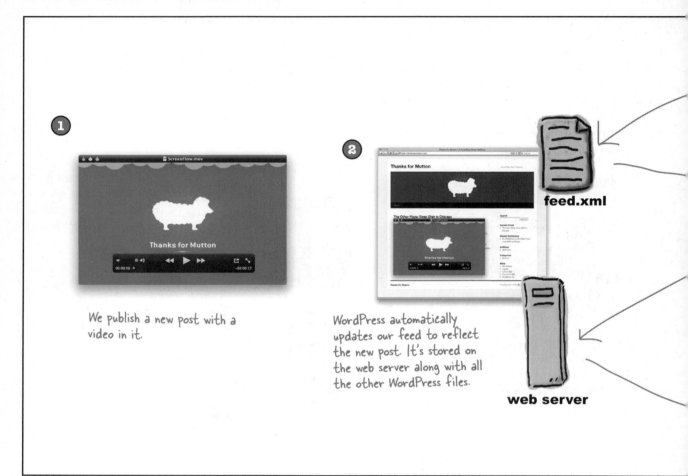

We publish a new post with a video in it.

WordPress automatically updates our feed to reflect the new post. It's stored on the web server along with all the other WordPress files.

feed.xml

web server

Don't worry about XML

We will look at what is in the XML feed file in a minute, but the good news is that WordPress automatically creates the feed.xml file for you every time you create a new post. That leaves you free to focus on adding content to your WordPress site!

3

iTunes checks regularly for changes to our feed, and when there is one, it updates the podcast list to reflect our new video.

iTunes

4

Here's the important part: the post content (in this case a video podcast) still lives on our site, and iTunes actually grabs it from our WordPress server, and downloads it to the subscriber's computer. The podcast is not hosted on any iTunes servers.

People that subscribe to our podcast through iTunes will get our new video downloaded automatically to their computer.

Exercise

To see how this works, find a video podcast you might be interested in and subscribe to it using iTunes (*http://apple.com/itunes*) or Google Reader (*http://google.com/reader*).

Both iTunes and Google Reader can handle podcast feeds. Use whichever you like.

Exercise Solution

To see how this works, find a video podcast you might be interested in and subscribe to it using iTunes (*http://apple.com/itunes*) or Google Reader (*http://google.com/reader*).

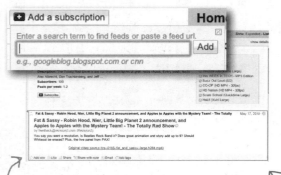

① Add a subscription.
You can just type the URL of the site or feed you want to subscribe to—Google Reader will handle the audio and video from the podcast.

② Browse for a podcast.
Reader also allows you to search for podcast feeds and subscribe if you don't know the site of the feed URL.

Google Reader is a fast and simple way to consume podcasts. It's also a standard news reader and has cool sharing features.

Searching in Google Reader isn't as nice as iTunes. It's better to find the site and paste it in to the subscribe field.

③ Search and subscribe.
iTunes has a huge catalog of audio and video podcasts all categorized to make it easy to find something you like.

④ Download to iTunes.
Once you subscribe to a podcast, new episodes will automatically be downloaded to your computer.

iTunes has a great interface for finding new content and because it downloads podcasts on to your computer, you can take then with you on your portable media player of choice.

XML feeds Up Close

As we saw earlier, the feed file is an XML document, which is a file containing data and tags much like HTML. Think of the RSS feed as a version of your blog that is only read by other computer programs, like feed readers and other websites.

```xml
<?xml version="1.0" encoding="UTF-8"?>
<rss version="2.0"
        xmlns:content="http://purl.org/rss/1.0/modules/content/"
        xmlns:wfw="http://wellformedweb.org/CommentAPI/"
        xmlns:dc="http://purl.org/dc/elements/1.1/"
        xmlns:atom="http://www.w3.org/2005/Atom"
        xmlns:sy="http://purl.org/rss/1.0/modules/syndication/"
        xmlns:slash="http://purl.org/rss/1.0/modules/slash/">
        <channel>
                <title>Thanks for Mutton</title>
                <atom:link href="http://thanksformutton.com/?feed=rss2"
rel="self" type="application/rss+xml" />
                <link>http://thanksformutton.com</link>
                <description>A Food Blog About Nothing</description>
                <language>en</language>
                <item>
                        <title>Sea Bass Fish and Chips</title>
                </item>
        </channel>
</rss>
```

This area is the "head" of the XML file and references other specifications used later in the file.

Notice our blog title and links pointing back to the Thanks for Mutton site.

Each post we write shows up in our RSS feed as a new <item>.

Just like in HTML, we have to close all our tags.

feed.xml

The name of the feed file doesn't matter much—it's what's inside that's important.

there are no Dumb Questions

Q: So is RSS only for podcasts?

A: No, RSS can tell subscribers about any kind of new content published to a blog or website.

Q: Do I have to use iTunes?

A: Not necessarily. It is one of the main ways to get podcasts, but if you only want to subscribe to a blog to find out when new posts get published, you can use any number of feed services, or most web browsers.

Q: So I can use RSS to find out when my favorite blogs get updated too, not just to let people know when mine is updated?

A: Exactly! RSS is an easy way to stay up-to-date on all your favorite sites without having to remember to go visit each one individually—you can see all their new content right in your feed reader or a single browser window.

WordPress publishes an RSS feed automatically

As we said earlier, WordPress handles much of the RSS functionality automatically—updating your feed every time you add a new post. On top of that, most modern browsers like Firefox, Google Chrome, and Safari will detect any site's feed automatically and display an "RSS" icon in the address bar. Clicking on that allows you to read the feed in your browser window.

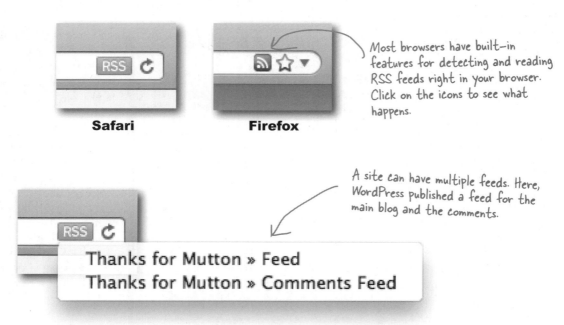

Safari   **Firefox**

Most browsers have built-in features for detecting and reading RSS feeds right in your browser. Click on the icons to see what happens.

A site can have multiple feeds. Here, WordPress published a feed for the main blog and the comments.

Thanks for Mutton » Feed
Thanks for Mutton » Comments Feed

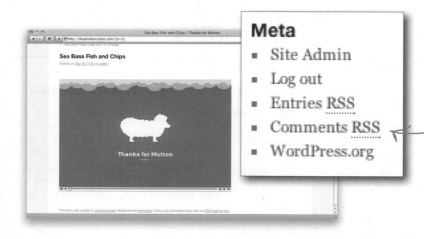

You can also access the RSS feed links in the WordPress sidebar under the "Meta" title. You'll notice again both the main blog and comment feeds.

TEST DRIVE

Let's try our RSS feed with iTunes and to see if we can use that for our podcast feed.

1 **Find your RSS feed.**

Before we can test our feed we need to find the URL to paste into iTunes. You can find links to your RSS feeds in the Meta sidebar on the home page of your blog. They should look something like this:

You can also click on the RSS icon in your browser, as shown on the previous page...

http://thanksformutton.com/?feed=rss2

Depending on your permalink settings, your feed URL should look something like this.

http://thanksformutton.com/feed

2 **Add the feed to iTunes.**

From the "Advanced" drop-down menu in iTunes, select "Subscribe to Podcast..." and enter the feed URL in the pop up.

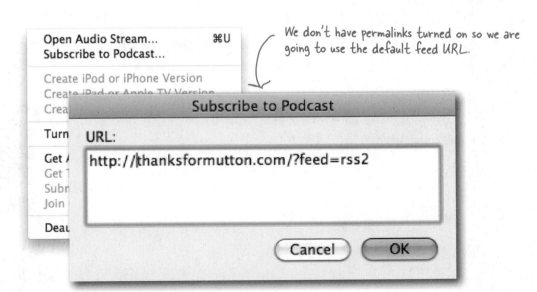

We don't have permalinks turned on so we are going to use the default feed URL.

Open Audio Stream... ⌘U
Subscribe to Podcast...

Create iPod or iPhone Version
Create iPad or Apple TV Version
Crea

Turn

Get

Get
Subm
Join

Deau

Subscribe to Podcast

URL:

http://thanksformutton.com/?feed=rss2

Cancel   OK

Test Drive

Let's try our RSS feed with iTunes and see if we can use that for our podcast feed.

Once you add the feed, it should show up in your podcast list.

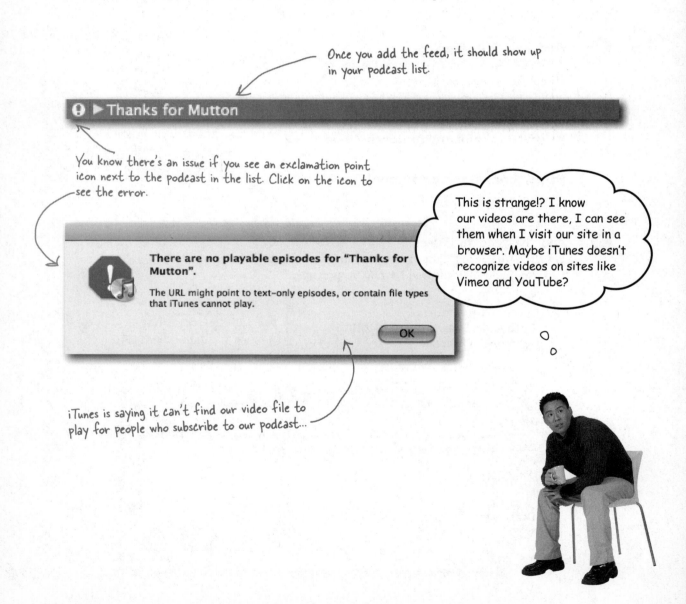

You know there's an issue if you see an exclamation point icon next to the podcast in the list. Click on the icon to see the error.

There are no playable episodes for "Thanks for Mutton".

The URL might point to text-only episodes, or contain file types that iTunes cannot play.

OK

This is strange!? I know our videos are there, I can see them when I visit our site in a browser. Maybe iTunes doesn't recognize videos on sites like Vimeo and YouTube?

iTunes is saying it can't find our video file to play for people who subscribe to our podcast...

Vimeo doesn't work well with podcasting

Now that we want to start syndicating our videos as a podcast, Vimeo is no longer the ideal solution for video hosting. It's worked great up until now, but the main reason it won't work for podcasting is you can't download videos from Vimeo, and that's just what iTunes does—it downloads the video from the site providing the RSS feed. So we'll need to find another solution.

We want visitors to be able to subscribe to our videos in iTunes, but right now, it's not recognizing our videos.

BRAIN BARBELL

What other option might exist for hosting our videos instead of something like Vimeo?

Vimeo is a great service for sharing videos through a browser, but it's not designed to be a platform to host podcasting media (audio or video) that allows people to download files. The whole idea of a podcast is that your viewer or listener should be able to take that media with them and consume it anywhere. In order to facilitate that, we have to make our videos available for download over the Web and not just for viewing. We can use our own web server for that.

Self-hosted

Vimeo-hosted

When we host the video on our own servers, we take responsibility for the space and bandwidth, but we can be more flexible about how we deliver the media to our viewers.

Vimeo only allows us to watch and share videos on the Web from our browser. We can't take these with us on our iPod.

Exercise

Before our subscribers can download our video podcast, we need to get it up on our WordPress web server. Use the same process you did in the last chapter to upload a ZIP file to the WordPress Media Gallery, only this time, tell WordPress you want to upload a video.

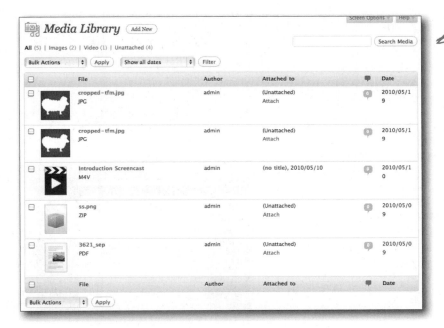

The media gallery holds all the media and files that have been uploaded to our WordPress site. This is where the video for our podcasts will be stored.

Upload the same sample video we put on Vimeo in the last chapter. You can find it at www.headfirslabs.com/WordPress.

Exercise Solution

Before our subscribers can download our video podcast, we need to get it up on our WordPress web server. Use the same process you did in the last chapter to upload a ZIP file to the WordPress Media Gallery, only this time, tell WordPress you want to upload a video.

① Upload the video from within a post.

From within a post you can select which type of media you want to upload. Just like we did in the last chapter—select the "video" icon to bring up the media gallery uploader.

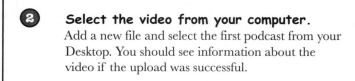

② Select the video from your computer.

Add a new file and select the first podcast from your Desktop. You should see information about the video if the upload was successful.

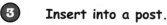

③ Insert into a post.

Once you have all the settings added, click "Insert into Post" to add the file to the WordPress editor and your post.

Watch it!

Hosting your own videos takes up a lot more space on your server.

Depending on how many videos (or other media files) you plan to create, you'll want to check with your hosting provider and be sure you have enough space on your server for everything. You can always purchase more space, but that can also start to get more costly...

Where's the video?

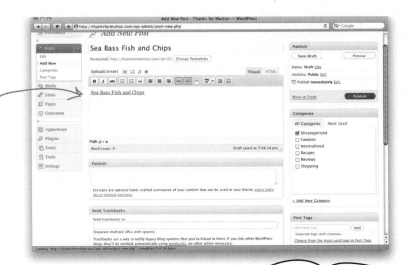

Here's the uploaded video showing in the Visual editor for our new post; we're almost there....

Well, before we used the code from Vimeo to embed the video. Maybe we need to do something similar here too?

But when we take a look at that post on the site, we only get a link inserted into our post—the video is there, but not quite how we wanted it!

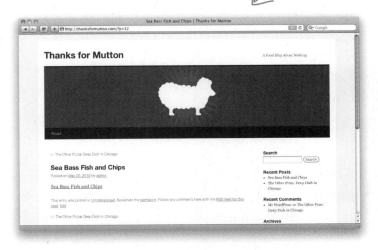

WordPress embeds its own videos too

If we want our videos to look like the Vimeo videos we were using, we'll need to use the Embed feature in WordPress. Embedding media in WordPress is basically taking the uploaded video and wrapping it in HTML that will allow it to play in the browser, just like we did with Vimeo. Even though it involves HTML, we can do this in the Visual editor. However, WordPress hides this feature in the expanded menu, so let's find it and put it to use.

1 **Copy the URL for your video.**
You can find this from within the post editor.

Either right click on the link in the Visual editor, or you can find the full link in the HTML editor instead.

2 **Expand the editor.**
In order to get to the embed functionality, we need to expand the editor.

This icon will show the second level of editor options below.

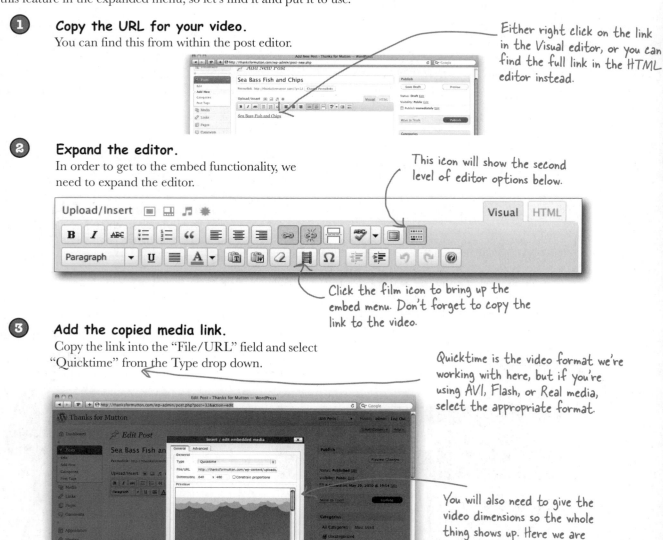

Click the film icon to bring up the embed menu. Don't forget to copy the link to the video.

3 **Add the copied media link.**
Copy the link into the "File/URL" field and select "Quicktime" from the Type drop down.

Quicktime is the video format we're working with here, but if you're using AVI, Flash, or Real media, select the appropriate format.

You will also need to give the video dimensions so the whole thing shows up. Here we are using the full size of our video, but feel free to size this proportionally any way you like.

④ Get meta.

You can add even more metadata in the "Advanced" tab (which we always recommend), but for now we are just going to de-select the auto-play feature.

Having any kind of media—audio or video—start playing when a visitor loads a web page can be annoying and make your site unusable. Be courteous to your visitors and let them decide when they should click "Play."

⑤ Click insert when you're ready.

Once you have all the information and links entered, go ahead and insert the video into your post. We should see our whole video properly embedded in the post, not just a link.

You may have to click Preview to make sure the video was embedded properly.

Exercise

Now that we have the embedded video in our post, give the iTunes subscription another try.

Now that we have actual embedded video in our post, give the iTunes subscription another try.

Our blog page should look a lot like Vimeo except this time we're hosting our own videos.

▼ **Thanks for Mutton**
  🔊 ☑ **Sea Bass Fish and Chips**

➜		5/20/10	A Food Blog About Nothing
🖥	0:18	5/20/10	

When we test the new feed in iTunes, it should work. You should be able to download and play the video inside of iTunes.

The only problem now is that iTunes doesn't seem to have the summary info (excerpt) about our video that we learned how to include in the previous chapter. It's going to be hard to get subscribers when they don't even know what the show is about.

It would also be nice to be able to show a special image for the podcast, instead of just a default image from iTunes.

Add some info to your iTunes feed

Although iTunes can handle standard RSS feeds, it needs extra information about the podcast to provide a solid summary about your video for users browsing for your shows (or similar shows). What we need is a special feed just for our podcast, one that has all the information iTunes needs to show our logo and extra information about our show.

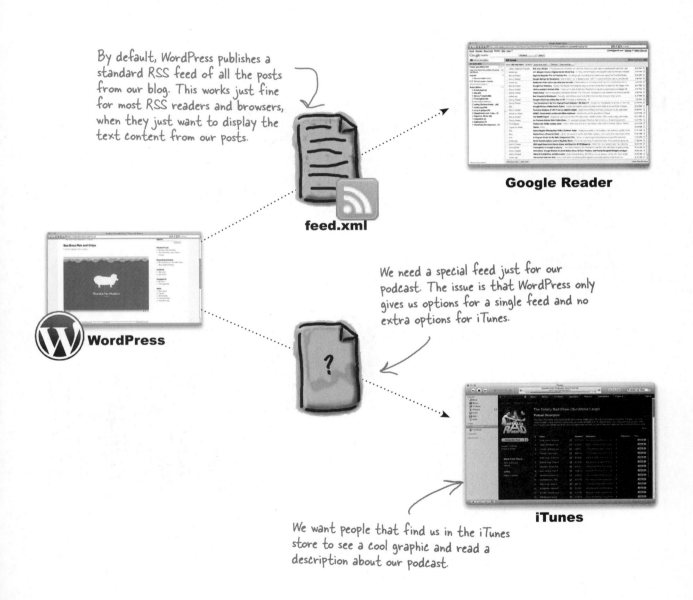

By default, WordPress publishes a standard RSS feed of all the posts from our blog. This works just fine for most RSS readers and browsers, when they just want to display the text content from our posts.

Google Reader

feed.xml

WordPress

We need a special feed just for our podcast. The issue is that WordPress only gives us options for a single feed and no extra options for iTunes.

iTunes

We want people that find us in the iTunes store to see a cool graphic and read a description about our podcast.

Use a plug-in to build a special feed for iTunes

Creating an extra feed is the perfect task for a plug-in. It's not essential to WordPress—not everyone wants to publish a podcast—but enough people do podcast that there are plenty of options when it comes to podcasting plug-ins. It will create a special podcast feed for you as well as help you manage all the extra information you need to supply to podcasting providers like iTunes.

Most plug-ins embed media and generate a special feed

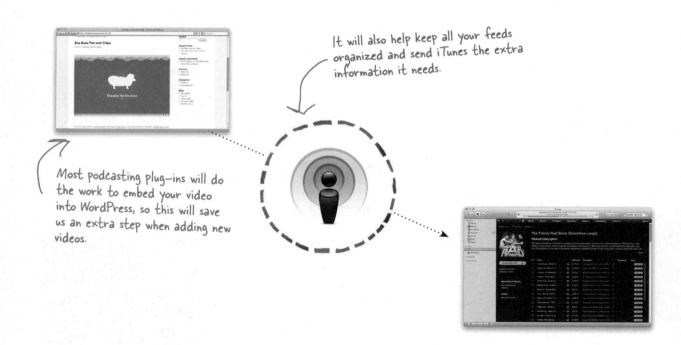

It will also help keep all your feeds organized and send iTunes the extra information it needs.

Most podcasting plug-ins will do the work to embed your video into WordPress, so this will save us an extra step when adding new videos.

TSG Podcasting Plug-in

One of the easiest podcasting plug-ins to use is the TSG Podcasting Plug-in. It's simple and doesn't have a ton of features, but it's easy to use and just works. TSG gives us a single interface in the administrative window to add details about our podcast and automatically handles the publication of our iTunes feed.

TSG handles embedding audio and video for us and even gives us a nice media player for the blog pages.

Another feature of TSG is that it only has one administrative window—just a simple set of options for iTunes.

Sharpen your pencil

Find the TSG Podcasting Plug-in on the WordPress plug-in page (*http://WordPress.org/extend/plugins/*) and install it on Thanks for Mutton.

Sharpen your pencil
Solution

Find the TSG Podcasting Plug-in on the WordPress plug-in page (*http://WordPress.org/extend/plugins/*) and install it on Thanks for Mutton.

1 **Copy the plug-in directory to Thanks for Mutton.**

Just like before, all we have to do is add the downloaded plug-in directory to the */wp-content/plugins/* folder in our WordPress folders.

You may need to upload this using your FTP client. Either way, this needs to be in the /wp-content/plugins/ directory of your active WordPress installation.

You can also use the "Add New" feature within the WordPress dashboard to install the plug-in.

2 **Activate**

In the Plug-ins menu on the WordPress Dashboard, activate the TSG Podcasting Plug-in by clicking the "activate" link.

3 **New Podcasting menu**

You should see a new option in the Settings menu called Podcasting. This menu allows you to edit all the different iTunes settings.

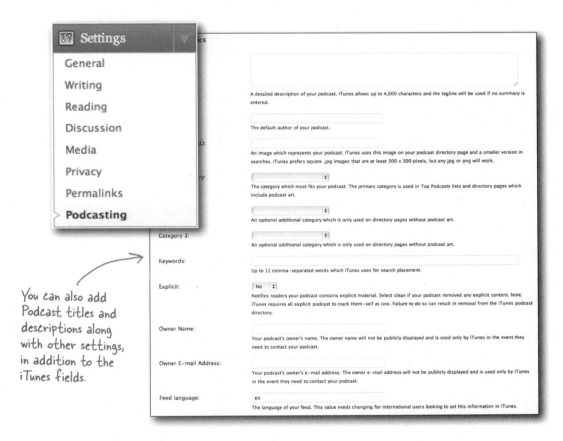

A detailed description of your podcast. iTunes allows up to 4,000 characters and the tagline will be used if no summary is entered.

The default author of your podcast.

An image which represents your podcast. iTunes uses this image on your podcast directory page and a smaller version in searches. iTunes prefers square .jpg images that are at least 300 x 300 pixels, but any jpg or png will work.

The category which most fits your podcast. The primary category is used in Top Podcasts lists and directory pages which include podcast art.

An optional additional category which is only used on directory pages without podcast art.

Category 3:

An optional additional category which is only used on directory pages without podcast art.

Keywords:

Up to 12 comma-separated words which iTunes uses for search placement.

Explicit: No

Notifies readers your podcast contains explicit material. Select clean if your podcast removed any explicit content. Note: iTunes requires all explicit podcast to mark them-self as one. Failure to do so can result in removal from the iTunes podcast directory.

Owner Name:

Your podcast's owner's name. The owner name will not be publicly displayed and is used only by iTunes in the event they need to contact your podcast.

Owner E-mail Address:

Your podcast's owner's e-mail address. The owner e-mail address will not be publicly displayed and is used only by iTunes in the event they need to contact your podcast.

Feed language: en

The language of your feed. This value needs changing for international users looking to set this information in iTunes.

You can also add Podcast titles and descriptions along with other settings, in addition to the iTunes fields.

Watch it!

TSG Podcasting Plug-in and WordPress 3

At the time of writing, the TSG Podcasting Plug-in doesn't work with WordPress 3 Beta when using pretty URLs. You have to use the default permalink settings.

Use the Podcasting Plug-in to embed videos for podcasts

Aside from providing all the appropriate data to iTunes and other podcasting directories, TSG Podcasting also helps us embed our audio and video in blog posts. Much like how the Vimeo Short code plug-in worked in the last chapter, all we need is the URL for the video file that we uploaded earlier.

① **Copy your video's URL.**
You did this previously, the first time you uploaded a video and wanted to embed it directly into a post.

File name:	sea-bass-fish-and-chips.mov
File type:	video/quicktime
Upload date:	May 20, 2010

Title	Sea Bass Fish and Chips
Caption	
Description	
File URL	http://thanksformutton.com/wp-content/uploads/2010/05/sea-bass-fish-.
	Location of the uploaded file.

Here's the URL in the listing for the file in the Media Gallery. This is another way to get it instead of right-clicking...

② **Podcasting post options**
With TSG Podcasting installed we now have a new window at the bottom of our "New post" page. All we have to do is paste in our video and link and click "Send to editor."

This isn't the same "Editor" as in the workflow from Chapter 4. Instead this just means that the plug-in is going to put the video embedding code in the Visual editor for you to work with it.

Podcasting					
File	http://thanksformutton.com/wp-content/uploads/2010/05/sea-bass-fish-and-chips.mov				Send to editor »
Format	Default Format ⬍	**Keywords**			
Author		**Length**		**Explicit** ⬍	Delete Enclosure
File URL			Default Format ⬍		Add

TSG Podcasting adds a new window that will help us add podcast media to our posts.

Here's that "short code" again...

Just like with our Vimeo plug-in, TSG Podcasting adds short code to our post
that will get interpreted by the browser when the post is published.

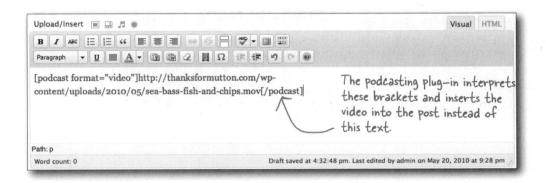

The podcasting plug-in interprets these brackets and inserts the video into the post instead of this text.

④ Check your post.

Just to make sure that everything is working, check out the post from a visitor's
point of view and make sure you can see the video embedded in the post.

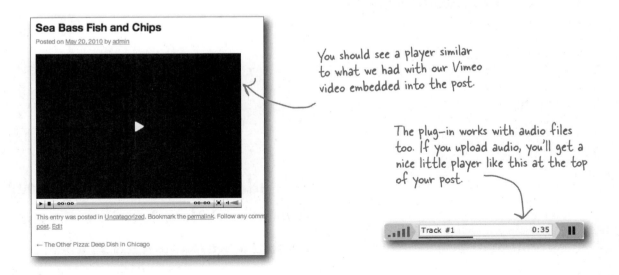

You should see a player similar to what we had with our Vimeo video embedded into the post.

The plug-in works with audio files too. If you upload audio, you'll get a nice little player like this at the top of your post.

In the same RSS drop down in your browser (in Safari and Firefox only) you should now see a third podcast feed in addition to the main blog and comment feeds.

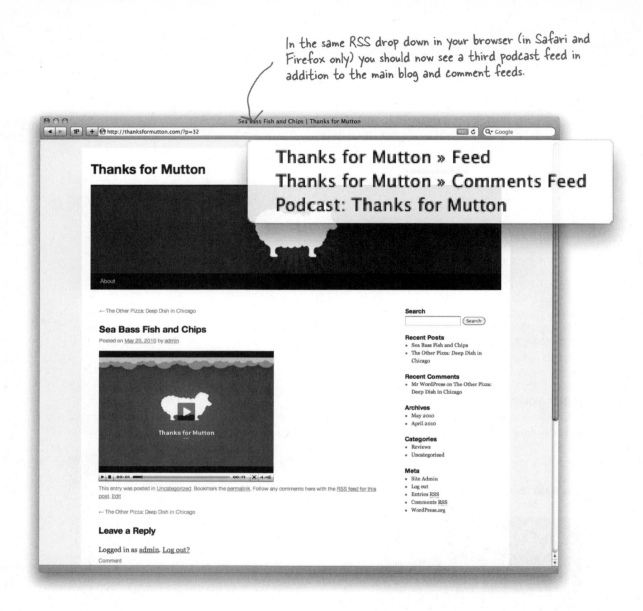

Let's add some metadata about our podcast and then test this out and see if it's working with iTunes...

Exercise

Before we test our new podcast feed, we need to add all the extra information for iTunes. That is why we installed this plug-in, right? Also, let's include the podcast banner image for display on the Thanks for Mutton iTunes page.

iTunes Specifics

Summary:

A detailed description of your podcast. iTunes allows up to 4,000 characters and the tagline will be used if no summary is entered.

Author:

The default author of your podcast.

Podcast Art (URL):

An image which represents your podcast. iTunes uses this image on your podcast directory page and a smaller version in searches. iTunes prefers square .jpg images that are at least 300 x 300 pixels, but any jpg or png will work.

Primary Category:

The category which most fits your podcast. The primary category is used in Top Podcasts lists and directory pages which include podcast art.

Category 2:

An optional additional category which is only used on directory pages without podcast art.

Category 3:

An optional additional category which is only used on directory pages without podcast art.

Keywords:

Up to 12 comma-separated words which iTunes uses for search placement.

Explicit: No

Notifies readers your podcast contains explicit material. Select clean if you
iTunes requires all explicit podcast to mark them-self as one. Failure to do
directory.

Owner Name:

Your podcast's owner's name. The owner name will not be publicly displa
need to contact your podcast.

Owner E-mail Address:

Your podcast's owner's e-mail address. The owner e-mail address will
in the event they need to contact your podcast.

Feed language: en

The language of your feed. This value needs changing for internationa

Thanks for Mutton

We'll need to upload this image and include it in the podcast information for iTunes.

Exercise Solution

Before we test our new podcast feed, we need to add all the extra information for iTunes. That is why we installed this plug-in, right? Also, let's include the podcast banner image for display on the Thanks for Mutton iTunes page.

① **Upload our TFM logo and copy its URL.**
We'll need this to include in our iTunes podcast feed settings. You should be a whiz at this by now...

Just like any other file we need to use on our site, we have to upload the iTunes image to the site before we can include it in anything.

We want to remember this link because we'll need to use it when we add the iTunes information to the podcasting plug-in.

http://thanksformutton.com/wp-content/uploads/2010/05/tfm.jpg

Update the podcast settings in iTunes.

We can include a lot of info here, some of it will be useful for people searching iTunes, and some of it is categorical info that will help iTunes organize our podcast with similar shows in their directory.

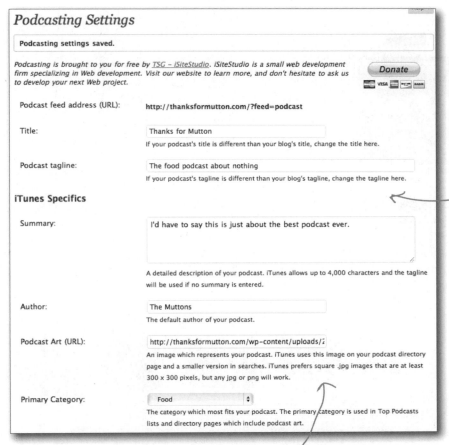

Podcasting Settings

Podcasting settings saved.

Podcasting is brought to you for free by *TSG – iSiteStudio*. iSiteStudio is a small web development firm specializing in Web development. Visit our website to learn more, and don't hesitate to ask us to develop your next Web project.

Donate

Podcast feed address (URL): http://thanksformutton.com/?feed=podcast

Title: Thanks for Mutton
If your podcast's title is different than your blog's title, change the title here.

Podcast tagline: The food podcast about nothing
If your podcast's tagline is different than your blog's tagline, change the tagline here.

iTunes Specifics

Summary: I'd have to say this is just about the best podcast ever.
A detailed description of your podcast. iTunes allows up to 4,000 characters and the tagline will be used if no summary is entered.

Author: The Muttons
The default author of your podcast.

Podcast Art (URL): http://thanksformutton.com/wp-content/uploads/z
An image which represents your podcast. iTunes uses this image on your podcast directory page and a smaller version in searches. iTunes prefers square .jpg images that are at least 300 x 300 pixels, but any jpg or png will work.

Primary Category: Food
The category which most fits your podcast. The primary category is used in Top Podcasts lists and directory pages which include podcast art.

We can provide all sorts of different information to iTunes, from podcast title and author to multiple categories for our shows to fit into.

Add the URL of the artwork we just uploaded to the Podcast Art section and also make sure you specify at least one category. This will help people find our podcast on iTunes.

Feedburner gives you podcast stats

Feedburner is a service from Google that allows you to promote your feed to a wider audience and see statistics on how many people subscribe to your podcast. The service uses the RSS feed you already publish and gives you a feedburner URL to hand out to subscribers. Your viewers and readers can then choose how they get your content and Feedburner keeps track of everything for you. It's kind of like the FeedBurner version of your feed becomes the actual main feed for your site's content, and your original feed becomes a private feed that only you and FeedBurner know about.

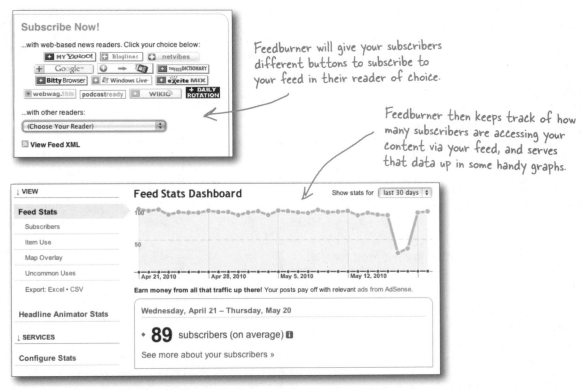

Feedburner will give your subscribers different buttons to subscribe to your feed in their reader of choice.

Feedburner then keeps track of how many subscribers are accessing your content via your feed, and serves that data up in some handy graphs.

Exercise

Create a Feedburner account for your blog. You'll need a Google Account to use Feedburner (*http://feedburner.google.com*). Make sure you add the Podcast feed, not the main blog feed.

http://thanksformutton.com/?feed=podcast

FeedBurner will prompt you for the feed from your blog.

Exercise Solution

Create a Feedburner account for your blog (you already have one if you have a Google account)

It's quick and easy to create a Google account if you don't already have one.

<image name="google_signin" />
Sign in with your
Google Account
Email: [   ]
Password: [   ]
☑ Stay signed in
[Sign in]
Can't access your account?

Don't have a Google Account?
[Create an account]

① Add the podcast feed to Feedburner.
You might be tempted to click the "I'm a podcaster" button—but don't! That's a whole other way of sending feeds to iTunes and we've already got that taken care of.

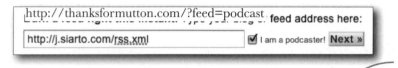

http://thanksformutton.com/?feed=podcast **feed address here:**

http://j.siarto.com/rss.xml   ☑ I am a podcaster! **Next »**

Make sure you make note of this new URL. We need to make that our feed URL in WordPress.

② Pick a title URL.
Here we add just one more title and the last part of our Feedburner URL.

Welcome! Let us burn a feed for you.

The original blog or feed address you entered has been verified.

Here is what happens next in the setup process:

▸ FeedBurner will apply some of our most popular services to your new feed to get you started. (You can always modify or remove them later.)
▸ This new feed will be activated in your FeedBurner account.
▸ You may also set up some optional traffic stats tracking and podcasting services.

Give your feed its title and feedburner.com address:

Feed Title: | Jeff Siarto
Thanks for Mutton   feed in your account.

Feed Address: | http://feeds.feedburner.com/
jsiarto
.tfm   can find your new feed.

All Feedburner feeds start with "http://feeds.feedburner.com." We get to choose the last part of the URL, so pick something short that identifies your feed easily.

③ Burned
That's it. We're now "burning" (or running) our feed through Feedburner.

| 1. Claim your feed | 2. Set up podcast | 3. Analyze traffic |

Congrats! Your FeedBurner feed is now live. Want to dress it up a little?

Subscribe to your feed (and share with others!) at:
http://feeds.feedburner.com/tfm

For your convenience, FeedBurner has applied the following services to your new feed:

▸ **SmartCast** makes your feed podcast-ready
▸ **BrowserFriendly** improves your feed's appearance in most web browsers and makes it easier to subscribe to
▸ **FeedBurner Stats** tracks basic feed traffic statistics

You control your feed. All services are optional and can be changed at any time.

You have completed step 1 of 3. In the next steps, you may customize the applied FeedBurner services to:

▸ Provide a more detailed podcast listing at iTunes and Yahoo! search
▸ Add additional free **FeedBurner Stats** options for a more richly detailed view of your feed readership

Next » or Skip directly to feed management.

http://feeds.feedburner.com/tfm

OK, so knowing how many people use our feed sounds nice, but why is the RSS link on the site still the old one? How is anybody supposed to find and use the new Feedburner feed?

Good point.

The podcast feed from Thanks for Mutton still points to our old feed URL. We need to change this so visitors subscribe using the Feedburner link. Otherwise we can't track our feed subscribers.

http://thanksformutton.com/?feed=podcast

Override feeds in the header of our theme

It's great that WordPress handles all the RSS file updates automatically, but now we have to dig into how it does that so we can update them to use the Feedburner URL instead. WordPress builds all of the RSS links automatically and places them in the <head> of your blog so that RSS services like Google Reader (and many others) can manage subscriptions to your content. We need to override the that link and place our Feedburner link in its place so that visitors subscribe using the new service.

Ready Bake Code

/themes/your-theme/header.php

1 **Add a new link.**
Add the new feed URL to your header.php theme file right below the <?php wp_head(); ?> line.

header.php

```
<?php wp_head(); ?>

<link rel="alternate" type="application/rss+xml" title="Podcast:
Thanks for Mutton" href="http://feeds.feedburner.com/tfm" />

</head>
```

Here's where you put in your new Feedburner URL

/plugins/podcasting/podcasting-feed.php

2 **Find podcasting-feed.php.**
In the TSG Podcasting plug-in folder there will be a file called podcasting-feed.php, which sends our podcasting link to WordPress. Open this file in your favorite text editor.

podcasting-feed.php

Ready Bake Code

3 **Comment out a few lines.**
Find the two bolded areas below and "comment" them out by preceding them with two forward slashes (//). These are single-line comments in PHP and will keep those feeds from displaying.

```php
    function addFeedDiscovery() {
        global $wp_rewrite;
        $podcast_url = ($wp_rewrite->using_permalinks()) ? '/feed/podcast/'
: '/?feed=podcast';
        $podcast_url = get_option('home') . $podcast_url;
        // echo '    <link rel="alternate" type="application/rss+xml"
title="Podcast: ' . htmlentities(stripslashes(get_option('pod_title')), ENT_
COMPAT, "UTF-8") . '" href="' . $podcast_url . '" />' . "\n";

        // Formats
        $pod_formats = get_terms('podcast_format', 'get=all');
        if ( is_array($pod_formats) && count($pod_formats) > 0 ) {
            foreach ($pod_formats as $pod_format) {
                if ( 'default-format' != $pod_format->slug ) {
                    $podcast_format_url = ($wp_rewrite->using_
permalinks()) ? $podcast_url . "?format=$pod_format->slug" : $podcast_url .
"&format=$pod_format->slug";
                    // echo '    <link rel="alternate"
type="application/rss+xml" title="Podcast: ' . htmlentities(stripslashes(get_
option('pod_title'))) . " ($pod_format->name)" . '" href="' . $podcast_format_
url . '" />' . "\n";
                }
            }
        }
    }
```

This is a PHP comment too. Anything that follows the two forward slashes gets ignored by WordPress. It's a safe way to disable any code without deleting it in case you need it later.

All this code does is display the same link we already added to header.php.

Relax

You usually don't have to do this much "hacking."

There are plenty of plug-ins that integrate Feedburner into WordPress—just not any good solutions for our podcasting plug-in. You'll sometimes find there are trade-offs for simplicity when using WordPress and you often have to get your hands dirty with themes and plug-ins. If you want to learn enough to really start putting PHP to work on your WordPress site, we definitely recommend *Head First PHP & MySQL*.

Welcome to the Thanks for Mutton podcast

You've got Chapter 6 under your belt and now you've added podcasting, syndication, and Feedburner to your tool box. Next up, how not to get hacked and backing up your WordPress site.

BULLET POINTS

- WordPress can act as your central hub for online content distribution.

- Any video and audio that you want to use for podcasting must be stored on your web server, not on hosted services like Vimeo and YouTube.

- RSS, or Real Simple Syndication is a way for blogs for syndicate content to other services on the Web.

- WordPress publishes a standard RSS feed for you blog by default.

- Use a podcasting plug-in like TSG Podcasting to make embedding and syndicating podcast content easier.

- Feedburner can help you manage your feeds and keep track of how many subscribers your blog and podcast have.

7 securing wordpress

Locking things down

Not everyone on the Internet is nice.

It's a fact of modern life on the Internet: there are people who spend their time trying to break into, or *hack*, other people's websites. Some do it just for the thrill, others to cause chaos, and some are simply after *sensitive information* like **credit card numbers**, social security numbers, and other **personal information**. Now, you'll learn how to make your WordPress site *more secure*, with unique **usernames**, **strong** passwords, and more. You'll also kick off **automatic backups** of all your WordPress files so you can **restore your site** if it ever does get hacked, or goes down for other reasons.

Something's not right here...

Just as Thanks for Mutton was starting to pick up steam, all the posts and pages are gone—including the podcasts. Luckily, we still have the video files in our Media Gallery, but the WordPress posts all show *page not found* errors.

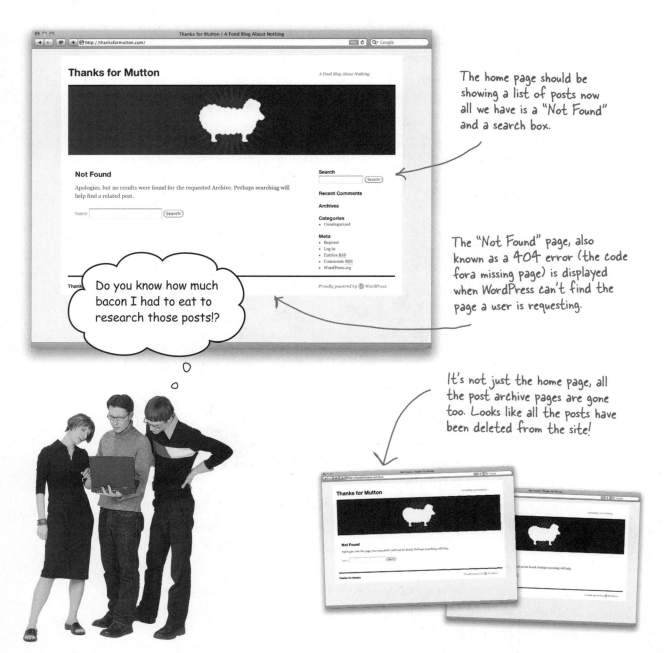

Edit Posts (Add New)

All (0)

No Posts found.

The post page in the admin section shows nothing—how did these posts get deleted?

It looks like someone else just logged in and deleted the posts. Could they have guessed the admin password?

BRAIN POWER

One of the easiest ways to secure your WordPress blog or site is to use *strong* passwords—specifically, passwords that can't easily be guessed and that don't show up in dictionaries. Think about other ways someone might try to break into your site and cause damage. Is creating a secure password the only thing you can do? What about servers, commenters, and spam?

You've been hacked

Believe it or not, there's a good chance that your blog or website has been on the receiving end of some type of malicious behavior. These attacks are occasionally undertaken by people themselves (or *hackers*), but they are mostly performed by "bots" (or robots, which are really just computer programs written by hackers) that scan sites for vulnerabilities. It sounds bad, but the good news is they aren't usually successful if you have a few safeguards in place. Let's take a look the most common attacks and then we'll see what we can do prevent them.

Brute force attacks

These types of attacks are very common and consist simply of a person or a computer program trying to access your admin dashboard by repeatedly trying different passwords until the correct one is found. This becomes even easier if you still use the default "admin" username and have a weak password that's easily guessed. **Best protection:** Change your username to something other than "admin" when you install WordPress, and use strong, secure passwords.

Brute force attacks can be used on any system with a username and password—this includes your web server and MySQL database.

Server attacks

Hackers don't need to gain access to your WordPress dashboard to cause problems either. If they can get access to the servers that your site is *hosted* on they can change information through the database or just bring your entire site down altogether. **Best protection:** Use reputable, reliable hosting and make sure your account passwords are strong and secure. Use SFTP to transfer files between your local computer and web server.

SFTP is a secure form of FTP which encrypts data communications between client and server.

Denial of Service (how dare they!)

Another way web hooligans can try and mess with your site is with a *denial of service* (or DoS) attack. DoS attacks work by flooding a web server with requests (also typically via a computer program) until it can no longer handle the load and crashes. While in most cases your data will be safe (though it's not guaranteed), your site will be inaccessible to the public until you can find and block the offending traffic. **Best protection:** Firewalls can help block traffic, but not until after you have identified the source of the DoS. We're not going to cover firewalls in any detail here, but your hosting provider should be able to help you get those set up too.

Hackers Exposed

**This week's interview:
We interview a hacker serving
time for credit card theft**

Head First: Welcome Mr. Hacker, thanks so much for coming out.

Hacker: Yeah, thanks. Real quick—just wanted to let you know that there are more than just those three ways to hack a website.

Head First: Well those are just some of the more popular ways—we could have a whole a Head First book on website security. [Ed note: *Interesting...*] Anyway, tell us how you got into hacking in the first place.

Hacker: Well, it started out as just a hobby. I'd break into websites just by trying default usernames and passwords. You'd be surprised how many people leave their websites wide open for attack like that. It was too easy, I'd hardly even call what I was doing *hacking* it was more like *guessing*. So easy my 2 year-old nephew could do it...

Head First:: Wow, that simple, huh? What did you do to the site once you broke in?

Hacker: Oh, usually I'd just delete some things, maybe swap out an image for one that's—how do I say this—not as "family friendly?"

Head First: So then what happened? Did you get bored with that?

Hacker: It was just too easy; I needed more of a challenge so I started trying to just break right into servers. There are lots of folks out there that manage their own servers and don't know what they're doing. Again, most of the time I could just guess their usernames and passwords. Once I was into the server I had full control over every aspect of the site—I could just turn it all off or find where they store credit card numbers...

Head First: Again, bad passwords? This is all hacking is, right? It's just guessing usernames and passwords. I've got to say, I don't know what's more shocking: how easy this seems to be or how bad we are at choosing secure passwords.

Hacker: Don't get me wrong, it can be a lot more difficult then that—but why try the hard stuff if there's a good chance a few guesses will work. Most of my, ahem, *colleagues* even have some software now that will try almost every word in the dictionary as a password. It's all automated too; I just sit back and wait for it to find a match.

Head First: You said there was some hard stuff? Can you give me an example?

Hacker: Well, there is a technique called Cross-site scripting, or XSS. These attacks require us to exploit a flaw in a website by inserting bad code into a website URL. If the website is not checking its data and input correctly, we could change records in the database or even remove data altogether.

Head First: Why is this more difficult?

Hacker: You just need to spend a little more time learning about the site and checking and testing flaws. It's just not as easy as trying passwords. The thing is though, once we know what type of site you're using (WordPress, Drupal, Joomla, etc.) It's easier to target the security holes.

Head First: This is just fascinating stuff. Any final words for our readers? Tips on making sites more secure?

Hacker: Use strong passwords everywhere. Make the hackers try the hard stuff; they'll usually just move on to the next easy target—there are plenty of them out there.

Head First: Great advice; always a pleasure having you in for a chat. Good luck with all those license plates...

Keep your WordPress installation and plug-ins up-to-date

Before you consider any other ways to secure your WordPress site, the first thing you need to do is make sure that your WordPress installation and plug-ins are all current. A large percentage of attacks on WordPress sites happen to blogs that are using out-of-date software. When WordPress finds security flaws and bugs, they are patched with updates regularly—don't ignore the pleas to update your software. The same logic applies to any plug-ins you have installed.

The update menu item will show how many updates are available for WordPress.

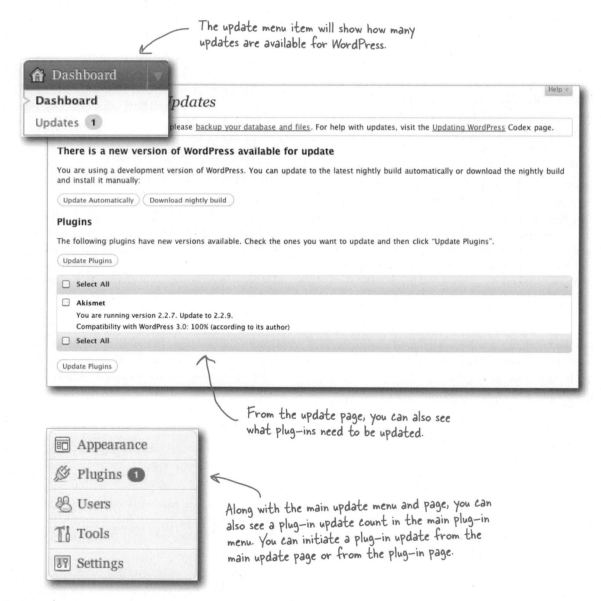

From the update page, you can also see what plug-ins need to be updated.

Along with the main update menu and page, you can also see a plug-in update count in the main plug-in menu. You can initiate a plug-in update from the main update page or from the plug-in page.

Avoid file uploads with automatic updates

Depending on your WordPress setup and your server configuration, you might be able to use the WordPress automatic updater to install updates. Just like we saw earlier with uploading images and video, the updater needs to be able to write to the file system. If it's not able to, it will ask for FTP connection information. WordPress recommends that you not use this method and instead change the file permissions on your web server.

There is a new version of WordPress available for update

You are using a development version of WordPress. You can update to the la
and install it manually:

(Update Automatically) (Download nightly build)

Depending on your WordPress version you will see an automatic update button along with a nightly build button (if you have a development version).

(Update Plugins)

☐ **Select All**

☐ **Akismet**
You are running version 2.2.7. Update to 2.2.9.
Compatibility with WordPress 3.0: 100% (according to its author)

☐ **Select All**

Auto-updating plug-ins can also be initiated from the update page. Here, Akismet, the spam plug-in, has a new version available.

Watch it!

Don't use the Connection Information update method.

If the automatic updater can't access the file system when attempting to update, it will ask you for FTP information and attempt to connect that way. According to WordPress, this won't work and you'll need update WordPress manually. Don't panic, we're about to get to that...

🏠 *Connection Information*

To perform the requested action, connection information is required.

Hostname

Username

Password

Connection Type   ◉ FTP ○ FTPS (SSL)

(Proceed)

If you see this screen, you'll need to update WordPress manually.

Use FTP to update WordPress if automatic updates don't work

Updating WordPress is pretty easy, even if you aren't using automatic updates. All we need to do is download the newest version of the WordPress system (or a specific plug-in that needs updating), and copy the new files up to the web server.

① **Download most current WordPress and plug-in files.**
For both plug-ins and WordPress itself, you need to download the updated files to your local computer before you can do anything else. You'll be able to find their most curent versions on their respective websites.

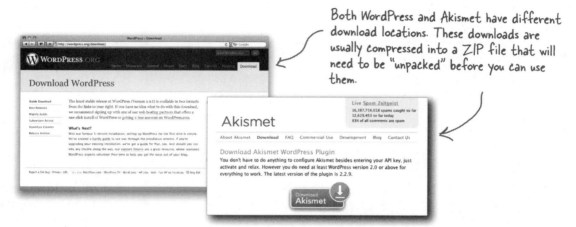

> Both WordPress and Akismet have different download locations. These downloads are usually compressed into a ZIP file that will need to be "unpacked" before you can use them.

② **Back up your original files.**
Before you install the new files, back up what you've got right now. Backing up WordPress and plug-ins before we upgrade will ensure that we can "undo" the changes if something goes wrong.

> To be safe, copy your entire WordPress installation down to your local computer. Stash it in a easily recongizable folder in case you have to replace anything.

backup

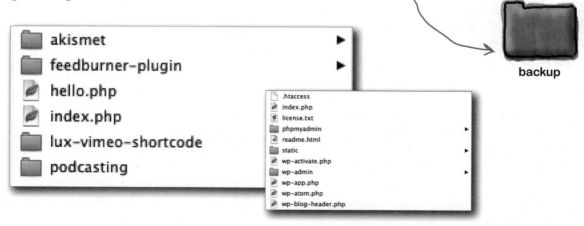

③ ### Upload the new files to WordPress.

When updating plug-ins, you can replace the entire folder. For example, Akismet is installed in */wp-content/plugins/akismet*. When we upgrade, we can just overwrite the /akismet folder. For a full WordPress system update, you want to replace every file and folder *except* your **wp-config.php** and **.htaccess** files and the **/wp-content** directory (this is where all of our uploaded files, themes, and plug-ins live—we want to keep those the same).

When updating plug-ins it's usually OK to just replace the entire directory. If you're not sure, back up first and then check the plug-in author's documentation.

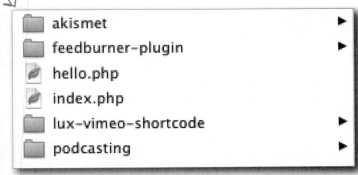

Don't delete or replace your /wp-content directory unless you want to lose all of your plug-ins and themes You can also leave wp-config.php alone to avoid having to re-type all of your database information.

When copying new files, select everything but the configuration file and wp-content. We want to leave those alone.

Watch it!

Be extra careful with /wp-content if you have custom themes.

If you accidently replace /wp-content and all you have is downloaded plug-ins and themes–those can be replaced. But if you made your own theme, it might not be as easy. Exercise caution when you update WordPress and mind your custom files.

Secure users make secure websites

Now that your WordPress installation and plug-ins are up-to-date, you can focus your attention on the next most vulnerable aspect of your WordPress site: your users. Users need to gain access to WordPress for many different functions, most of which involve modifying the system (adding a post, changing an email address, moderating a comment). Because of this, you need to make sure everyone is using secure usernames and passwords and that they only have access to the functions they need (see previous chapters on user roles).

☐ Make sure usernames are unique and never use the "admin" default for administration accounts. If you're really paranoid, don't use the same username you use on other web applications or social networking sites.

The main reason you want to change your username is that it's well known as the default one for WordPress, which makes brute force attempts on your site even easier as the hacker only has to guess your password.

☐ Always use strong passwords. You should strive to get the WordPress password meter into the green and avoid dictionary words whenever possible. Weak passwords can become your biggest security headache.

The WordPress password meter will tell you how strong your password is and give you tips on how to write strong passwords.

•••••••••••	*If you would like to change the password type a new one. Otherwise leave this blank.*
•••••••••••	*Type your new password again.*
Strong	*Hint: The password should be at least seven characters long. To make it stronger, use upper and lower case letters, numbers and symbols like ! " ? $ % ^ &).*

☐ Be smart about user roles. Only give users as much access as they require to do their job. Keep access to administrative user accounts to one or two people and limit the number of users that can publish content or modify the live site.

For Thanks for Mutton, our users are spread out across the roles to limit who can publish to the blog.

👥 *Users* (Add New)

All (3) | **Administrator** (1) | **Editor** (1) | **Contributor** (1)

Do this!

The admin user wasn't changed when Thanks for Mutton was first created. Log in to the WordPress dashboard and change the "admin" username in the user settings.

Profile

It looks like the username field is disabled in the profile settings. Looks like we can't change our username from here.

Name

Username   admin   *Usernames cannot be changed.*

First Name

Last Name

Nickname *(required)*   admin

What gives? I can't edit the username.

admin

Authors & Users

Add New

> **Your Profile**

The profile page is the only place in the admin dashboard that displays our user information, and it won't let us change our username...

⚛ BRAIN POWER

Where are your username and password actually *stored*? Could that help you figure out another way to change your admin username?

Edit your database to change usernames

Once you've created a user in WordPress—*any* user, not just the admin—you can't change their username from the dashboard any longer. You can change how a user's First and Last names appear on the live site, but the username they log into the site with isn't editable. In order to modify the username after it has been created, we need to edit our database and user table directly.

If your using Media Temple, you can get to phpMyAdmin by clicking on the admin button next to your database.

We took a quick peek at phpMyAdmin in Chapter 1 as a way to check our new database—now we're going to need it again.

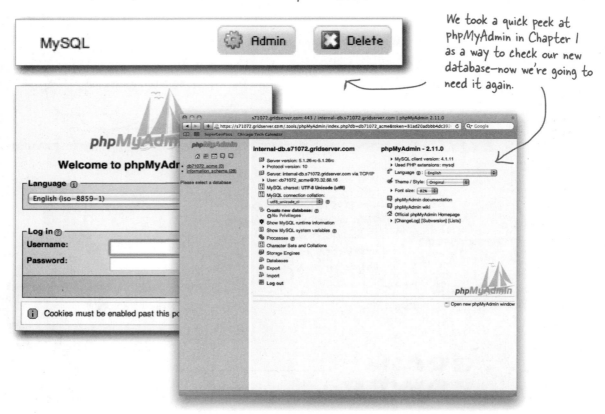

You don't have to be a database or MySQL ninja to do this.

Relax

Tools like phpMyAdmin help you work with databases using familiar interfaces that look a lot like web forms. You're able to access your database, look at all your tables (more on that in a second), and change things easily. We'll take a quick look at how a database is set up in general before diving in and changing our admin username.

Databases are made up of tables

So all along we've been referring to the web server that hosts WordPress, but in reality, the computer that runs the web server also runs what we call a database server. That's where your MySQL database lives (or multiple databases, in many cases). You communicate with a database server in a language it can understand, which in this case is SQL. A database server typically runs alongside a web server on the same server computer, working together in concert reading and writing data, and delivering web pages.

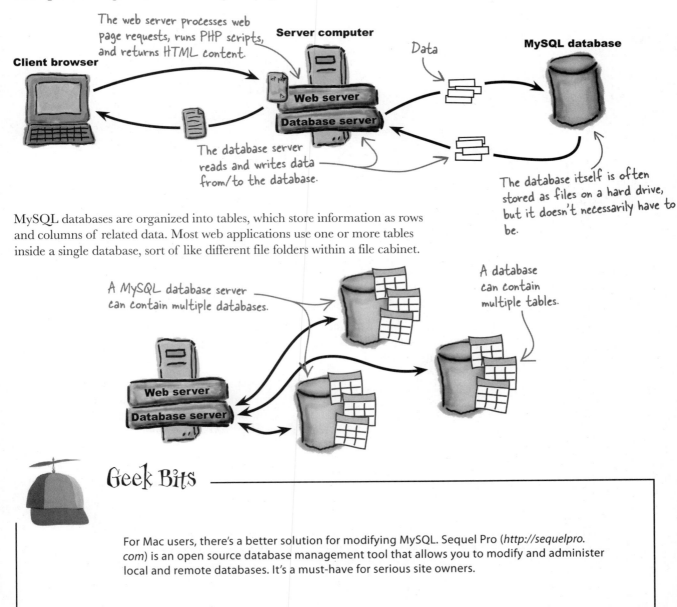

The web server processes web page requests, runs PHP scripts, and returns HTML content.

Client browser

Server computer

Web server

Database server

Data

MySQL database

The database server reads and writes data from/to the database.

The database itself is often stored as files on a hard drive, but it doesn't necessarily have to be.

MySQL databases are organized into tables, which store information as rows and columns of related data. Most web applications use one or more tables inside a single database, sort of like different file folders within a file cabinet.

A MySQL database server can contain multiple databases.

A database can contain multiple tables.

Web server

Database server

Geek Bits

For Mac users, there's a better solution for modifying MySQL. Sequel Pro (*http://sequelpro. com*) is an open source database management tool that allows you to modify and administer local and remote databases. It's a must-have for serious site owners.

On most web hosts, the easiest way to change data in your database is to use the MySQL administration tool that comes with your hosting. For most of us that's going to be phpMyAdmin—a browser-based tool that allows use to see a visual representation of our database and it's tables, and then make modifications accordingly.

① **Log in to phpMyAdmin.**
Before we can do anything to our database, we need to log in to phpMyAdmin using our database username and password.

Your hosting company may have different procedures for using phpMyAdmin. If you're not on Media Temple, check their documentation before moving forward.

② **Back up your database.**
This database holds all the content for our entire site—it's important. As we saw earlier, the best way to make sure important files stay safe is to back them up, and databases are no exception. We'll cover this in more detail later in the chapter.

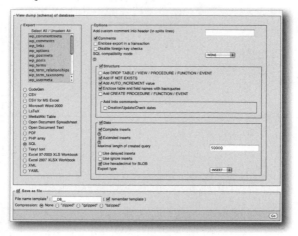

a Select your database from the main dropdown in the left sidebar.

b At the top of the window, click the tab that says "Export." You'll then see a list of all the tables in your database in the left column.

c Make sure all the tables are selected and that both "data" and "structure" are checked for export. Then click "Go" and save the exported file to your computer for safe keeping. We can re-import this later if need be, and we'll have our database restored to how it was before the backup.

③ Show the `wp_users` table.

Once you have a backup safely stowed on your local machine, go back to the "Structure" tab, open up the wp_users table and find the admin user. The user is one row in the wp_users table.

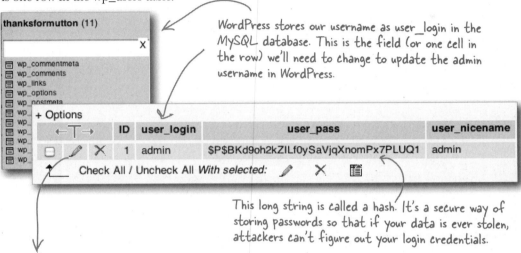

WordPress stores our username as user_login in the MySQL database. This is the field (or one cell in the row) we'll need to change to update the admin username in WordPress.

This long string is called a hash. It's a secure way of storing passwords so that if your data is ever stolen, attackers can't figure out your login credentials.

④ Update the admin username.

Clicking the pencil icon will take you to an edit form for that table row. Change the user_login field to something other than "admin" and click Go. We now should be able to log in to WordPress using our new username. Remember, pick a unique username that isn't in the dictionary and would be very difficult to just guess!

Field	Type	Function	Null	Value
ID	bigint(20) unsigned			1
user_login	varchar(60)			tfmadministrator
user_pass	varchar(64)			PBKd9oh2kZILf0ySaVjqXnomPx7PLUQ1
user_nicename	varchar(50)			admin
user_email	varchar(100)			admin@thanksformutton.com
user_url	varchar(100)			
user_registered	datetime			2009-12-28 16:03:03
user_activation_key	varchar(60)			
user_status	int(11)			0
display_name	varchar(250)			admin

Browse · Structure · SQL · Search · Insert · Export · Import · Operations · Empty · Drop

Go

Once our database is updated we can log in to Thanks for Mutton using the new username. No more insecure admin!

Notice that changing the username didn't alter any of the "display name publicly as" settings. These remain the same and can be changed from within the dashboard.

there are no Dumb Questions

Q: Why can't you just change the username from the dashboard?

A: That's a great question. This was a design decision by WordPress programmers and that functionality never made it to the dashboard. Our guess is it was done for security and administrative purposes.

Q: Can't hackers just guess my new username too? How is this more secure?

A: Yes, hackers could just guess your username but that's twice as hard as just guessing only your password. By adding another variable (the unknown username) brute force attacks become less effective.

Q: Are there other "insecure" usernames like admin?

A: The only reason "admin" is insecure on WordPress is that it's well known as the default username. Other systems may have different known defaults and pose different security risks to the site owner. Best case is to never use the default.

Add more security to WordPress by protecting wp-admin

There is one final thing we can do to make the WordPress dashboard and all your user accounts a little more secure. As you might remember, the /wp-admin directory is actually accessible in a browser window if someone knows how to navigate to it. It's another well-known vulnerability for WordPress sites. By adding a second layer of authentication to the /wp-admin directory, we can force users to enter two sets of credentials to gain access to the site. That alone should ward off many potential hackers.

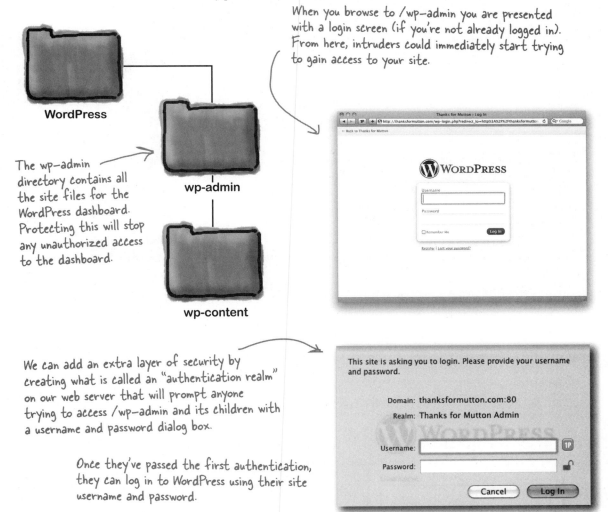

WordPress

The wp-admin directory contains all the site files for the WordPress dashboard. Protecting this will stop any unauthorized access to the dashboard.

wp-admin

wp-content

When you browse to /wp-admin you are presented with a login screen (if you're not already logged in). From here, intruders could immediately start trying to gain access to your site.

We can add an extra layer of security by creating what is called an "authentication realm" on our web server that will prompt anyone trying to access /wp-admin and its children with a username and password dialog box.

Once they've passed the first authentication, they can log in to WordPress using their site username and password.

Seem like too much hassle? It's much easier to type two sets of usernames and passwords than it is to rewrite a year's worth of posts and pages...

Create a new authentication realm

The easiest way to create a new authentication realm (also known as HTTP Basic Authentication) on your web server is to use your hosting panel. Most hosts—Media Temple included—allow you to create these from within your account settings.

1 **Log in to your web host and find the password protect directory option.**
This should be located in your primary domain settings.

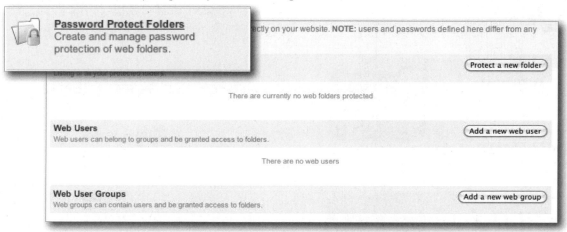

2 **Add a user for the new realm.**
We need to create a new "user" for our realm. This is really just the username/ password combination that people will use to log in to the realm.

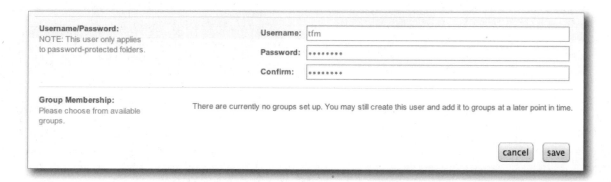

3 **Choose a folder to protect.**

We need to select a folder (in our case /wp-admin) that will be protected by the realm. All files and folders within this folder will also be protected

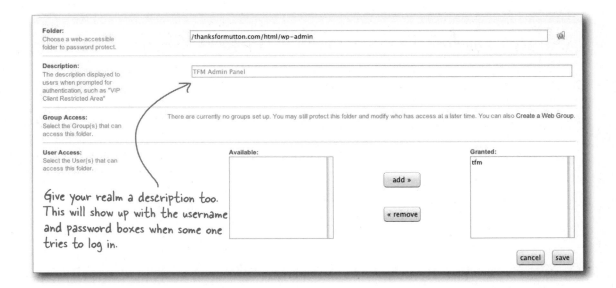

4 **Confirm your settings.**

Before you leave your web server control panel, make sure your new realm settings are correct.

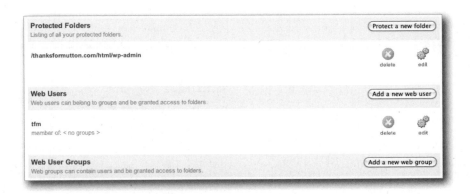

TEST DRIVE

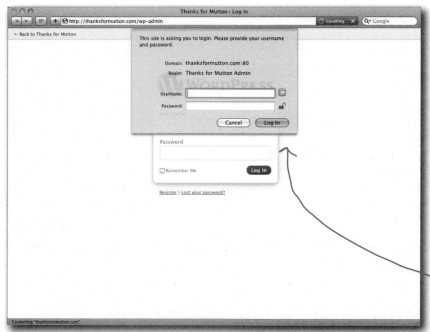

If you navigate to /wp-admin on your blog's URL, you should be presented with a drop down authentication box (this may look slightly different depending on your browser).

Once they pass the HTTP authentication, users can continue logging in to the main WordPress dashboard.

Geek Bits

You don't need to use your hosting panel to add an HTTP authentication realm. In fact, you can add the all necessary info right to your .htaccess file. For more information on creating your own authentication realms, check out the Apache manual pages: *http://httpd.apache.org/docs/2.2/howto/auth.html*.

```
<Location /wp-admin>
    AuthType basic
    AuthName "TFM Admin Panel"
    AuthUserFile /passwds
    Require valid-user
</Location>
```

Security by obscurity

WordPress sometimes gets a bad rap for security—some of it founded in actual vulnerabilities, but most of it is based on exaggeration and/or people not doing the work to secure their WordPress sites properly. Security is not something most web frameworks are good at, especially not without some forethought from programmers and site administrators. Websites also become more vulnerable when the attacker knows what type of system the site is running on and can try specific hacks for that platform. Basically, if a hacker knows we're using WordPress, he knows where to start breaking in. What's the best way around this? Make WordPress act like something other than WordPress.

Exercise

Identify parts of the (hacked) Thanks for Mutton site that might identify it as a WordPress blog. Hint: don't be afraid to check out the "view source" option for your site in a web browser to see if there is anything under the hood that might identify TFM as WordPress-powered.

Exercise Solution

Identify parts of the (hacked) Thanks for Mutton site that might identify it as a WordPress blog. Hint: don't be afraid to check out the "view source" option for your site in a web browser to see if there is anything under the hood that might identify TFM as WordPress-powered.

If pretty permalinks aren't enabled, the URL of our site can give away the fact that we're using WordPress to power the site.

Using the default WordPress theme is also a clue that we might be, well, using WordPress. We're not going to change that right now, but we can still make it a bit less obvious.

Not Found | Thanks for Mutton

`http://thanksformutton.com/?p=2`

Thanks for Mutton

A Food Blog About Nothing

Not Found

Apologies, but the page you requested could not be found. Perhaps searching will help.

Search [   ] (Search)

Thanks for Mutton

Proudly powered by WordPress.

The Powered by WordPress logo is pretty much a dead giveaway that we're using WordPress.

If you look at the page source you can see other meta tags that may also give us away.

```
<link rel="EditURI" type="application/rsd+xml" title="RSD" href="http://
thanksformutton.com/xmlrpc.php?rsd" />

<link rel="wlwmanifest" type="application/wlwmanifest+xml" href="http://
thanksformutton.com/wp-includes/wlwmanifest.xml" />

<link rel='index' title='Thanks for Mutton' href='http://thanksformutton.com' />

<meta name="generator" content="WordPress 3.0-beta1" />
```

You can learn a lot about a site by looking at its head

You can learn a lot about a site and how it works by viewing the source in a browser and checking out the link and meta tags in the <head> section of the HTML.

We're looking at the browser source of the TFM home page, but the code that generates this HTML is located in the header.php theme file so you could look there instead.

```
<link rel="EditURI" type="application/rsd+xml" title="RSD" href="http://
thanksformutton.com/xmlrpc.php?rsd" />

<link rel="wlwmanifest" type="application/wlwmanifest+xml" href="http://
thanksformutton.com/wp-includes/wlwmanifest.xml" />

<link rel='index' title='Thanks for Mutton' href='http://thanksformutton.com' />

<meta name="generator" content="WordPress 3.0-beta1" />
```

The most obvious clue that we're running WordPress is the HTML tag that tells, in fact, that we are using WordPress version 3.0 Beta 1. That's like leaving the key to your house under the front doormat...

Anytime you have a link or file that references "wp" it's a good bet that WordPress is involved.

Sharpen your pencil

Let's get rid of the most obvious WordPress give-away, the meta tag "generator." Examine header.php in your template directory to see if you can remove it from the page.

Sharpen your pencil
Solution

Let's get rid of the most obvious WordPress giveaway, the meta tag "generator." Examine header.php in your template directory to see if you can remove it from the page.

```php
<?php
/**
 * The Header for our theme.
 *
 */
?>
<!DOCTYPE html>
<html <?php language_attributes(); ?>>
<head>
<meta charset="<?php bloginfo( 'charset' ); ?>" />

<link rel="profile" href="http://gmpg.org/xfn/11" />
<link rel="stylesheet" type="text/css" media="all" href="<?php bloginfo(
'stylesheet_url' ); ?>" />
<?php if ( is_singular() ) wp_enqueue_script( 'comment-reply' ); ?>
<link rel="pingback" href="<?php bloginfo( 'pingback_url' ); ?>" />

<?php wp_head(); ?>

<link rel="alternate" type="application/rss+xml" title="Podcast: Thanks for
Mutton" href="http://feeds.feedburner.com/mmmmmutton" />
```

Remember, the header.php file contains the templates for the head of our HTML, exactly where that generator tag is located.

header.php

It looks like all those meta and link tags are being generated by a PHP function called wp_head().

We're not going to be able to turn off the generator tag from the header.php file. We'll need to find the file where the PHP functions are coded instead...

① Open the functions.php theme file.

Scroll all the way to the bottom (especially if you're using the twentyten theme). If you don't have a functions.php file you can create one in the main theme directory.

```php
/**
 * Removes the default styles that are packaged with the Recent
Comments widget.
 */
function twentyten_remove_recent_comments_style() {
      global $wp_widget_factory;
      remove_action( 'wp_head', array( $wp_widget_factory-
>widgets['WP_Widget_Recent_Comments'], 'recent_comments_style' ) );
}
add_action( 'widgets_init', 'twentyten_remove_recent_comments_style
```

functions.php

② Add a remove action call to disable the generator tag.

WordPress allows us to add and remove actions within the system, including the wp_head(). We can use the remove_action() function to disable the meta generator tag.

```php
function twentyten_remove_recent_comments_style() {
      global $wp_widget_factory;
      remove_action( 'wp_head', array( $wp_widget_factory-
>widgets['WP_Widget_Recent_Comments'], 'recent_comments_style' ) );
}
add_action( 'widgets_init', 'twentyten_remove_recent_comments_style' );

remove_action('wp_head', 'wp_generator');
```

This function will remove the single generator meta tag but leave the rest of the document head intact. This will ensure that other services, like the podcast, stay functional.

functions.php

BULLET POINTS

- Good security starts with good passwords.

- A strong password is a word or phrase that is longer than eight characters, contains some special symbols, and isn't a standalone dictionary word.

- Always keep WordPress and any installed plug-ins up-to-date so your software reflects the latest security updates.

- Avoid using the default WordPress "admin" username. Make sure you change it during the initial install of WordPress or use a database manager like phpMyAdmin or Sequel Pro to change it after the fact.

- Use security by obscurity to keep would-be hackers from attempting WordPress-specific attacks on your site.

I feel better already. You know, given that this could happen anytime— we really should have a backup plan for the site. It would have been nice to just replace the posts that got deleted.

Back up early, back up often

Backups are probably the single most important security measure you can take for your site. In the rare event that your site is irreversibly hacked or suffers a server crash, a backup may be the only recovery option. They are often overlooked by new site owners who are just concerned with getting their blogs off the ground and are not worrying about replacing a broken database or files that have gone missing. Everyone from the novice blogger to the professional webmaster should be backing up all important data and files regularly, and to a location that's ***not*** on the main web server.

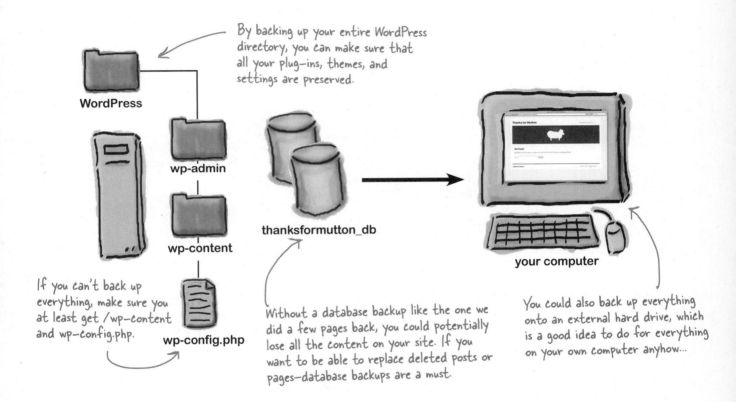

By backing up your entire WordPress directory, you can make sure that all your plug-ins, themes, and settings are preserved.

WordPress

wp-admin

wp-content

thanksformutton_db

your computer

If you can't back up everything, make sure you at least get /wp-content and wp-config.php.

wp-config.php

Without a database backup like the one we did a few pages back, you could potentially lose all the content on your site. If you want to be able to replace deleted posts or pages—database backups are a must.

You could also back up everything onto an external hard drive, which is a good idea to do for everything on your own computer anyhow...

Exercise

If you didn't do this earlier when we covered installing WordPress updates manually, then log in to your site using your FTP client and copy your main WordPress directory down to your local computer.

Exercise Solution

If you didn't do this earlier when we covered installing WordPress updates manually, then log in to your site using your FTP client and copy your main WordPress directory down to your local computer.

1 **Login to your web server using FTP.**

One you're on the server, navigate to the main WordPress installation directory.

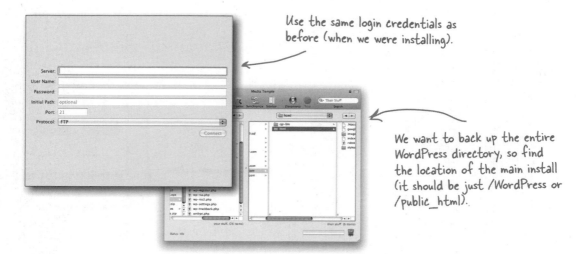

Use the same login credentials as before (when we were installing).

We want to back up the entire WordPress directory, so find the location of the main install (it should be just /WordPress or /public_html).

2 **Download the entire WordPress installation to your local computer.**

Copy your WordPress installation to your desktop by dragging the directory that contains all your WordPress files from your FTP client to your computer's desktop or another location on your computer. This will capture your entire WordPress installation, including any themes, plug-ins, or special settings you've made.

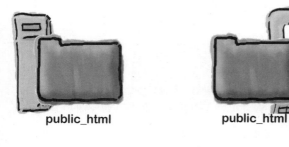

public_html   public_html

Depending on how many uploads, plug-ins, and themes you have, this download could take a bit of time. Be patient—this is an important step.

> This is your backup solution? I have to manually do this every time?! Now I see why no one ever backs up their blogs.

Use plug-ins for remote, automated backups

Although downloading files manually is a safe, simple way of backing up your files, it can be come cumbersome as your site gets larger and you begin to require more frequent backups. You also have to remember to do it frequently! The best way to manage WordPress backups is with a plug-in. Just as they can be useful for functionality on our blog, plug-ins can also help us manage backups by automatically copying site and database files to a remote storage location.

automatic-WordPress-backup

We are going to use the Automatic WordPress Backup plug-in to take care of our automated backups. You can download and install this plug-in from: http://WordPress.org/extend/plugins/automatic-WordPress-backup/.

Backup schedule: Daily ▾

Parts of your blog to back up
☑ Config file and htaccess
☑ Database dump
☑ Themes folder
☑ Plugins folder
☑ Uploaded content

☑ Delete backups older than one month
   ☑ Keep a monthly backup for one year
   ☐ Keep manual backups forever

(Save Changes) (Save Changes and Backup Now)

This plug-in will take care of everything we need in terms of backup. It will even back up our MySQL database so we don't have a repeat of the latest Thanks for Mutton missing content issue.

Don't store backups on your web server

One way for your site to go "down" is for your hosted web server to fail. If you have your backups stored there then, well...that won't help you very much. Once of the best features of the Automatic WordPress Backup (AWB) plug-in is that it stores your backups on Amazon's Simple Storage Service. At its basic level, Amazon Simple Storage (or S3) is a giant hard drive that's distributed across thousands of servers all over the world. You can put as much data on the service as you wish and you only pay for the storage and transfer that you use.

Amazon S3

In order for our Automatic WordPress Backup plug-in to work, we need to have Amazon S3 configured. Think of S3 as just another web server with FTP access—you can read and write files just like you do when you install or backup WordPress.

Amazon calls their folders "buckets" and you have to set up at least one bucket to store your files. Pick a unique name; each bucket must be different.

Amazon has a ton of servers that they use to store all your data. They call this redundancy—if one (or more) of the servers fails, there's still plenty of servers available to keep your stuff.

Our web server (or any other computer) can write files to Amazon S3 just like any other file system.

If you don't already have an S3 account, you can create one at http://aws.amazon.com/s3.

Geek Bits

If you've heard people talking about "**the cloud**" this is what they're referring to: shared but distributed resources, like software, server space, and even data are provided to computers and other devices "on demand." Think of it like the **electricity grid**, where power is diverted/moved around based on where it is currently needed most.

Connect automated backups to Amazon S3

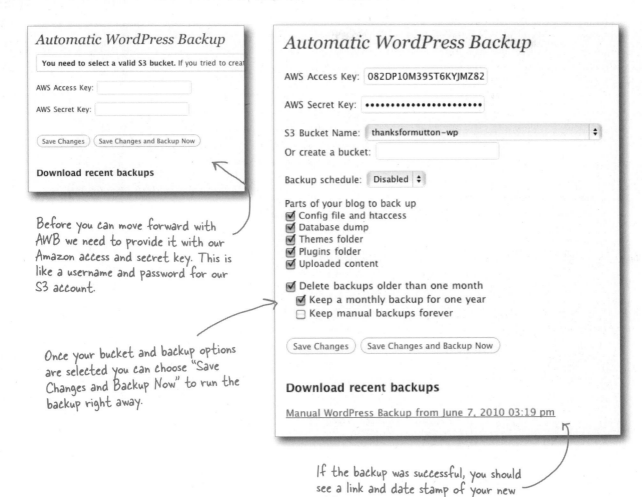

Before you can move forward with AWB we need to provide it with our Amazon access and secret key. This is like a username and password for our S3 account.

Once your bucket and backup options are selected you can choose "Save Changes and Backup Now" to run the backup right away.

If the backup was successful, you should see a link and date stamp of your new S3 backup.

Restoring your backups

Restoring files is as easy as pulling down your backups from S3 (some FTP clients, like Transmit, will allow you to connect directly to S3). The database, on the other hand, will take a bit more work. Thankfully you're already somewhat familiar with the phpMyAdmin interface, which is what we'll use to get our data back on Thanks for Mutton. Let's get that going...

Import a backed-up database using phpMyAdmin

In the case of Thanks For Mutton, all would not be lost if we'd just
backed up our database. To finish the chapter, let's say we did have
that handy backup stored on S3, and now we just need to get it
back onto our database server. We can do this using phpMyAdmin's
import feature.

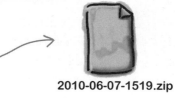

2010-06-07-1519.zip

The main backup comes in a single ZIP archive.
We need to double-click that file to get to the
directory of backups underneath. They're all
labeled by the date they were created.

2010-06-07-1519

① Log in to phpMyAdmin.
Just like you did when you we're backing up the database earlier in the
chapter...

② Select the Thanks for Mutton database.
We don't want to import this to the wrong table so make sure you are
replacing the right one.

③ Select the import tab and upload your SQL file.
The SQL files contains the structure and data from our database and
will restore our site to the state it was when the backup was taken.
Once this import is finished, we should see the original Thanks for
Mutton site.

wp-s3-database-backup.sql

We need to find the SQL file, as
this is the backup for our database.

Once your backup is restored, the site should be
just like it was before you lost everything.

Phew! Now we can get back
to writing that big article
on inhalable coffee...

Your WordPress Toolbox

You've got Chapter 7 under your belt and now you've added security and backups to your tool box. Next up, making your WordPress site run super fast!

BULLET POINTS

- Unfortunately, not everyone (or everything) on the Web has good intentions. Although it's rare for sites to be completely taken down by "hackers," it's still smart to protect your site from some of the more well-known attacks.

- Keeping your WordPress installation, plug-ins, and themes up-to-date is one of the best security measures you can take.

- Using strong, secure passwords is your first line of defense against brute-force attacks—people or robots simply guessing your login information.

- Change the default admin username to something else, using phpMyAdmin or some other database management tool.

- Creating an additional authentication "realm" (or an .htacess password) in addition to your WordPress authentication can add an extra layer of protection between your dashboard login and rest of the world.

- Always back up your files. Even if you have the most secure installation available, things can still happen and data can be lost.

- Automate backups using a plug-in and store your backups off site (or "in the cloud") for extra protection.

8 making wordpress fast

Time for the passing lane

Speed is important online.

A fast-loading site isn't just about keeping visitors around. Yes, if your site doesn't load quickly then people might just wander off, but a slow site also gets dinged in search results from the likes of Google, meaning fewer people will actually find your site in the first place. Beyond just increasing your horsepower, you'll also learn how to use caching, database optimization, and additional hosting options to beef up your site to handle more traffic, too.

Not again...

Just as things were starting to settle down, it looks like Thanks for Mutton is having some problems again.

Laura

Bob

Mark

Laura: Wait, how do you know how many people have been visiting the site? I thought the Feedburner stats only told us about our RSS feed subscriptions, not the visitors to the site overall.

Mark: Oh yeah, I didn't get that from Feedburner, I'm getting our site stats from Google.

Bob: Google? OK, I know that Google does a lot of things, but how in the world does it know how many people are visiting our site?

Mark: Well, you have to sign up for it as a service from Google, but when a visitor comes to Thanks for Mutton, our web server "logs" a whole bunch of information about that person.

Laura: Information? What kind of information? Like their name and where they live? That seems a bit creepy...

Mark: Not quite. We don't know specifically *which* people come to the site, but we do know a whole bunch of useful stuff: what kind of computer/browser they are using, where in the world they live (their general area, not an address or the like), and how long they stayed on the site.

Bob: Oh, that's pretty cool. So we could even look at which pages they visit the most (or which ones people hardly visit at all)?

Mark: Exactly. And not only does that allow us to help decide which content is most popular so we can plan future articles and videos, but it might also provide some clues about why the site isn't showing up at all right now...

Laura: Oh, I get it. If we look at traffic from before today, we typically have a couple hundred visitors a day, maybe close to a thousand max if we write a really popular article. But today we just had 15,000 visitors in 10 minutes. What could cause a spike like that?

 **BRAIN POWER**

Think back to how your web server handles web page requests, and what it has to do to put together a WordPress page (you can also take a look at Chapter 1 again for a refresher). How do you think a sudden "spike" (or increase) in visitors to your site might affect the web server? Before we solve that mystery, let's get Google Analytics rolling for Thanks for Mutton...

Keep an eye on your traffic with Google Analytics

Every time a user visits a page on your site, a whole host of information is made available to the web server about where that person came from, what type of computer and browser they use and how long they stayed on the site. This information is important in helping us figure out both who our audience is and what their technical requirements are, but it's also super helpful in deciding and how much server space and power we need to handle the traffic. Google Analytics is a service that easily integrates into WordPress and will give us all the data we need about our site visitors.

This is our dashboard in Google Analytics (don't worry, we'll get it set up in a second).

The main line graph in the dashboard shows daily "traffic" to our site over the past 30 days. It's like the counter at the entrance to a store, but we have it for every page on our site. We can use this information to help us make the site perform better.

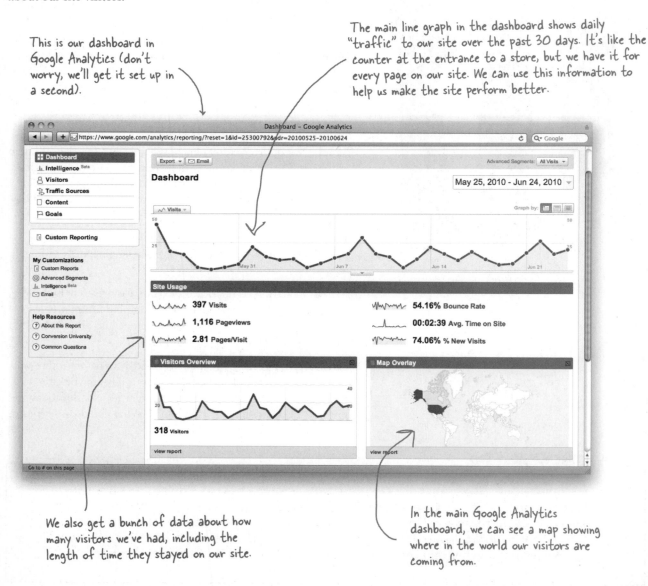

We also get a bunch of data about how many visitors we've had, including the length of time they stayed on our site.

In the main Google Analytics dashboard, we can see a map showing where in the world our visitors are coming from.

Integrating Google Analytics with WordPress

The only thing you need to do to get your site to work with Google Analytics is to add a small bit of JavaScript to the header of every page that you want tracked. This can be done by copying code that Google gives you to the header.php template file. To make things even easier, we'll give you the code here and show you where to put it.

1 **Sign up for Google Analytics.**
You should already have a Google account from when you installed Feedburner. You can use the same login info to create an account at *www.google.com/analytics*. From there, add your WordPress site as a "Website Profile."

1 **Copy/paste the tracking code.**
You can find your code in the "Profile Settings" page for your site. It is the same code that any other site would use to implement tracking, except it has a user ID specific to your site. We've provided the code below, and all you have to do is change the ID to match what Google gave you in your site profile.

Ready Bake Code

We want to place the Google Analytics code (in bold) just above the closing </head> tag in the header template. This bit of code will be run every time a user visits a page on our site.

header.php

```php
<?php wp_head(); ?>
<script type="text/javascript">
  var _gaq = _gaq || [];
  _gaq.push(['_setAccount', 'UA-XXX']);
  _gaq.push(['_trackPageview']);


  (function() {
    var ga = document.createElement('script'); ga.type = 'text/javascript'; ga.async =
true;
    ga.src = ('https:' == document.location.protocol ? 'https://ssl' : 'http://www') +
'.google-analytics.com/ga.js';
    var s = document.getElementsByTagName('script')[0]; s.parentNode.insertBefore(ga,
s);
  })();
</script>
</head>
```

Replace this text (UA-XXX) with your own user ID. Google uses this to know that the traffic it is tracking is associated with your site.

Make sure the code is pasted just above the closing </head> tag.

Your site traffic has a lot to say...

There's a ton more we could get into about analyzing your site traffic, but for now we're just going to step back and look at the bigger picture. A bird's-eye view can help you spot interesting trends (hot topics as they start to emerge on your site), or significant trouble spots.

This is a graph from Google Analytics showing our website traffic for the last 30 days.

On the most recent day, you can see the huge spike in traffic. Is it a hacker (DoS) attack, or maybe something else?

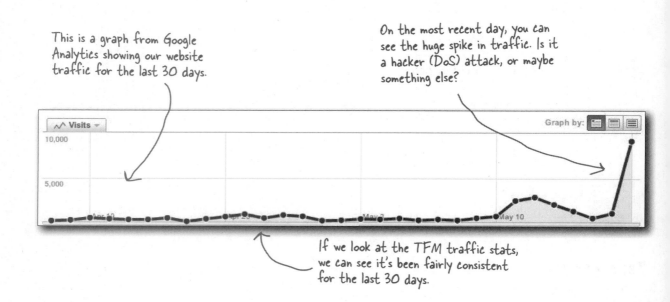

If we look at the TFM traffic stats, we can see it's been fairly consistent for the last 30 days.

... but it can't tell you everything

Google Analytics is a great tool, but it's not a mind reader. Once you've found some trends (or a big change) in your site traffic, you may need to use other tools or approaches to figure out what is causing the traffic changes on your site. This could include site surveys, customer research, and more. (Check out *Head First Web Design* for some great techniques to learn more about your site visitors).

Looks like it's time to start digging...

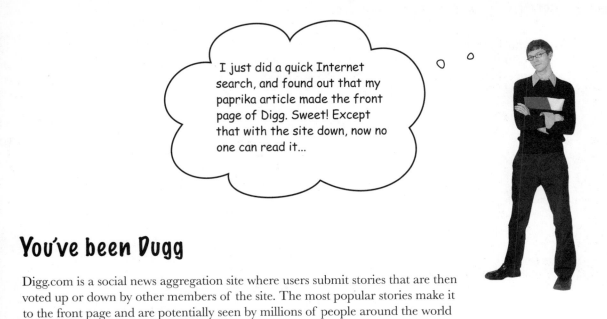

> I just did a quick Internet search, and found out that my paprika article made the front page of Digg. Sweet! Except that with the site down, now no one can read it...

You've been Dugg

Digg.com is a social news aggregation site where users submit stories that are then voted up or down by other members of the site. The most popular stories make it to the front page and are potentially seen by millions of people around the world (people call this getting "Dugg"). Sites featured on the home page could see 100s or even 1000s of page views per second—traffic that could bring even the most well-prepared sites to their knees.

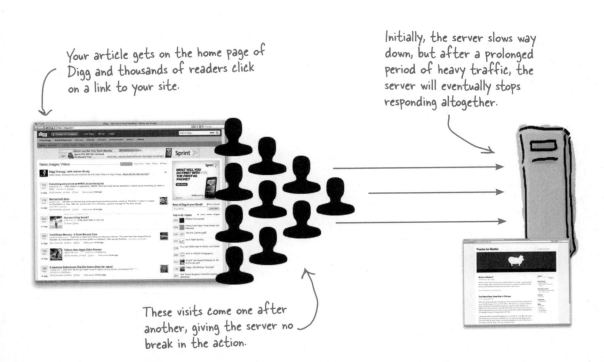

Your article gets on the home page of Digg and thousands of readers click on a link to your site.

Initially, the server slows way down, but after a prolonged period of heavy traffic, the server will eventually stops responding altogether.

These visits come one after another, giving the server no break in the action.

The anatomy of a web page request

In order to find ways to help Thanks for Mutton stand up to the heavy traffic of the Digg Effect (or any other rush of traffic to the site), we first need to look ever deeper into the details of what's happening when someone types your site's URL into the address bar of their web browser.

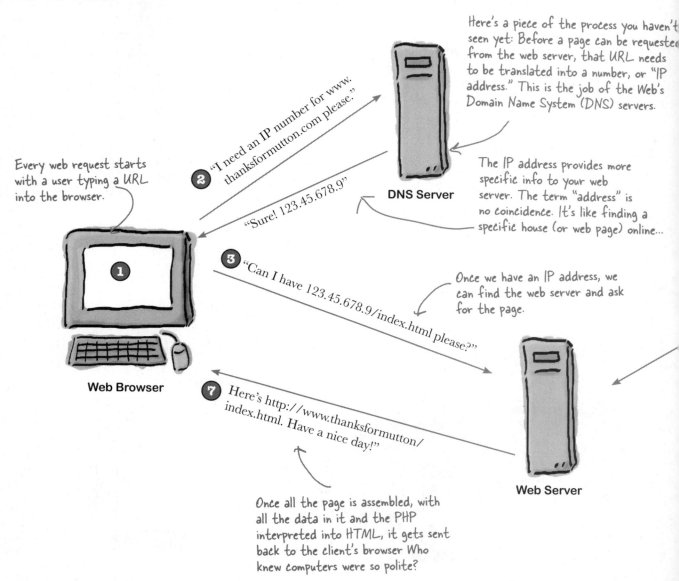

Here's a piece of the process you haven't seen yet: Before a page can be requested from the web server, that URL needs to be translated into a number, or "IP address." This is the job of the Web's Domain Name System (DNS) servers.

Every web request starts with a user typing a URL into the browser.

2 "I need an IP number for www.thanksformutton.com please."

"Sure! 123.45.678.9"

DNS Server

The IP address provides more specific info to your web server. The term "address" is no coincidence. It's like finding a specific house (or web page) online...

1

3 "Can I have 123.45.678.9/index.html please?"

Once we have an IP address, we can find the web server and ask for the page.

Web Browser

7 Here's http://www.thanksformutton/index.html. Have a nice day!"

Once all the page is assembled, with all the data in it and the PHP interpreted into HTML, it gets sent back to the client's browser Who knew computers were so polite?

Web Server

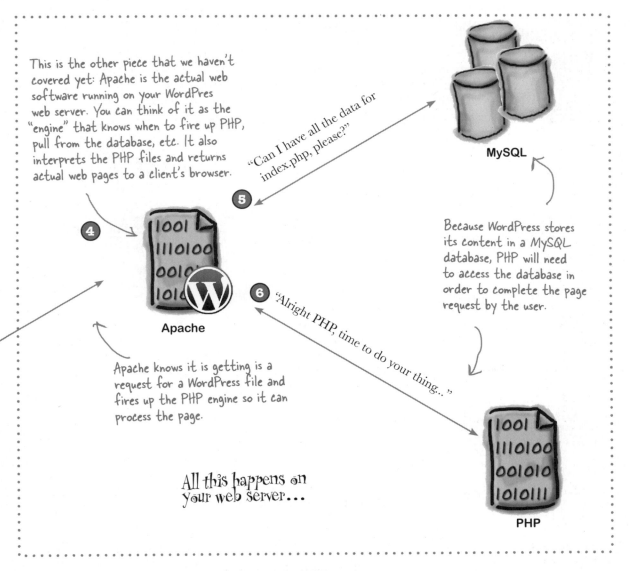

This is the other piece that we haven't covered yet: Apache is the actual web software running on your WordPres web server. You can think of it as the "engine" that knows when to fire up PHP, pull from the database, etc. It also interprets the PHP files and returns actual web pages to a client's browser.

"Can I have all the data for index.php, please?"

5

MySQL

4

Because WordPress stores its content in a MySQL database, PHP will need to access the database in order to complete the page request by the user.

Apache

6 "Alright PHP, time to do your thing..."

Apache knows it is getting is a request for a WordPress file and fires up the PHP engine so it can process the page.

All this happens on your web server...

PHP

Based on the the diagram above, identify three areas you think might be bottlenecks for a website slowdown or even a crash. Why those particular areas?

PHP

Even though PHP is well-integrated into Apache, it still has to start up and shut down the PHP interpreter on each request. This can add up over 1,000s of requests per minute.

Web servers were built to serve static HTML files—plain text documents that simply need to be returned to the browser. However, WordPress is written in PHP which needs to be *processed* and converted into HTML before it can be sent along. This takes time and although it's still relatively fast, it's not nearly as fast as just sending a plain old HTML file.

MySQL Database

The database—in our case, MySQL—is another step in between turning PHP in HTML that can be sent back to the browser. Some of the pages in WordPress need content that's stored in the database. In order to render the page correctly, PHP needs to talk to MySQL so that our post about the etymology of paprika shows in its entirety.

HTTP Communication

Finally, the last slow-down in our request chain is HTTP itself, or the protocol by which all this stuff works together. Depending on how many "assets" (images, media, scripts) need to be returned via an HTTP request, the browser may need to make several requests to several different web servers. This can also slow a site down if not watched carefully.

By default, most browsers will only download two assets per domain, meaning that if you have more than two images on your web page, the browser will need to make multiple requests to the server for content. That right there will start to slow things down....

there are no
Dumb Questions

Q: OK, isn't there just a plug-in for the Google Analytics stuff?

A: Yes, there's a plug-in for this too... although a plug-in can be overkill for a simple service like Google Analytics. If you don't wish to modify your theme, there are plenty of plug-ins that will automatically integrate WordPress with Google Analytics.

For details about these plug-ins, look for Google Analytics at *http://wordpress.org/ extend/plugins*.

Q: Do I really have to worry about all this performance stuff? I just have a nice little site that not so many people visit every day...

A: Well, you certainly don't have to, but an ounce of web performance prevention is worth a pound of sleepless nights dealing with crashed servers. And you never know when your little niche site might become an overnight sensation. Aside from that, dealing with the potential performance trouble spots on your site in advance means it will run faster in general, which will be a nice thing for those select visitors that do come to your site.

WordPress performance checklist

Obviously we'd like to have Thanks for Mutton be fast and efficient, but before we look at making it run even faster, let's start by dealing with the things we need to do to keep our site from crashing when the next big blog post hits the front page of Digg. We'll dig into (ha!) each of the checklist items below in more detail. and have the site humming along in no time.

☐ ## Caching

Most WordPress pages, as we've seen, are served up "dynamically," meaning WordPress assembles them from a variety of sources and uses PHP to create an actual HTML page on demand. When we "cache" a page in WordPress, it stores the rendered HTML as a static (pre-built) file and then serves that up on the next request—this speeds up response times considerably, allowing our web server to handle more requests in a given period of time.

Creating static HTML isn't the only way to cache a page. Web servers and browsers also have built-in caching—but that's another book...

☐ ## Database optimization

Although caching is easy to implement in WordPress, at some point you're going to have to talk to the database. Because of this, we shouldn't neglect MySQL and we should do everything we can to make sure it's running as fast as possible.

We can also bring in some other online services to help us store and serve up all those images and other site assets.

☐ ## Reduce server requests

Another slow point in our request path is the time it takes your web browser to download all the images, scripts, and content to your computer for display. If we can limit the number of times the browser has to make a request, we can speed up our pages.

These services are sometimes called "cloud" hosting. They let you add virtual servers to your site.

☐ ## The web server

Finally, even if we have all the caching, database optimization, and limited requests in place our server could still be slow (and possibly crash).

Speed up WordPress with caching

One of the best ways to make WordPress more snappy and to save your server from being overworked by requests is to set up some form of *caching*. Caching is the process by which web servers and browsers keep a pre-rendered copy of a page handy so that the next time it's requested it can be served immediately to the user—without having to talk to PHP, MySQL, or even the web server in some cases.

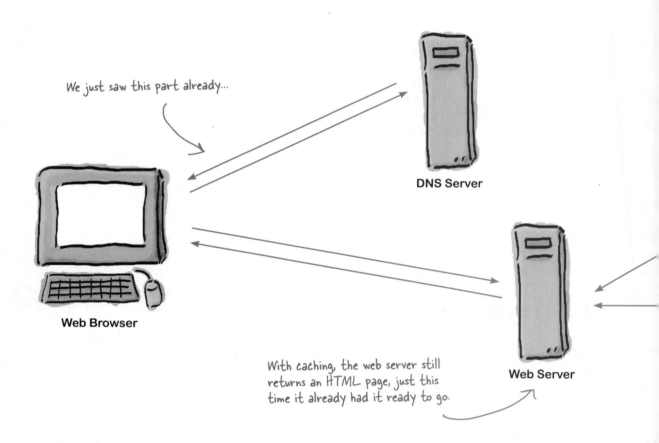

We just saw this part already...

DNS Server

Web Browser

With caching, the web server still returns an HTML page, just this time it already had it ready to go.

Web Server

The important caching stuff all happens on the web server...

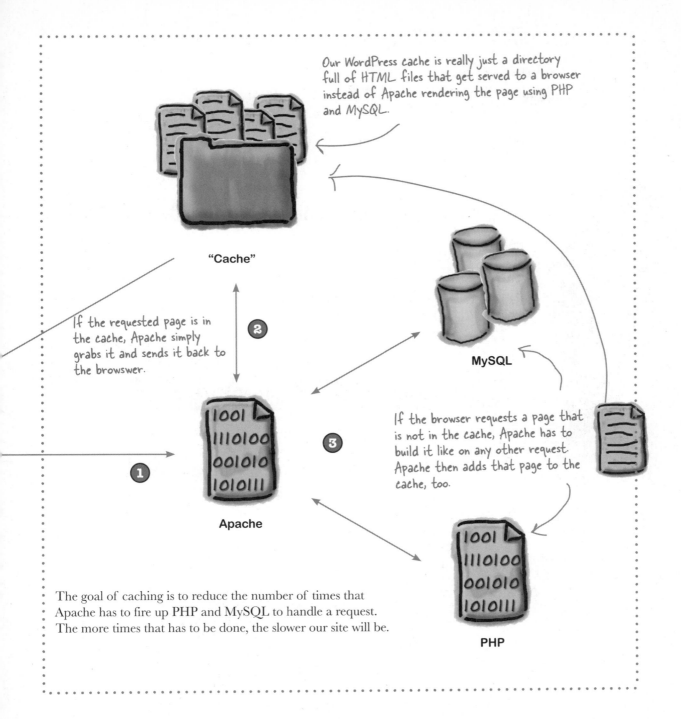

Our WordPress cache is really just a directory full of HTML files that get served to a browser instead of Apache rendering the page using PHP and MySQL.

"Cache"

If the requested page is in the cache, Apache simply grabs it and sends it back to the browswer.

②

MySQL

If the browser requests a page that is not in the cache, Apache has to build it like on any other request. Apache then adds that page to the cache, too.

1001
1110100
001010
1010111

①

③

Apache

The goal of caching is to reduce the number of times that Apache has to fire up PHP and MySQL to handle a request. The more times that has to be done, the slower our site will be.

1001
1110100
001010
1010111

PHP

This is great and all, but why aren't there any caching settings in WordPress? Shouldn't this be on by default?

Start caching with the WP Super Cache plug-in

Unfortunately, the type of caching we need—which is really just storing static HTML files—isn't handled by WordPress out-of-the-box. So, like most other add-on features we find ourselves using a plug-in. In this case, the best option is the WP Super Cache plug-in. It handles creating all the static files, setting up the caching process, and even some extra goodies that will make our site even faster.

WP Super Cache is a bit more complex than some of the other plug-ins we've been using, but the basic installation procedures are still the same.

WP-Super Cache turns your blog into a bunch of HTML files

Don't worry! This is a good thing. HTML files are what web servers were built to serve—and serve fast! WP Super Cache does the work for Apache, saving an HTML version of a page on your blog the first time it's requested by a user. Any requests that come in for that same page later on will be quickly served the HTML file without loading PHP or making a connection to a database—both of which increase page load time.

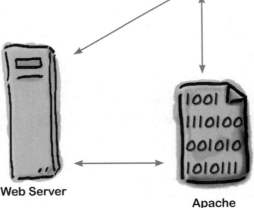

Serving cached files can be 2–3x faster than the standard WordPress setup.

Cache

Web Server

Apache

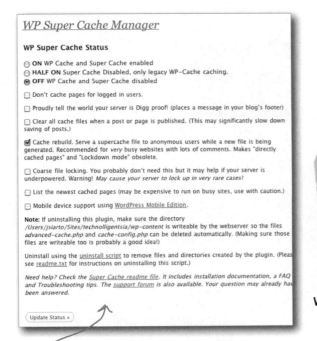

WP Super Cache Manager

WP Super Cache Status

○ **ON** WP Cache and Super Cache enabled
○ **HALF ON** Super Cache Disabled, only legacy WP–Cache caching.
◉ **OFF** WP Cache and Super Cache disabled

☐ Don't cache pages for logged in users.

☐ Proudly tell the world your server is Digg proof! (places a message in your blog's footer)

☐ Clear all cache files when a post or page is published. (This may significantly slow down saving of posts.)

☑ Cache rebuild. Serve a supercache file to anonymous users while a new file is being generated. Recommended for *very* busy websites with lots of comments. Makes "directly cached pages" and "Lockdown mode" obsolete.

☐ Coarse file locking. You probably don't need this but it may help if your server is underpowered. Warning! *May cause your server to lock up in very rare cases!*

☐ List the newest cached pages (may be expensive to run on busy sites, use with caution.)

☐ Mobile device support using WordPress Mobile Edition.

Note: If uninstalling this plugin, make sure the directory */Users/jsiarto/Sites/technolligentsia/wp–content* is writeable by the webserver so the files *advanced–cache.php* and *cache-config.php* can be deleted automatically. (Making sure those files are writeable too is probably a good idea!)

Uninstall using the uninstall script to remove files and directories created by the plugin. (Pleas see readme.txt for instructions on uninstalling this script.)

Need help? Check the Super Cache readme file. It includes installation documentation, a FAQ and Troubleshooting tips. The support forum is also available. Your question may already have been answered.

[Update Status »]

WP Super Cache gives us tons of options for handling cached files and site performance—more on this after we install it.

Exercise

Install WP-Super Cache (*http://wordpress.org/extend/plugins/wp-super-cache/*) just like you have with other plug-ins throughout the book.

Exercise Solution

Install WP Super Cache (*http://wordpress.org/extend/plugins/wp-super-cache/*) just like you have with other plug-ins throughout the book.

① **Install the plug-in.**

WP Super Cache installs just like any other WordPress plug-in—use the Add New plug-in feature in the Dashboard or download and install the files manually.

plug-ins

Remember, if you're not using the Add New plug-in feature, all plug-ins go in the /plugins directory inside /wp-content.

② **Enable and configure.**

Makes sure you enable the plug-in from the dashboard plug-in menu. Don't worry if you see a disabled warning—we'll take care of that in a minute.

Once you activate the plug-in you will see what looks like an error—this is just telling you that WP Super Cache needs to be turned on to start working.. (We know, "activating" should do that so it's a bit weird...)

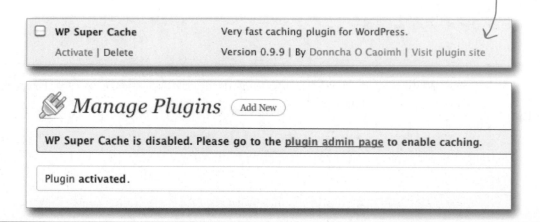

☐ **WP Super Cache**   Very fast caching plugin for WordPress.

Activate | Delete   Version 0.9.9 | By Donncha O Caoimh | Visit plugin site

Manage Plugins (Add New)

WP Super Cache is disabled. Please go to the <u>plugin admin page</u> to enable caching.

Plugin **activated**.

③ **Start the plug-in.**

Turn on WP Super Cache to make sure everything is running properly.
If all is well, you should see a message to update your .htaccess file.

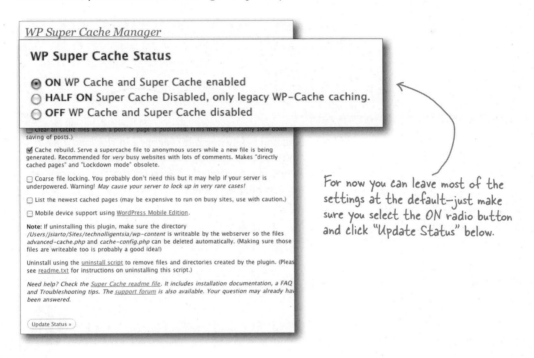

WP Super Cache Manager

WP Super Cache Status

⦿ **ON** WP Cache and Super Cache enabled
◯ **HALF ON** Super Cache Disabled, only legacy WP–Cache caching.
◯ **OFF** WP Cache and Super Cache disabled

☐ Clear all cache files when a post or page is published. (This may significantly slow down saving of posts.)

☑ Cache rebuild. Serve a supercache file to anonymous users while a new file is being generated. Recommended for *very* busy websites with lots of comments. Makes "directly cached pages" and "Lockdown mode" obsolete.

☐ Coarse file locking. You probably don't need this but it may help if your server is underpowered. Warning! *May cause your server to lock up in very rare cases!*

☐ List the newest cached pages (may be expensive to run on busy sites, use with caution.)

☐ Mobile device support using WordPress Mobile Edition.

Note: If uninstalling this plugin, make sure the directory /Users/jsiarto/Sites/technolligentsia/wp-content is writeable by the webserver so the files *advanced-cache.php* and *cache-config.php* can be deleted automatically. (Making sure those files are writeable too is probably a good idea!)

Uninstall using the <u>uninstall script</u> to remove files and directories created by the plugin. (Pleas see <u>readme.txt</u> for instructions on uninstalling this script.)

Need help? Check the <u>Super Cache readme file</u>. It includes installation documentation, a FAQ and Troubleshooting tips. The <u>support forum</u> is also available. Your question may already hav been answered.

(Update Status »)

For now you can leave most of the settings at the default—just make sure you select the ON radio button and click "Update Status" below.

④ **Don't forget about .htaccess rules.**

Click "Update Mod_Rewrite Rules" at the bottom of the long yellow
box to write the appropriate lines to your .htaccess.

This button will write the .htaccess for you—if it fails you can always go in and add the rules yourself. The installation docs will help too: http://wordpress.org/extend/plugins/wp-super-cache/installation/.

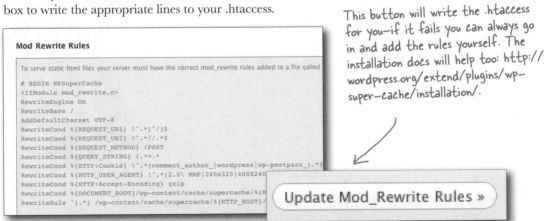

Mod Rewrite Rules

To serve static html files your server must have the correct mod_rewrite rules added to a file called

```
# BEGIN WPSuperCache
<IfModule mod_rewrite.c>
RewriteEngine On
RewriteBase /
AddDefaultCharset UTF-8
RewriteCond %{REQUEST_URI} !^.*[^/]$
RewriteCond %{REQUEST_URI} !^.*//.*$
RewriteCond %{REQUEST_METHOD} !POST
RewriteCond %{QUERY_STRING} !.*=.*
RewriteCond %{HTTP:Cookie} !^.*(comment_author_|wordpress|wp-postpass_).*$
RewriteCond %{HTTP_USER_AGENT} !^.*(2.0\ MMP|240x320|400X240
RewriteCond %{HTTP:Accept-Encoding} gzip
RewriteCond %{DOCUMENT_ROOT}/wp-content/cache/supercache/%{H
RewriteRule ^(.*) /wp-content/cache/supercache/%{HTTP_HOST}/
```

Update Mod_Rewrite Rules »

```
</body>
</html>

<!-- Dynamic page generated in 1.083 seconds. -->
<!-- Cached page generated by WP-Super-Cache on 2010-06-08 13:52:19 -->
```

WP Super Cache gives us a little insight into load times at the bottom of the HTML page (you can see these by viewing the page sources in your browser).

You can really see a difference in the load times, and the site already feels much faster. I wonder if there is also a way to speed up the database when the caching isn't used?

Caching

Caching speeds up pages because the web server has to do less work for each request. When we cache a page in WordPress, it stores the rendered HTML as a file and then serves that file up on the next request—speeding up response time considerably and allowing our web server to handle more requests in a given period of time.

Don't forget about your database

Even though we have caching enabled with WP Super Cache, our database is still going to get used on a daily basis. Not all our content is cached and some data, especially for items in the dashboard and pertaining to comments, is not cached at all. In these cases, we want to make sure that our database is running at optimal performance. And guess what? Another plug-in to the rescue!

WP-Optimize is a WordPress optimization plug-in that will help us keep our MySQL database in good working order. You can download and install this plug-in from: http://wordpress.org/extend/plugins/wp-optimize/

Status	Space Save
Already Optimized	0 Kb
Already Optimized	0 Kb
Already Optimized	0 Kb
Need to Optimize	0.086 Kb
Already Optimized	0 Kb
Already Optimized	0 Kb
Already Optimized	0 Kb
Already Optimized	0 Kb
Already Optimized	0 Kb
Already Optimized	0 Kb
Already Optimized	0 Kb
Status	**Space Save**

The WP-Optimize menu might be hard to find initially. They've stuck it underneath the "Updates" option in the main Dashboard menu.

WP-Optimize checks our MySQL tables to see if it can free up any space. This may not seem like a big change now, but once you get a few 100 posts and 1,000s of comments, these tables can become quite large.

① **Optimization Options**

The top half of the plug-in admin screen gives you options for what will happen when you click the "Process" button. The last checkbox will optimize our database but there are other options as well, including a way to clear out post revisions (WordPress saves a snapshot of your post every time you save or publish).

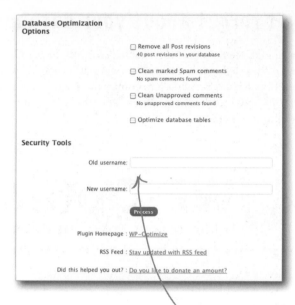

Fight post revision bloat

Every time you create a new post or page, WordPress creates a "revision" file for it. If you tend to go back and edit/revise your posts, or your posts are just generally longer to begin with, those revision files can add up fast, and make your database sloooow.

And since this plug-in works directly with your database, you can also change usernames, something we previously had to do in PHPMyAdmin.

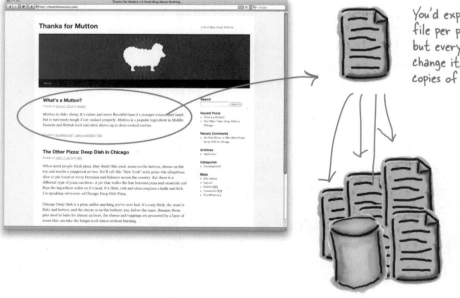

You'd expect there to be only one file per post or page that you create, but every single time you edit or change it, WordPress saves "revision" copies of the file.

WP Optimize removes old revision files, and gives you options to remove spam and un-approved comments from your database too.

Database Report

WP-Optimize tells us if our database tables need to be optimized. Tables needing work will be flagged in red and will also show how much space can be saved by optimization. It's beyond the scope of this book to go into how it does this, but if we run the "*Optimize database tables*" option, we should see an entire table full of "Already Optimized" statuses. Everything may look good now, but after you start to get a lot of posts and comments, these tables can become large and optimization will result in more space being saved. So be sure to return to this option after your site has been running for a few months.

Table	Size	Status	Space Save
wp_commentmeta	4 Kb	Already Optimized	0 Kb
wp_comments	7.242 Kb	Already Optimized	0 Kb
wp_links	3.543 Kb	Already Optimized	0 Kb
wp_options	338.059 Kb	Need to Optimize	0.086 Kb
wp_postmeta	13.738 Kb	Already Optimized	0 Kb
wp_posts	41.664 Kb	Already Optimized	0 Kb
wp_term_relationships	3.369 Kb	Already Optimized	
wp_term_taxonomy	4.27 Kb	Already Optimized	
wp_terms	11.195 Kb	Already Optimized	
wp_usermeta	11.949 Kb	Already Optimized	

Hmm. So how do we really know this stuff is working?

✓ Database optimization

Although caching is easy to implement in WordPress, at some point you're going to have to talk to the database. Because of this, we shouldn't neglect MySQL and we should do everything we can do make sure it's running as fast as possible.

Check performance issues with YSlow

Now that we have WP Super Cache saving the HTML files of our site pages to serve them quicker, we can check out what other aspects of our site might be slowing it down. There are plenty of tools out there to check the performance of web pages in a browser, one of the best being YSlow. YSlow is a Yahoo tool that can check everything from load times to HTTP requests and report back where the slow areas on your site are.

YSlow runs as a plug-in for Firefox—it's like your WordPress plug-ins, just for a browser instead! Once installed, it gives you detailed site information to help understand which pages on your site are working well, and which aren't so hot...

YSlow also produces a report card of sorts outlining the areas of site performance that need improvement.

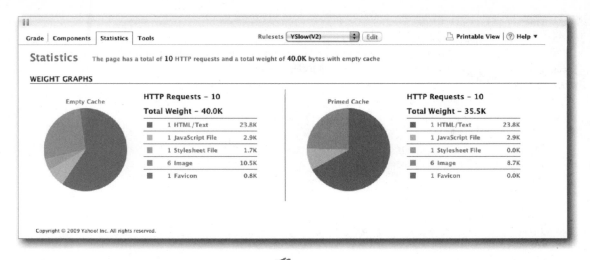

In addition to the site report card, YSlow gives you detailed graphs on how long HTTP requests take for your cached and non-cached pages.

YSlow also requires the Firebug extension for Firefox.

You'll have to use Firefox in order to run YSlow, and before you do that, you'll need to install the Firebug extension as well.

Install Firebug and YSlow in Firefox and check *http://thanksformutton.com* to see how it does on the YSlow test. **Firebug** can be installed at *http://getfirebug.com/* and then **YSlow** can be installed at *https://addons.mozilla.org/en-US/firefox/addon/5369/*.

Install Firebug and YSlow in Firefox and check *http://thanksformutton.com* to see how it does on the YSlow test. **Firebug** can be installed at *http://getfirebug.com/* and **YSlow** can be installed at *https://addons.mozilla.org/en-US/firefox/addon/5369/*.

① **Install Firebug**

YSlow is a plug-in for the Firebug Firefox plug-in. You need to install Firebug before YSlow will work with the browser.

When you navigate to the Firebug site in Firefox you can initiate the install from within the browser window. Once it's installed it may need to restart your browser to become active.

② **Install YSlow**

YSlow installs just like Firebug—once it's set up you can start profiling site performance.

You should see a YSlow and Firebug icon in the status bar of Firefox.

So much for being class valedictorian...

If you run YSlow on http://thanksformutton.com you'll notice that we haven't scored well on a few of the tests—mom and dad are not going to be happy about this!

Content Delivery Networks give your web server a break

A content delivery network (or CDN) is a global network of servers that serve static files, (images, stylesheets, scripts, video, etc.) on the Web. They remove the responsibility of serving static files from your cache on the web server. A big hindrance to your site's speed is the number of requests the browser has to make for *assets* (images, zip files, etc) on a page. If there's more than two per page, your browser is going to have to go back to the web server for each additional asset, and that slows everything down.

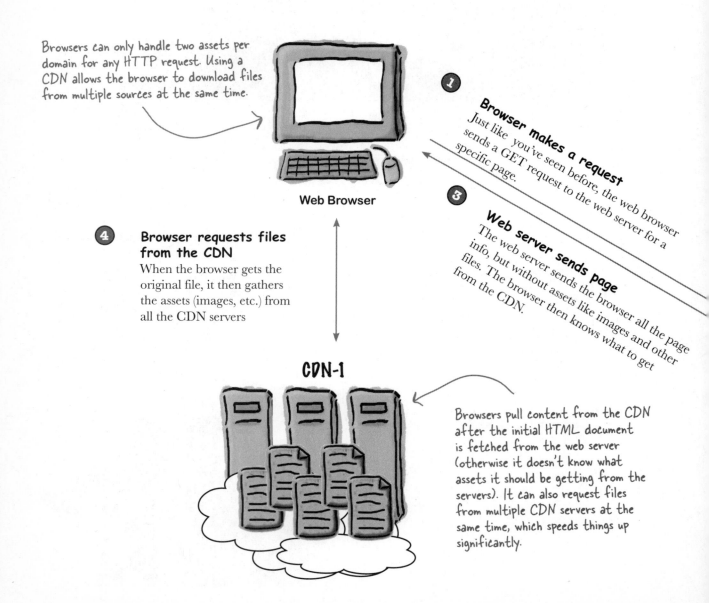

Browsers can only handle two assets per domain for any HTTP request. Using a CDN allows the browser to download files from multiple sources at the same time.

Web Browser

①

Browser makes a request
Just like you've seen before, the web browser sends a GET request to the web server for a specific page.

③

Web server sends page
The web server sends the browser all the page info, but without assets like images and other files. The browser then knows what to get from the CDN.

④ **Browser requests files from the CDN**
When the browser gets the original file, it then gathers the assets (images, etc.) from all the CDN servers

CDN-1

Browsers pull content from the CDN after the initial HTML document is fetched from the web server (otherwise it doesn't know what assets it should be getting from the servers). It can also request files from multiple CDN servers at the same time, which speeds things up significantly.

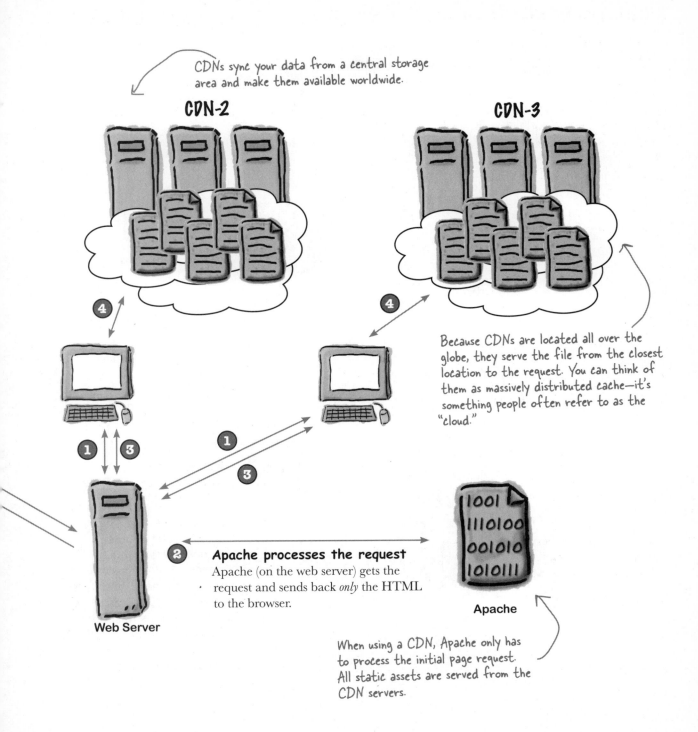

CDNs sync your data from a central storage area and make them available worldwide.

CDN-2

CDN-3

④

④

Because CDNs are located all over the globe, they serve the file from the closest location to the request. You can think of them as massively distributed cache—it's something people often refer to as the "cloud."

① ③

① ③

Apache processes the request
② Apache (on the web server) gets the request and sends back *only* the HTML to the browser.

1001
1110100
001010
1010111

Apache

Web Server

When using a CDN, Apache only has to process the initial page request. All static assets are served from the CDN servers.

Float around in the Amazon cloud

Amazon Web Services (AWS) is a suite of hosting services designed for people who build websites and web applications on the Internet. The services include S3, a web-based storage solution that we learned about in the previous chapter, EC2, a cloud computing "platform," and CloudFront, a content delivery network built on top of the 3S service. Such hosting platforms have become known as "cloud" services, because they often comprise tens of thousands of individual computers, connected together to share resources. Oftentimes your data is duplicated across hundreds of machines—or in our case "floating" in the cloud.

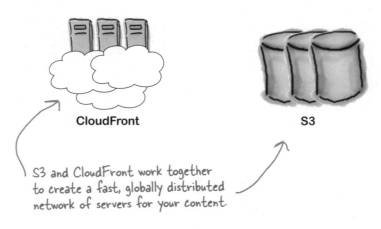

CloudFront

S3

S3 and CloudFront work together to create a fast, globally distributed network of servers for your content.

We're not using it here, but think of EC2 as a way to rent time on a giant super computer. You can run math problems, solve the energy crisis, or just build a web server.

EC2

Watch it!

Amazon's web services aren't free

Although creating an AWS account is free, using services like S3 and CloudFront are not. Make sure you check out the pricing before you start using the service. Also, because this is a hosting-related service, check out your current web host's services to see if they offer a CDN as well—many do. Finally, if your looking for a free solution, try Coral CDN. Coral is a free CDN that is simple to use.

Amazon CloudFront CDN

Amazon's CloudFront works just like any other CDN except all your files are pulled from their S3 service (remember, that's where we're storing our backups). You simply upload your wp-content folder to your S3 storage and then setup a CDN distribution with CloudFront. Within minutes your static files are around the world and ready for browser requests.

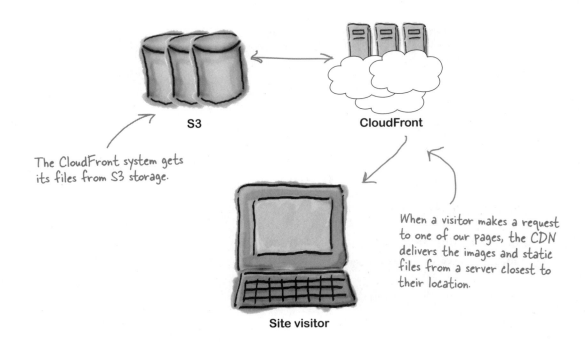

S3

CloudFront

The CloudFront system gets its files from S3 storage.

Site visitor

When a visitor makes a request to one of our pages, the CDN delivers the images and static files from a server closest to their location.

Geek Bits

Using a content delivery network may seem like a lot of work for a small performance gain–but having a fast site can make it easier for people to find you. Search engines like Google take load times into consideration when deciding where to rank your page. The closer you can get to the first page of results in a search the more people will find your site. And then you will be happy you made all these great performance enhancements! It'a a very non-vicious cycle...

Link Amazon S3 and CloudFront to complete the CDN

1 **Sign up for AWS and activate S3 and CloudFront.**
If you don't already have one, sign up for an AWS account at *http://aws. amazon.com*. You'll also need to activate the S3 and CloudFront service once your account is set up and ready.

2 **Make sure you create at least one access key.**
Access keys and secret keys are your username and password for the S3 storage system. We'll use these to get our files uploaded to Amazon.

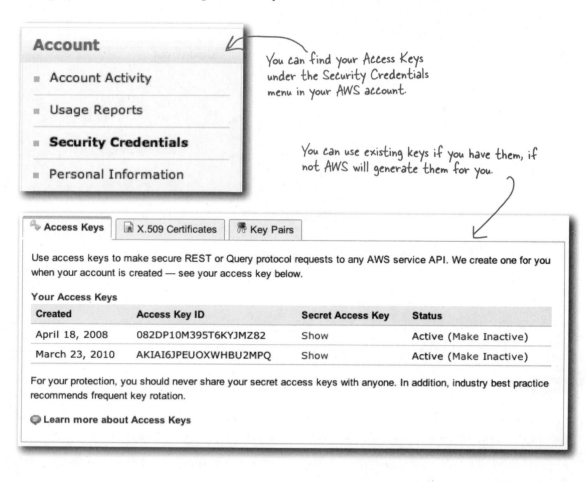

You can find your Access Keys under the Security Credentials menu in your AWS account.

You can use existing keys if you have them, if not AWS will generate them for you.

3 **Connect to S3.**

Use an FTP client that supports S3 to connect to the service. Once you've authenticated you can move files to and from your S3 storage just like you do with the web server.

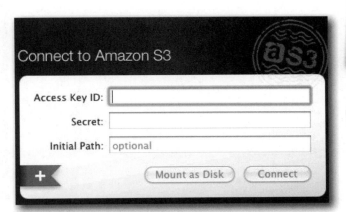

If you don't have an FTP client that supports S3, you can use the Firefox S3 organizer (https://addons.mozilla.org/en-US/firefox/addon/3247/).

4 **Add a bucket for the Thanks for Mutton CDN.**

Just as we did for our S3 backup last chapter, we need a separate bucket for our CloudFront CDN.

Distribute your site's files

1 **Open your AWS console.**

The AWS console is where you can control all of your services through Amazon. Once you create a distribution, you can manage and monitor it through this screen.

2 **Create a new distribution.**

Click "Create Distribution" and select your CDN bucket as the origin. Leave the other options in the default state. Think of a distribution as a little web server in the cloud that serves up all your images and scripts stored on S3.

3 **Finish the distribution.**

You should see the status of your distribution once its created. Here you can enable and disable it and modify settings. Make note of the domain name as we'll need that for our WordPress plug-in momentarily (oh yes, another plug-in!).

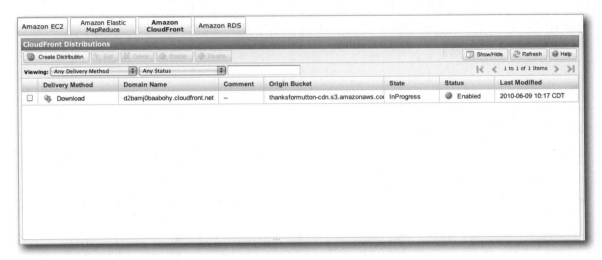

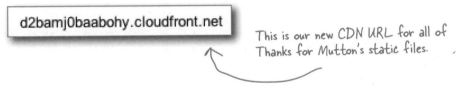

d2bamj0baabohy.cloudfront.net

This is our new CDN URL for all of Thanks for Mutton's static files.

4 **Upload wp-content to S3.**

Using an FTP client that supports S3 or the Firefox organizer plug-in, upload your whole wp-content directory to Amazon.

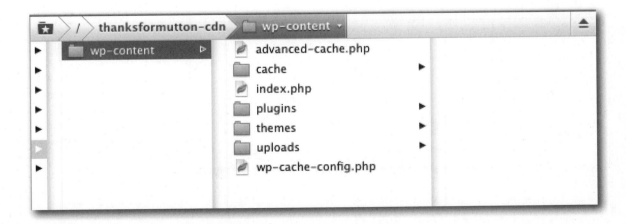

Using the CDN in WordPress

To use the CloudFront CDN with WordPress, we need to use our special CDN URL to retrieve the files. Depending on how customized your theme is, you may want to add this manually. If you're using a default theme or a theme from the gallery, you can use a CDN plug-in like My CDN to change those links automatically (don't worry, because we're using caching, adding this plug-in won't harm the performance of our site).

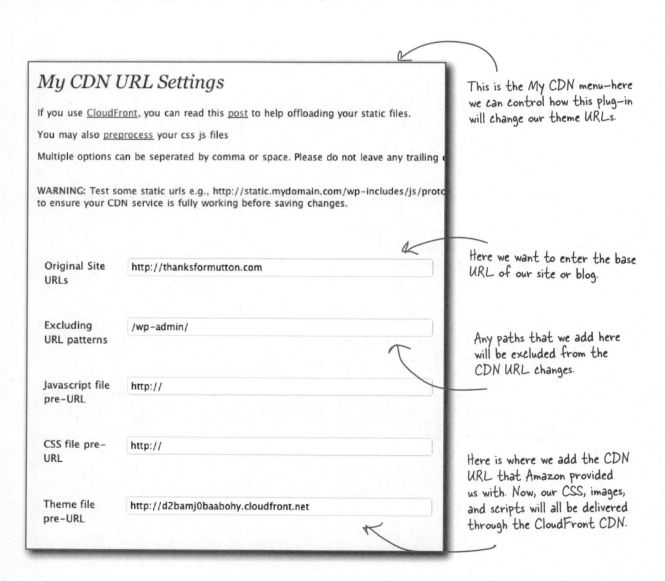

My CDN URL Settings

If you use CloudFront, you can read this post to help offloading your static files.

You may also preprocess your css js files

Multiple options can be seperated by comma or space. Please do not leave any trailing

WARNING: Test some static urls e.g., http://static.mydomain.com/wp-includes/js/proto
to ensure your CDN service is fully working before saving changes.

Original Site URLs
http://thanksformutton.com

Excluding URL patterns
/wp-admin/

Javascript file pre-URL
http://

CSS file pre-URL
http://

Theme file pre-URL
http://d2bamj0baabohy.cloudfront.net

This is the My CDN menu—here we can control how this plug-in will change our theme URLs.

Here we want to enter the base URL of our site or blog.

Any paths that we add here will be excluded from the CDN URL changes.

Here is where we add the CDN URL that Amazon provided us with. Now, our CSS, images, and scripts will all be delivered through the CloudFront CDN.

```
<link rel="stylesheet" type="text/css" media="all" href="http://
d2bamj0baabohy.cloudfront.net/wp-content/themes/twentyten/style.css" />
```

If you view the source of Thanks for Mutton, you should see the new CDN path in link elements in the head of the HTML.

 ### Reduce server requests

Another slow point in our request path is the time it takes your web browser to download all the image, scripts, and content to your computer for display. If we can limit the number of times the browser has to make a request, we can speed up our pages.

 ### The web server(s)

Finally, even if we have all the caching, database optimization, and limited requests in place, our server could still be slow (and possibly crash). Depending on your hosting, your physical server just may not be powerful enough to handle your site traffic and no amount of tweaking will change that.

Usng a CDN helps take some of the load off your servers, but there's even more robust cloud hosting options available. Check out the Appendix for more info on that.

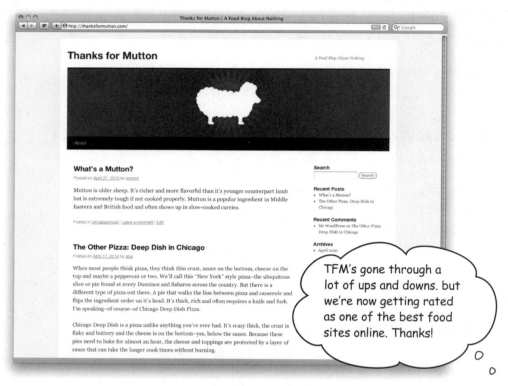

Thanks for Mutton

A Food Blog About Nothing

About

What's a Mutton?

Posted on April 27, 2010 by gwjont

Mutton is older sheep. It's richer and more flavorful than it's younger counterpart lamb but is extremely tough if not cooked properly. Mutton is a popular ingredient in Middle Eastern and British food and often shows up in slow-cooked curries.

Posted in Uncategorized | Leave a comment | Edit

The Other Pizza: Deep Dish in Chicago

Posted on April 27, 2010 by aba

When most people think pizza, they think thin crust, sauce on the bottom, cheese on the top and maybe a pepperoni or two. We'll call this "New York" style pizza–the ubiquitous slice or pie found at every Dominos and Sabaros across the country. But there is a different type of pizza out there. A pie that walks the line between pizza and casserole and flips the ingredient order on it's head. It's thick, rich and often requires a knife and fork. I'm speaking–of course–of Chicago Deep Dish Pizza.

Chicago Deep Dish is a pizza unlike anything you've ever had. It's crazy thick, the crust is flaky and buttery and the cheese is on the bottom–yes, below the sauce. Because these pies need to bake for almost an hour, the cheese and toppings are protected by a layer of sauce that can take the longer cook times without burning.

Search

[   ] (Search)

Recent Posts

- What's a Mutton?
- The Other Pizza: Deep Dish in Chicago

Recent Comments

- Mr WordPress on The Other Pizza: Deep Dish in Chicago

Archives

- April 2010

TFM's gone through a lot of ups and downs. but we're now getting rated as one of the best food sites online. Thanks!

Your Theme Toolbox

You've got Chapter 8 under your belt and now you've added a high-performance, super fast WordPress site to your tool box.

- Because WordPress is powered by PHP and MySQL, the web server sometimes has to do a lot of work to keep up with the requests. This can often slow down your site.

- Having a slow site can hurt your rankings on search engines and can be a bad user experience for your visitors.

- Caching is one way you can take some of the workload off your web server. Cached files don't require the web server to talk to PHP and MySQL to deliver a page. Instead, they are served like any other HTML file.

- Use a plug-in like WP Super Cache to automatically control the caching of pages within WordPress.

- YSlow and Firebug can help you determine what areas of optimization you should focus on. Every site has different needs.

- Use a content delivery network (CDN) to serve your static files to visitors. This will cut down on the amount of requests your web server has to make and speed up the load time of the site.

Wouldn't it be dreamy if this were the end of the book? If there were no bullet points or exercises or PHP files? But that's probably just a fantasy...

Congratulations!
You made it to the end.

Of course, there's still an appendix.

And the index.

And then there's the website...

There's no escape, really.

appendix: leftovers

The Top Ten Things (we didn't cover)

We've really covered a lot of ground in this book.

The thing is, there are some important topics and tidbits that didn't quite fit into any of the previous chapters. We feel pretty strongly about this, and think that if we didn't at least cover them in passing, we'd be doing you a disservice. That's where this chapter comes into the picture. Well, it's not really a chapter, it's more like an appendix (OK, it *is* an appendix). But it's an awesome appendix of the top ten best bits that we couldn't let you go without.

① **Managing comments**

Comments are an essential part of any online community or blog and WordPress makes it easy manage reader comments and deal with spam (unwanted comments often come from "bots" as well). Depending on your settings, comments are either automatically posted to your blog (unless they are spam) or held for *moderation*, which requires the site administrator to approve the comment before it gets posted on the live site.

Comments can be managed from within the comments menu or quickly handled from the main dashboard page.

From the dashboard page you can see the current status of discussions on your site. This panel will let you know if there are any comments awaiting moderation and if anything has been flagged as spam.

From the comment menu you can read and moderate comments and control if they show up on the live site. Any comments marked as spam will help Akismet (a plug-in installed by default to handle comment spam) learn to better handle your spam comments.

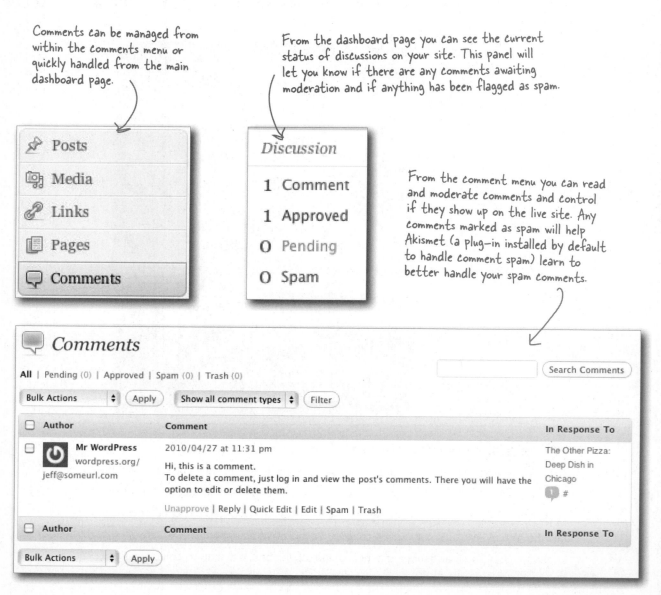

② Migrating from WordPress.com

One powerful feature of WordPress is its ability to import and migrate content (and much more) from other blogging platorms—including WordPress.com. WordPress.com is a "hosted" version of WordPress, similar to Blogger, that allows users to sign up and create a free blog online. You have a similar interface to the downloaded version of WordPress and your own URL, but it's on the WordPress domain, like *yourblog.wordpress.com*. If you want to do custom themes, create your own plug-ins, and start working more with PHP, you're going to outgrow the hosted service eventually. And once you do, you can export all your content and import it into your own WordPress installation, preserving posts, pages, settings and comments.

From the tools menu on Wordpress.com, you can export all your content as a "WXR" file that can be read by other WordPress installations.

Exporting is also a great way to backup your content for a quick and easy restore.

WordPress   Install the WordPress importer to import posts tags from a WordPress export file.

Depending on whether you are importing from WordPress.com or not, you may need to install a plug-in to properly import your file.

Howdy! Upload your WordPress eXtended RSS (WXR) file and we'll import the posts, pages, comments, custom fields, categories, and tags into this site.

Choose a WordPress WXR file to upload, then click Upload file and import.

Choose a file from your computer: (Maximum size: 2MB)

(Choose File) no file selected

Once the importer plug-in is set, you can upload your WXR file to the new WordPress installation.

(Upload file and import)

❸ Theme Library

We briefly mentioned the theme library erlier in the book, and it functions just like the plug-in library within WordPress. The concept is simple: designers build themes that work withim the WordPress system and make them available for free in the library. You can browse and download themes from the website or browse and install themes from the WordPress dashboard just like plug-ins. All the themes available in the library are free to use and are a great way to quickly change the look and feel of your site. In addition to the free themes, there are also high-quality commercial themes (at a cost) that are available outside the theme library.

Themes can be install directly from the WordPress dashboard. You can even preview the new style before you make it live.

Browsing for themes can be done through the WordPress dashboard or online at http://wordpress.org/extend/themes/.

Install "Motion"

Motion

by Sam07

Version: 1.0.7

Cancel

Install Now

Manage Themes | **Install Theme**

Search | Upload | **Featured** | Newest | Recently Updated

Mystique

Install | Preview

Feature-packed theme with a solid design, built-in widgets and a intuitive theme settings interface... Designed by digitalnature.

Details

Constructor

Install | Preview

Wordpress Constructor Theme, it's many-in-one theme (six layouts, configured colors, fonts and slideshow, widget ready). Build your own theme on settings page. For Wordpress version 2.9+ (include 3.0)

Details

ChocoTheme

Install | Preview

Stylish WordPress theme with two columns, right-sidebar. 3 color schemes availible. Theme options panel for background and navigation configuration.

Details

❹ Theme Editor

WordPress gives you the option to edit your theme files and templates from within the dashboard. Here you can modify your own themes or make changes to an existing theme you've downloaded. It's a good idea to make a backup of the original theme before you start making changes just in case things don't go as planned. The easiset way to do this is to dupliate and rename the theme in your wp-content/themes/directory.

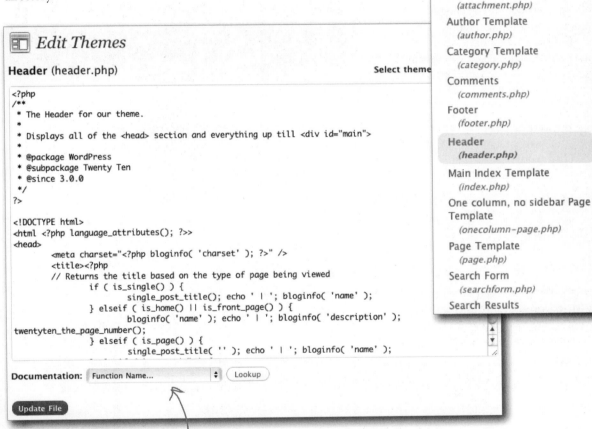

Templates

404 Template
(404.php)

Archives
(archive.php)

Attachment Template
(attachment.php)

Author Template
(author.php)

Category Template
(category.php)

Comments
(comments.php)

Footer
(footer.php)

Header
(header.php)

Main Index Template
(index.php)

One column, no sidebar Page
Template
(onecolumn–page.php)

Page Template
(page.php)

Search Form
(searchform.php)

Search Results

Edit Themes

Header (header.php)   Select theme

```php
<?php
/**
 * The Header for our theme.
 *
 * Displays all of the <head> section and everything up till <div id="main">
 *
 * @package WordPress
 * @subpackage Twenty Ten
 * @since 3.0.0
 */
?>

<!DOCTYPE html>
<html <?php language_attributes(); ?>>
<head>
        <meta charset="<?php bloginfo( 'charset' ); ?>" />
        <title><?php
        // Returns the title based on the type of page being viewed
                if ( is_single() ) {
                        single_post_title(); echo ' | '; bloginfo( 'name' );
                } elseif ( is_home() || is_front_page() ) {
                        bloginfo( 'name' ); echo ' | '; bloginfo( 'description' );
twentyten_the_page_number();
                } elseif ( is_page() ) {
                        single_post_title( '' ); echo ' | '; bloginfo( 'name' );
```

Documentation: [Function Name... ▲▼] (Lookup)

(Update File)

The theme editor shows your files just like a text editor would on your local computer. You can change the text, look up documentation, and save the file to disk.

Be careful! This feature modifies files directly on your web server, so the changes you make here are permanent and affect the live site.

⑤ WordPress MU (multi-user)

With the release of WordPress 3, the WordPress MU project is now incorporated directly into WordPress (it used to be a separate installation). This multi-site feature in WordPress 3 allows you to create a network of blogs under a common domain. For example, we could create the Thanks for Mutton nextwork where all of our users could have blogs under the thanksformutton.com domain (*bob.*thanksformutton.com, *jeff.*thanksformutton.com). What you're doing is basically creating a mini version of the hosted Wordpress.com service for your own authors.

Each user has their own "install" of WordPress allowing them to customize their blog and make it their own.

To enable the multi-site/multi-user features in WordPress you need to add the WP_ALLOW_MULTISITE directive to your wp-config.php file.

```
define('WP_DEBUG', false);
define('WP_ALLOW_MULTISITE', true);


/* That's all, stop editing! Happy blogging. */
```

Once the configuration directive is in place, you'll see a network option under the Tools menu, which will help you set up and manage the multi-site WordPress mode.

🍾 Create a Network of WordPress Sites

Welcome to the Network installation process!

Fill in the information below and you'll be on your way to creating a network of WordPress sites. We will create configuration files in the next step.

Network Details

Sub-domain Install	Because your install is not new, the sites in your WordPress network must use sub-domains. **The main site in a sub-directory install will need to use a modified permalink structure, potentially breaking existing links.**
Server Address	The internet address of your network will be `thanksformutton.com` .
Network Title	TFM Network What would you like to call your network?
Admin E-mail Address	admin@thanksformutton.com Your email address.

`Install`

See http://codex.wordpress.org/Version_3.0/ for more information on multi-site mode in WordPress 3.

⑥ BuddyPress social networking plug-in

BuddyPress is a large plug-in that transforms WordPress into an out-of-the-box social networking site. The addition of BuddyPress gives your visitors features like a public profile, friend news feed, messaging, microblogging, and groups. In addition, all the blogging features of WordPress work as well. This is a great plug-in if you're looking to implement your own personal social network for a group of friends, a book club, or even an office intranet. For more information, check out BuddyPress on the Web at *http://buddypress.org/*.

Even the BuddyPress site is run on WordPress—go figure!

See a list members on your network and click through to view their personal blogs or public profile pages.

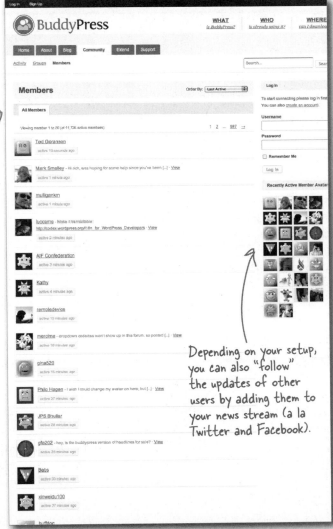

Depending on your setup, you can also "follow" the updates of other users by adding them to your news stream (a la Twitter and Facebook).

⑦ PHP

As you learned earlier, PHP (or PHP Hypertext Preprocessor), is an open source scripting language used in web development to create dynamic web pages. WordPress is built primarily with PHP and so are the plug-ins and themes that work along side it. You'll be able to extend the functionality of your site significantly if you start working with PHP. If, for example, you want to have different sidebars show up depending on which page someone is viewing, or (as we did in Chapter 3) make your main home page appear different from the rest of the site, you'll need to get more familiar with PHP.

homepage.php template file

Here's the code we used in Chapter 3. When you use PHP within an HTML file, all PHP code falls within the <?php ?> tags and the file needs to have a .php extension so the web server knows to process the code.

```php
<?php
/* Template Name: Homepage */
?>
<?php get_header(); ?>
<div id="content" class="wrap">
    <ul id="products">
        <li><p class="bit-16">16</p></li>
        <li class="center"><p class="bit-32">32</p></li>
        <li><p class="bit-64">64</p></li>
    </ul>
    <ul id="descriptions">
        <li><p><strong>16 Bits</strong> Lorem ipsum dolor sit amet,
consectetur adipisicing elit, sed do eiusmod tempor incididunt ut labore et
dolore magna aliqua. Ut enim ad minim veniam, quis nostrud exercitation ullamco
laboris.</p></li>
    </ul>
</div>
<?php get_footer(); ?>
```

This get_header() part is a function, meaning it calls code that is located elsewhere in the file or even in a completely different file. It's how you reuse code in PHP.

The get_footer() function actually inserts the content of the footer.php file into the index page.

Relax

Head First PHP & MySQL is a great way to get started with PHP.

From there, you can also check out the PHP home page at *http://php.net/index.php* and the W3C Schools tutorials: *http://www.w3schools.com/php/default.asp*.

⑧ Cloud Hosting

Cloud hosting is a term used to describe a type of virtual server technology that allows a website to use a pool of resources (hard disk space, processors, and memory) to help run their site, and also expand that pool of resources when the need arises. Before the advent of cloud hosting, scaling a website involved adding new physical hardware to a system to handle the load. Today, that can be done simple by allocating more resources to a particular cloud server without adding hardware. Another feature of these services is that they can be purchased by the hour, giving you the freedom to test and build without committing to months of service and long contracts.

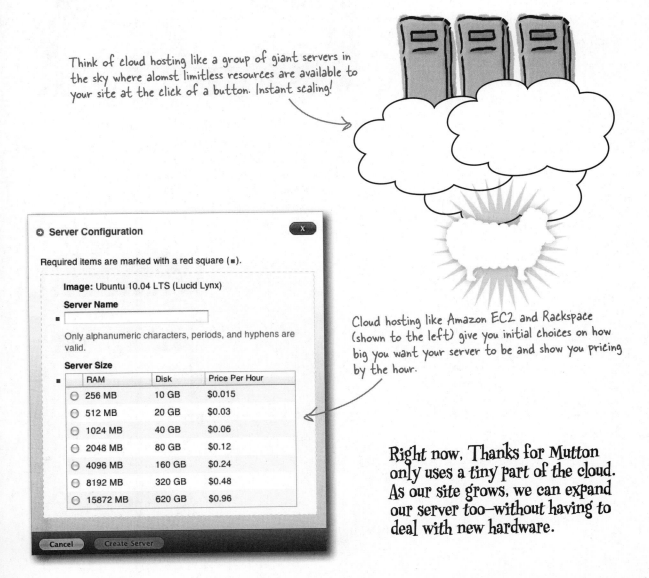

Think of cloud hosting like a group of giant servers in the sky where alomst limitless resources are available to your site at the click of a button. Instant scaling!

Cloud hosting like Amazon EC2 and Rackspace (shown to the left) give you initial choices on how big you want your server to be and show you pricing by the hour.

Server Configuration

Required items are marked with a red square (■).

Image: Ubuntu 10.04 LTS (Lucid Lynx)

Server Name

Only alphanumeric characters, periods, and hyphens are valid.

Server Size

RAM	Disk	Price Per Hour
256 MB	10 GB	$0.015
512 MB	20 GB	$0.03
1024 MB	40 GB	$0.06
2048 MB	80 GB	$0.12
4096 MB	160 GB	$0.24
8192 MB	320 GB	$0.48
15872 MB	620 GB	$0.96

Cancel   Create Server

Right now, Thanks for Mutton only uses a tiny part of the cloud. As our site grows, we can expand our server too—without having to deal with new hardware.

⑨ Mobile WordPress

With the advent of smartphones like the iPhone and Android handsets, mobile browsing and interaction with websites have become an important part of everyday life on the Internet. WordPress has many different options for integrating with mobile devices from a dedicated iPhone application that allows you to manage your blog from your phone, to plug-ins that optimize your site for viewing on the small screen of a mobile device. With the mobile space getting larger by the day, making your content accessible to smartphones isn't somthing to be overlooked any longer.

The WordPress iOS client allows you to manage your blog, write posts and moderate comments all from your iPhone.

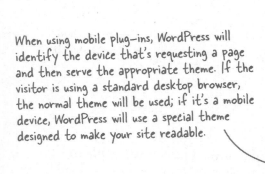

Some websites (WordPress themes included) don't display well on mobile devices because of the limited browser capabilities and the small screen. Special themes and plug-ins can help serve pages that look right on small screens.

When using mobile plug-ins, WordPress will identify the device that's requesting a page and then serve the appropriate theme. If the visitor is using a standard desktop browser, the normal theme will be used; if it's a mobile device, WordPress will use a special theme designed to make your site readable.

⑩ Search engine optimization (SEO)

Most of the time, visitors don't get to your site by typing a URL in to their browser windows. Instead, the visit a search engine like Google or Yahoo and search for a topic or phrase related to what they are looking for. Sometimes, they will even just type your name or the name of your blog in to a search engine in the hope that it comes up on the first page of results. And of course, you'd like to be there. Search engine optimization, also known as SEO, makes sure you are doing all you can to get your site and pages showing up in relevant search results. SEO has recieved a bit of a bad rap recently because of the proliferation of companies and people claiming to be "SEO experts" or guaranteeing "first page results" for specific keywords. These firms often use tricks to try and game the system and spam services to try and get your content on as many sites as possible. True, effective SEO starts with great content, and a well-designed, fast-running site.

Quick and dirty SEO checklist

☐ Use the pretty permalink feature in WordPress so that your URLs carry more meaning with the inclusion of post and category titles.

☐ Write good content. This is one of the most important things you can do. Write things that people want to read and that are relavent to the topic of your site–this includes page and posts titles.

☐ Use a well-designed theme that uses proper "semantic" markup like <strong>, <em> and heading levels that are relevant to content (e.g., only one <h1> per page). See *Head First HTML with CSS & XHTML* for more on this.

☐ Makes sure your page loads quickly. Use Google Webmaster Tools (and YSlow) to monitor the speed and performance of your site to make sure slow load times aren't hurting your search performance.

 Relax

Of course, there is a plug-in that can help you with some basic SEO.

Search the WordPress plug-in directory for "SEO." You should find a few options to help you with basics like page titles, meta tags, and avoiding content duplication.

Index

Numbers

1-Click Install 8, 9

777 permissions 35

A

About page 94

Acme Bit and Pixel 6–42, 44–88, 90–130
    changing background color and font for site 64
    home page 6, 45
        design elements 46–50
    identifying elements in blog theme 66–69
    Ready Bake Code
        making blog look like website 71–73
    Test Drive
        footer 74
        widgets 82

administrators
    multiple 143
    permissions 137–138
    reviewing pending posts from admin dashboard 142
    security 248

Akismet 178, 180

all access permissions 35

Amazon CloudFront 300–303
    linking S3 and 302–305
    using CDN in WordPress 306–307

Amazon EC2 300, 319

Amazon S3 268–269, 300–310
    linking CloudFront and 302–305

Amazon Web Services (AWS) 300

Apache
    caching 285
    CDNs 299
    manual pages 258

archives 2
    monthly 2

attacks 242–243

authentication
    new authentication realm 256–257

authors 2
    permissions 137–138
    profile page 2
    role 141

automatic updates 245

Automatic WordPress Backup plug-in 267

Automattic 156

avatars
    email address 156–157
    (see also Gravatar)

B

backups 265–272
    Amazon S3 268–269
    Bullet Points 271
    importing backed-up database using PHPMyAdmin 270
    remote, automated backups 267
    storing on web server 268

blogging videos (see videos)

blogs
    Acme Bit website
        changing background color and font for site 64
    author 2
    changing font across entire blog 63
    default WordPress blog design 44
    design (see design)
    home page options 123–124
    identifying elements in blog theme 66–69
    managing blog and content
        WordPress Dashboard 20
    monthly archives 2

X

Y

Z

Learning for the Way Your Brain Works

Learning isn't something that just happens to you. It's something you do. But all too often, it seems like your brain isn't cooperating. Your time is too valuable to spend struggling with new concepts. Head First books combine strong visuals, puzzles, humor, and the latest research in cognitive science to engage your entire mind in the learning process.

Also available:

Head First Design Patterns

Head Rush PMP

Head First PHP & MySql

Head First Javascript

Can't get enough Head First? Visit **www.headfirstlabs.com**, your resource and community for all things Head First. Learn about our current and upcoming books, get help from the experts on the Forums, get to know the people behind Head First, and find out what it takes to write a Head First book yourself!

Get even more for your money.

Join the O'Reilly Community, and register the O'Reilly books you own.It's free, and you'll get:

- 40% upgrade offer on O'Reilly books
- Membership discounts on books and events
- Free lifetime updates to electronic formats of books
- Multiple ebook formats, DRM FREE
- Participation in the O'Reilly community
- Newsletters
- Account management
- 100% Satisfaction Guarantee

Signing up is easy:

1. **Go to: oreilly.com/go/register**
2. **Create an O'Reilly login.**
3. **Provide your address.**
4. **Register your books.**

Note: English-language books only

To order books online:

oreilly.com/order_new

For questions about products or an order:

orders@oreilly.com

To sign up to get topic-specific email announcements and/or news about upcoming books, conferences, special offers, and new technologies:

elists@oreilly.com

For technical questions about book content:

booktech@oreilly.com

To submit new book proposals to our editors:

proposals@oreilly.com

Many O'Reilly books are available in PDF and several ebook formats. For more information:

oreilly.com/ebooks

O'REILLY®

Spreading the knowledge of innovators   www.oreilly.com

Buy this book and get access to the online edition for 45 days—for free!

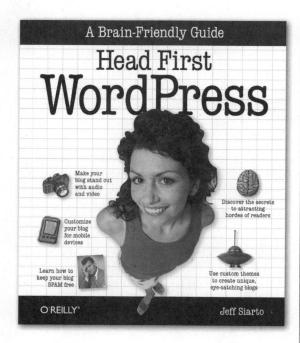

Head First WordPress

By Jeff Siarto
July 2010, $34.99
ISBN 9780596806286

With Safari Books Online, you can:

Access the contents of thousands of technology and business books

- Quickly search over 7000 books and certification guides
- Download whole books or chapters in PDF format, at no extra cost, to print or read on the go
- Copy and paste code
- Save up to 35% on O'Reilly print books
- **New!** Access mobile-friendly books directly from cell phones and mobile devices

Stay up-to-date on emerging topics before the books are published

- Get on-demand access to evolving manuscripts.
- Interact directly with authors of upcoming books

Explore thousands of hours of video on technology and design topics

- Learn from expert video tutorials
- Watch and replay recorded conference sessions

To try out Safari and the online edition of this book FREE for 45 days, go to **www.oreilly.com/go/safarienabled** and enter the coupon code OPNJZAA. To see the complete Safari Library, visit safari.oreilly.com.

O'REILLY®

Spreading the knowledge of innovators   safari.oreilly.com